DEVELOPING SCHOOL READINESS

SAGE was founded in 1965 by Sara Miller McCune to support the dissemination of usable knowledge by publishing innovative and high-quality research and teaching content. Today, we publish over 900 journals, including those of more than 400 learned societies, more than 800 new books per year, and a growing range of library products including archives, data, case studies, reports, and video. SAGE remains majority-owned by our founder, and after Sara's lifetime will become owned by a charitable trust that secures our continued independence.

Los Angeles | London | New Delhi | Singapore | Washington DC | Melbourne

Kathryn Peckham

DEVELOPING SCHOOL READINESS

CREATING LIFELONG LEARNERS

Los Angeles | London | New Delhi
Singapore | Washington DC | Melbourne

Los Angeles | London | New Delhi
Singapore | Washington DC | Melbourne

SAGE Publications Ltd
1 Oliver's Yard
55 City Road
London EC1Y 1SP

SAGE Publications Inc.
2455 Teller Road
Thousand Oaks, California 91320

SAGE Publications India Pvt Ltd
B 1/I 1 Mohan Cooperative Industrial Area
Mathura Road
New Delhi 110 044

SAGE Publications Asia-Pacific Pte Ltd
3 Church Street
#10-04 Samsung Hub
Singapore 049483

Assistant editor: George Knowles
Production editor: Tom Bedford
Copyeditor: Solveig Gardner Servian
Proofreader: Kate Campbell
Indexer: Anne Solamito
Marketing manager: Dilhara Attygalle
Cover design: Wendy Scott
Typeset by: C&M Digitals (P) Ltd, Chennai, India
Printed in the UK

First published 2017

Library of Congress Control Number: 2016948839

British Library Cataloguing in Publication data

A catalogue record for this book is available from the British Library

ISBN 978-1-4739-4724-5
ISBN 978-1-4739-4725-2 (pbk)

To James, Evelyn and Steven in thanks for their endless support and encouragement and whose love of learning are a testament to the experiences we all cherish.

CONTENTS

ABOUT THE AUTHOR

Kathryn Peckham, having initially trained as a secondary school teacher of mathematics, fell in love with the early years and made the move in 2005. Retraining by gaining her Early Years Professional Status and a Masters in Early Years, she worked within early years practice for many years, managing a number of settings and advising others through her monthly column in *Nursery World*. Going on to direct early years care and education at senior management levels, Kathryn combined practical experience with strong theoretical knowledge to lead practice throughout many settings.

With research interests in outdoor play and the effects of early experiences on children's lives, Kathryn is an active member of Early Childhood networks, a consultant to outdoor play designers and actively involved in the All Party Parliamentary Group on A Fit and Healthy Childhood, contributing to publications making a real difference in the lives of young children. Presenting research at international conferences and a keynote speaker, Kathryn's engaging style and delivery has inspired those interested in early childhood at all levels.

Having taught across under-graduate and post-graduate programmes at three universities, as a Senior Lecturer Kathryn has led the Foundation Degree in Early Years. Retaining her love of practice, Kathryn also guides and supports early years settings. For more information see www.kathrynpeckham.co.uk.

ACKNOWLEDGEMENTS

Great thanks goes to Jan White who gave me the early inspiration and encouragement to be a voice for children, exploring and realising the beliefs I hold dear, and to Dr Jane Murray for her encouraging interest and for reading my early work.

And also to the hundreds of children I have had the pleasure of playing with, observing and nurturing the curiosities that fuel their passions.

ABOUT THE BOOK

At a time of increased focus on the style and degree of 'school readiness' displayed within our young children, this book will promote thinking and debate around the issues concerned with preparing children for school. With reference to early years curriculum throughout the UK, the historic context of early years provision, political agenda and key research in the profession it will ask how we have arrived at this point, challenging current perceptions and refocusing attention on the holistic needs of the developing child.

Presenting ideas underpinned with consideration for how children grow and develop, the book will discuss the far-reaching potential of early childhood experiences to affect not only future academic success but also children's attitudes towards all learning and the degree to which any future opportunity will be embraced. In doing so it identifies the importance not of 'school readiness' but of preparing children for a lifetime of learning; a process begun from birth that continues throughout life, creating confident, courageous and self-motivated learners.

By recognising the unique potential of early childhood this book celebrates the diversity of children and their wide-ranging abilities and skills, suggesting that children's readiness for school cannot be ascertained through any pre-determined set of testable, quantifiable abilities, but through a plethora of characteristics, attitudes and frames of mind that develop through play-rich experiences throughout early childhood and beyond. By examining how intrinsic behaviours and approaches to deep thinking and learning can be nurtured within language and sensory-rich environments that promote social and experiential learning during these precious years, this book will present a new way of thinking that considers what it means to equip children with the vital foundations for all future learning, the features required for Lifelong Learning.

By focusing in turn on each of the familiar age groupings found within the early years (babies, under-twos and under-fives), Chapters 8, 9 and 10 consider how the features of Lifelong Learning can be developed and delivered, illustrating its influence on future learning. By demonstrating the impact of embedded practices throughout children's early years, these chapters demonstrate how preparation for formal education must be delivered not solely within the later stages of preschool but nurtured and promoted through every experience of young children's lives, cultivating deeper features of learning and thinking that grow with every future positive learning experience. Exploring the premise that these principles do not end as school begins, Chapter 11 looks at the importance of nurturing the features of Lifelong Learning throughout the practices of the school classroom.

However, none of this is possible without the informed understanding and conviction of key figures within children's lives. Celebrating the potential of effective practitioner and parental actions, attitudes and practice, Chapters 5 and 6 focus on these key groups, recognising the impact of effective guidance and support. Points of reflection throughout all chapters encourage consideration of current practice, suggesting ideas and alternative views to promote wider discussion amongst all involved with the care of children. Concluding remarks highlight 10 key concepts from the chapter and supplies recommendations for further reading to extend understanding. The conclusion also offers a practical project to explore the issues raised, future activities to allow the reader to relate these to practice and a work-based task to enable the concepts discussed to be used. To enable understanding and promote further study, a glossary is provided at the end of the book.

Intended for anyone concerned with offering children the best chance of future success during their early years, this book will appeal to practitioners, teachers, parents and students anywhere, offering a new lens to view children's achievements through and the rationale to promote and support further debate, ensuring they themselves can remain committed, Lifelong Learners.

1

UNDERSTANDING THE CONCEPT OF 'SCHOOL READINESS'; A JOURNEY ALREADY BEGUN AT BIRTH

THIS CHAPTER WILL

- define school readiness as a holistic process already begun at birth
- consider what school readiness means from the perspectives of early years practitioners, teachers, parents, children and the government
- invite practitioners to critically assess the traditional demand for demonstrated abilities to act as a measure of children's success
- consider instead the need for longer term, deep rooted features of learning.

The degree to which a child is ready for school depends on a multitude of factors that begin to take effect even before birth. Attempts at defining a list of attainable credentials to apply to all children is unfeasible, and efforts must therefore be centred around developing in all children the features required for a lifetime of effective and committed learning. When considering what school readiness is, it is this concept that above all else must remain central whilst remaining mindful of the agendas behind more traditional views and the lessons we can learn from others.

Characteristics of school readiness

Before we know it children are at the age of formal academic schooling and their early years are over. Preparation for this transition has been coined by the phrase 'school readiness'. However with little agreement on how this concept manifests itself in the life of the child, 'school readiness' is used ambiguously with many implications (Whitbread and Bingham, 2012). With no agreement on how, why or exactly what children should be prepared for, attempts at definition touch on deeper tensions regarding the purpose of the early years and arouses great debate throughout the sector (Whitbread and Bingham, 2012).

> The term 'school readiness' features in many reviews of education and statutory guidance. However, the precise characteristics of school readiness and the age of the child to which it applies are interpreted variously by the providers we visited. There is no nationally agreed definition. (Ofsted, 2014b)

SCHOOL READINESS

School readiness could be seen as:

- a culmination of all of the essential social, emotional, cognitive and autonomy building competences that have been developed during the child's early years
- the acquisition of the skills required to ensure that children can progress when starting formal schooling
- including achievements in speech, perception and the ability to understand numbers and quantities
- the skills that will enable children to adapt to the requirements of school, such as attitude to work, concentration, memory and social conduct
- the ability to engage positively and without aggression with other children and to respond appropriately to requests from teachers (Allen, 2011; Stefan and Miclea, 2014).
- including visual-motor maturities, such as the ability to accurately copy shapes, spot simple patterns and integrate information from multiple sources (Feinstein and Duckworth, 2006).
- considering visual perception, manual motor ability and memory skills, along with the temporal and spatial concepts of organisation which if lacking may indicate developmental delays.

However, some may say that laying the foundations for a deeper understanding of more complex skills and problem-solving abilities, such as encoding and decoding, are more beneficial and stand to yield higher gains in school (Feinstein and Duckworth, 2006).

With many differing views of school readiness presenting themselves through a variety of viewpoints, it is helpful to consider the nature of these various agendas and to look closely at where the impetus for school readiness originates from.

Are our current policies, provision and practice based on the lived experiences of young children today, or ideas derived from our own early experiences (Brooker, 2008)? Should school readiness be thought of as a child's status at a point in time, or is it more entwined with the objectives of family and school, developed and co-constructed by the home and setting (Dunlop and Fabian, 2007)? Or should we be concerned at all? Maybe all children should be permitted to start with a 'clean slate'? Certainly the evidence is clear that children ready to learn on entry to school have greater chances of future success (Wasik et al., 2011), but what attributes once secured could suggest that a child is now ready to embark on a formal academic journey set to last through the next decade? And what can determine this degree of 'readiness' more than the individual needs of the child?

REFLECTION

If not 'preparation for school', what is the purpose of early years provision?

What would you consider to be the most important skills a child can gain throughout the first five years of childhood?

Where and when are children prepared for school?

Children are participants in many interlocking 'microsystems', including their home, the homes of extended families, childminders and nursery, all of which have a direct and indirect contribution to their well-being during this time of transition to formal schooling. Through careful planning and preparation, links between familiar environments, routines and expectations, the unknowns to come can be identified and utilised, easing their transition and ultimate developmental outcomes. This period of transition cannot be viewed in isolation, represented by a day on the calendar, but rather as a continuum, aided by the actions of parents and both familiar and new adults. With full participation from the child, information regarding their needs and interests must be transferred and used effectively so that current enthusiasms can be utilised and familiar ideas of learning can be established and held by all those involved (House of Commons Education Committee, 2013).

Preparation for starting school should include experiences of relationships, behaviours and demands similar to those that will be encountered in the classroom, so that the *multidimensional* expectations to come will not be completely new, allowing children to behave naturally (Brooker, 2008; Wasik et al., 2011). Despite being part of the Early Years Foundation Stage (EYFS) within England, the reception class is often considered as much a part of formal schooling yet should be established through play-based approaches and playful adult-directed learning (Tickell, 2011) if children are to experience a smooth transition.

It is important to bear in mind that children experience the classroom from their own particular cultural background, identity, learning stance, interests and strategies (Brooker, 2002). When beginning school they will be presented with a range of developmental, individual, interactional and contextual challenges (Margetts, 2013), highlighting again the need for staff and parents to communicate with each other in order to co-construct transition activities and stimulate socio-emotional development (Fabian, 2002). Children's ability to rely on their inner resources and dispositions to integrate into the learning culture of the classroom successfully and access the knowledge and skills needed to succeed will be impacted further by feelings of self-esteem and well-being. If this environment or way of behaving is not familiar to their earlier experiences or compounded by cultural or language differences, this can have an immediate negative impact on classroom success and will be reflected in any attempts at early testing.

Attempts at measuring children's school success – or the success of the school – by comparing very early assessment of children (within the first six weeks of starting in reception, with later testing at the end of primary) has fuelled concerns regarding *Baseline Assessments*. Currently available from three named providers, the Baseline Assessment is a non-compulsory national testing of reception-aged children. First introduced by the government in 1997, plans were confirmed in 2014 for its use in measuring primary school accountability, to begin from September 2016. Following the reception baseline comparability study (Standards and Testing Agency, 2016) which concluded that results between trial schools were not comparable, this plan was scrapped. Whilst schools are still encouraged to assess children's 'baseline', the government (at the time of writing) does not plan on using these as a school accountability measure (DfE and STA, 2016).

REFLECTION

What are the expectations you have regarding the preparations children need for their first day of school?

Children develop at vastly different rates, with some more ready for school at age 5 than others. Variance in their experiences and the level of support gained from their families are influential, as are children's natural differences including any special educational needs. All have the potential to effect children's rates of development, which demonstrates the highly personal support children need in these formative years of early growth and development, highlighting the *parity* of quality required within children's early years experiences (Whitbread and Bingham, 2012).

In the current UK educational systems of England, Wales, Scotland and Northern Ireland (see Chapter 3 for their comparative approaches), there are five years for a child to grow in every way from a dependent new-born to being ready for the transition to formal schooling. A transition meaning so much more than a different place to learn: it has knock-on effects that shape children's future development and influences their ongoing school achievement as well as effecting their health and well-being (DfE and DH, 2011).

The five years preceding this transition are therefore staggeringly important, but for all the riches of opportunities available to children, they must not become distracted by demands of stages yet to come. The early years must be fully understood in their own right, harnessed and utilised before discrete *windows of opportunities* close if we are to establish key features of healthy growth and development.

Different perspectives of those involved

As we continue to establish a sense of what it means to be ready for school we need to remember that definitions of school readiness naturally differ, depending on whose lens the concept is viewed through.

Traditional views of school preparation include developing the competencies connected to the process of learning; approaches to understanding; taking responsibility for one's own learning and development (Margetts, 2013); and the fulfilling of school tasks (Brzeziska et al., 2012), including skills such as reading, writing, interacting with peers and the teacher, independent activity and the skills required for passing the inevitable tests (Margetts, 2013). If we are to assume that 'The skills a child needs for school are part of the skills they need for life' (Tickell, 2011), then we must strongly question the premise that the tasks demanded by the school curriculum are the most conducive to shaping the learners of the future as well as preparing the child to participate in the complex social and informational reality of a future yet unknown and that the process of learning is accurately matched for all children at all times.

For early years providers, concerns regarding the nature of learning, such as number and letter recognition and forming legible marks on the page, social emotional maturity, general knowledge and the ability to use a range of materials and strategies, are often given as factors in school readiness, with pre-literacy skills seen as particularly important in urban settings and by those working with large numbers of children where English is not their first language (Noel and Lord, 2014).

REFLECTION

Do you think that the concept of school readiness is affected by the objectives of the person considering it? As a practitioner, how do your views of how ready a child is for school differ from the parents and teachers that you work with?

For a primary school teacher tasked with logistical class management of September's intake and expectations of results to follow, demands of school readiness may be more likely to focus on children's abilities to engage in activities familiar to the primary classroom (e.g. sitting at a desk, self-managing trips to the toilet and changing for PE) as well as social skills required to engage well with others and respond to requirements of adults. Working in a system of standards, levels and accountability, teacher's may feel pressured to focus on children's development with the meeting of targets playing a central driver, rather than respecting children's right to learn in their own way and at their own pace (Brooker, 2008). Being able to integrate into the demands of the more regulated classroom is a focus from the beginning. For the parent, concerns may centre on separation anxiety, their child's ability to make a friend and to feel safe and confident within their new environment. For the child, this is a period of great emotional and physical transition – perhaps the first leap into an unknown, with an overwhelming sense of importance – which requires the mastering of new equipment, dress and practices in an environment that holds great yet unfamiliar demands, expectations and realities.

Through all these lenses one thing is clear: if a child is not ready for this transition or it does not go well, this will create obstructions to their own as well as other's learning (Tickell, 2011). In a formal education system where success builds *cumulatively*, a strong beginning enables children to build on initial success whilst disadvantages felt now will only intensify. Whilst there are undoubtedly expectations for physical, social and cognitive abilities within children's healthy development, questions need to be asked regarding the methods, practices and roles used to achieve these desired outcomes. Mindful that behaviours and *pedagogies* will likely differ according to the views of learning and level of knowledge held by practitioners (Karweit, 1998), a wide range of teaching methods and practices will undoubtedly be displayed (West et al., 1993). The understanding held by those responsible for these influential years must be considered and continuously developed if we are to ensure that practices are able to secure a quality foundation for our children.

REFLECTION

What are your own early memories of school? What preparations and experiences would have made this easier for you?

Having recognised that the key to an auspicious school start is the fostering of fundamental personal attributes from the earliest age, the starting place for any debate on school readiness must then be the child. However a school start characterised by effective skills is only secure in a minority of children; the vast majority are not being given the best opportunity for success (Fabian, 2002). Identifying and embedding key abilities, experiences and features into early childhood enables children to harness and utilise these finite years, not only preparing them for this significant transition but also securely laying the foundations to a continual life of enquiry, wonder and learning and establishing the building blocks for successful, healthy adult lives. Recognition of the staggering importance of the *foundation years* and the skilful managing of the years that follow are vital if we are not to disadvantage our children at a time when they have barely begun. All children must receive early experiences steeped in quality that not only secure the best start to formal education but which will also instil in them a love of enquiry and learning fuelled by a belief of their own abilities that will last a lifetime. However, this in itself is open to interpretation.

REFLECTION

How do you think a set curriculum could go about supporting you in preparing all children at all times?

What is quality in early years provision?

Looking at trends observed through a number of populations and types of provision, The Effective Provision of Preschool Education (EPPE) project (Sylva et al., 2004) and the subsequent Effective Preschool, Primary and Secondary Education (EPPSE) project (Sylva et al., 2014) examined the impact of specific elements of early childhood and their ability to afford children the best starting point. The quality of the provision, with its potential to identify and support all children, especially those from disadvantaged backgrounds and those with specific needs, was pivotal. Well-trained, committed, consistent, responsive, affectionate and readily available practitioners with appropriate adult–child interactions and the knowledge to deliver developmentally appropriate curriculum were instrumental in this quality (Sylva et al., 2004, 2014) and have a proportionate impact on children's education trajectory (Field, 2010) and their achievements in later life, even if their performance deteriorates during the school years (Whitbread and Bingham, 2012). Integrated, well-funded, socio-educational programmes were also seen to improve the cognitive and social functioning of children, particularly for those at risk, and specialised support for language and pre-reading skills were seen to have benefited where English was an additional language (Sylva et al., 2004, 2014).

REFLECTION

In the paragraph above there are several references to quality and appropriateness. What do these words mean to you in this context? How open to interpretation is this?

The depth of a child's vocabulary on starting school has a tremendous impact on their ability to access the experience and promotes ongoing enhanced learning. In order for children to develop a rich vocabulary, to have the opportunities to practice their speech and rehearse the interplays of communication, they must have an environment rich in language and experience. Where this is provided in the home, high levels of quality childcare is less essential; however, if the child is lacking in these experiences, providing them through other means will have a long-term effect on the child's life chances (Melhuish, 2003). This was seen in the Allen (2011) Report, which recommended 'early intervention' places and was also reflected in the Field (2010) review of child poverty, which considered the importance of improving parenting as a means of ending the *inter-generational* transmission of child poverty.

REFLECTION

What could you do to ensure that home environments are steeped in language?

Messages from around the world

So a picture is emerging of the importance of a highly specialised early years' experience on the life chances of children. Yet many of these play-based practices become lost to the demands of school. Whilst many different cultures and practices can be observed, evidence from across the world suggests that children should not leave the early years curriculum to begin formal teaching before the age of 7–8 (Bruce, 2011b; Hurst, 1997; Woodhead, 1986, 1989; Miller, 2010; Blakemore, 2000). The idea that 'earlier is better' when it comes to formal learning of an 'overly academic curriculum' (Sylva et al., 1999 in Broadhead, 2001) is misguided, with no long-term benefit (Whitbread and Bingham, 2012). Whilst direct instruction of numeracy and reading for some very young children may bring about initial advantages, for many the long-term effects are at best no different and at worse are seen to promote disengagement as children's opportunities to make decisions and self-direct are diminished (Broadhead, 2001). With significant effects on children's enjoyment of reading, as is demonstrated by the amount they actually read, together with potential psychological and social problems (Suggate, 2007; Schweinhart et al., 2005), this is an issue that requires further debate.

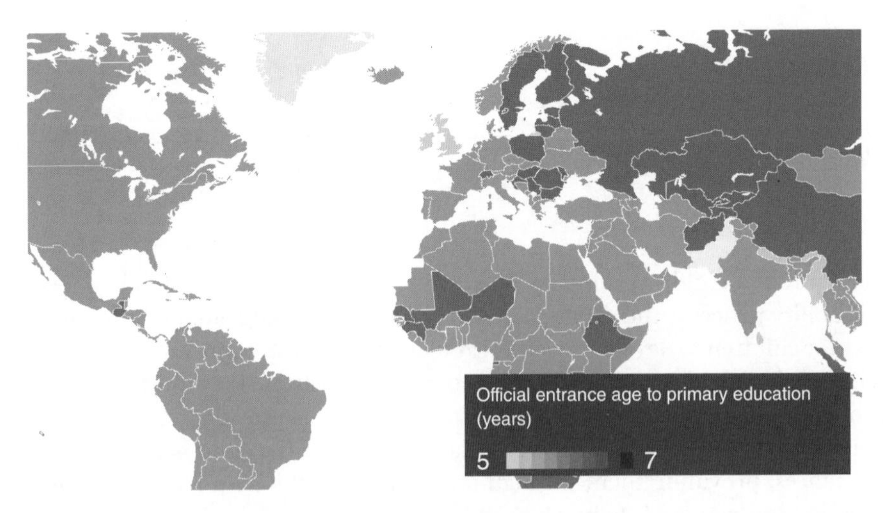

Figure 1.1 Official entrance age to primary education (years) 2011–2015 (World DataBank, 2016)

For children in Norway, Italy, France, Germany and America school starts at age 6, often with a 'preschool' year of informal activities (see Figure 1.1). In Finland, Hungary, Poland and China children do not begin formal education until the age of 7. In the UK, throughout the differing curricula of England, Wales, Scotland and Northern Ireland, the expectation of formal education comes at the earlier starting age of 5, bringing into sharp relief how out of step the UK is with other countries in introducing children to more formal learning in their early life (Sharp, 2002).

In Britain, as in all countries, we have our own clearly defined culture and set of values intrinsic within our eclectic customs and practices, formed through our diverse and growing population. We must be careful not to assume that what works well for others will have the same effect for all, or to try to 'borrow cultures' which is a complex yet common mistake (Wollens, 2000). That is not to say there isn't a great deal to be learnt by looking at the practices of others, not as a wholesale solution to be emulated within very different circumstances but as a well-developed case study. Provided that we look with eyes informed by our own identity and remain mindful of not assuming great insight from brief selected observations. Theories of learning viewed in context can demonstrate the effects of staff autonomy, where working in consultation with families can be seen to enable holistic practices fine-tuned to children's individual needs and curricula used as guidance rather than sets of standards to measure children against on starting school (Whitbread and Bingham, 2012).

Scandinavian countries are well known for offering heavily *subsidised* full-day care (OECD, 2006). With a maternal leave of 36 months (Finland) and a much older age at school entry, 'preschool' is a relaxed, playful environment based on social interaction and individual investigation with pedagogies that extend into early primary (Whitbread and Bingham, 2012). The early years curriculum for children under 6 follows a 'theme of interest' approach through play-based unstructured, semi-structured and structured activities connected with familiar home routines such as dressing, gardening and sharing meals, both indoors and outdoors. The objectives of the areas of learning must be covered (mathematics, natural sciences, historical-societal, aesthetic, ethical, religious-philosophical), but these are integrated so that the learning process is seen as more important than individual core elements. Language is then threaded throughout to support cognitive processes and children's abilities to learn (ECEC, 2004 in Bjorklund et al., 2014).

The ethos of the world renowned Reggio-Emilia setting in Northern Italy was developed by challenging the accepted practices and dominant discourse of the time and reconstructing ideas of children, teaching and curriculum practices; not by dismissing all that was familiar but by looking at practice in a different way, placing an articulated and distinctive vision of the child at the centre. Planning follows collaboration with the child and parents rather than following any pre-conceived goals (Miller, 2010) in a curriculum centred on the child's experiences, interests and choices (Whitbread and Bingham, 2012). Play is integrated throughout (Samuelsson and Carlsson, 2008) and children are celebrated for their abilities to think and act for themselves (Dahlberg and Moss, 2005).

As an alternative view, Eastern cultures can be observed teaching children within their early years to be capable of great feats in numeracy and literacy. In Hong Kong writing and correct stroke sequencing of Chinese characters has been seen for many years as effective preparation for school from three years old. Heavily academic approaches have been forced through correct holding of pencils and excessive print practice (Wong, 2003). With the belief that fluency and mastery will be achieved if enough effort is applied through repetition and hard work, it was believed that this must begin as early as possible. Repeated physical hand holding, testing and completion of daily written assignments was seen by many as effective and appropriate (Wong, 2008). In fact, the Chinese term for learning consists of two characters: 'to study' and 'to practice repeatedly' (Dahlgaard-Park, 2006). However, more recently quality assurance inspectors have questioned the appropriateness of these techniques (Education and Manpower Bureau, 2005) and the tide is changing (Wong, 2008).

REFLECTION

Who decides on the attributes that school readiness should contain, and where do we go looking for them?

Is school readiness a defined set of skills mastered (or not) by the child waiting for their first day of school?

Should we be looking at the transition preparations of the school in collaboration with key figures in the child's life?

Or is school readiness tied into the cultural practices and family attitudes shaping the experiences of the child to date?

CHAPTER SUMMARY

This chapter has attempted to unpick the concept of school readiness by considering it from various points of view. It has invited debate on the key attributes required by children and has suggested that these must centre around the characteristics of the individual child, forming part of an ongoing continuum of development that has already begun at birth.

By looking at the effect of early childhood experiences on the future lives of children, the chapter has focused on the importance of ensuring that these experiences are of the highest quality and is fully understood by those delivering them.

Ten Key Concepts

1. A strong school beginning has the potential to affect the child and their endeavours well into adulthood. (Brooker, 2008)
2. Children need to be viewed holistically. To ensure their well-being we must consider the various aspects of family, setting, culture and home life, making sure to establish and nurture these links. (Tickell, 2011)
3. Transitions to reception will be aided by practices that fully embrace learning through play during this continuing phase of the foundation stage. (Grauberg, 2014)
4. School readiness needs to stem from the needs of the child. (Claxton, 2008a)
5. The greatest gift we can give our children as they prepare for starting school is a love of learning and a belief in their own capabilities. (Ramey and Ramey, 1998)
6. Views of school readiness will differ depending on the role of the person giving them; to understand what is needed by the child we must look to the child. (Wasik et al., 2011)
7. Skills needed for life are embedded in the experiences afforded during the early years. (Dombey, 2010)
8. Deeper rooted skills and abilities of children must be recognised, valued and celebrated. (Whitbread and Bingham, 2012)
9. Dispositions towards enquiry and investigation must be nurtured and developed. (Rayna and Laevers, 2014)
10. The knowledge and skills of the adults in the lives of our young children are key. (Nutbrown, 2012)

IDEAS FOR PRACTICE

Practical Project

Gain an understanding of the beliefs and expectations held with regard to school readiness by seeking out the opinions of early year's practitioners, teachers, parents and children.

Future Activities

Establish a forum where these views can be shared, exchanged and understood. This could be achieved through a PTA Group, a notice board or an online blog.

(Continued)

(Continued)

Work-based Tasks

Establish your own rationale and suggested plan for school readiness with reference to the importance of developing the long-term characteristics of children. Sensitively bearing in mind existing opinions, communicate your intentions to those who will be affected by it.

FURTHER READING

Boivin, M. and Bierman, K. (Eds.) (2014) *Promoting School Readiness and Early Learning: Implications of Developmental Research for Practice.* New York: Guilford Press.

Through developmental knowledge and research this book considers what school readiness entails and the skills and practices required for improving it.

Brown, C.P. (2010) 'Balancing the readiness equation in early childhood education reform', *Journal of Early Childhood Research*, 8 (2).

This American study looks at the difficulties of trying to define the school-ready child within a standards-based educational system, calling for a balanced view of school preparation that considers not only academic skills and knowledge but also the abilities of families, schools and communities to prepare children for school success.

Evans, M. (2011) 'What does "ready for school" mean?', *Nursery World*, 111 (4255): 10–11.

This article discusses the concerns raised by the phrase 'readiness for school' in government and policy documents and the lack of clear definition of the term when children are to be assessed with new readiness for school measures at the age of 5. The disparity between Great Britain and the rest of Europe in starting formal education is also discussed.

Kirkup, C. (2016) 'Baseline assessment', *Research Insights*. Available at www.nfer.ac.uk/schools/baseline-assessment.pdf (accessed 21/6/16).

This discusses some of the big questions raised regarding the introduction of Baseline Assessment. The press release following the comparability study can be found at www.gov.uk/government/news/reception-baseline-comparability-study-published (accessed 22/6/16).

Ofsted (2014) *Are You Ready? Good Practice in School Readiness.* Manchester: Ofsted. Available at www.gov.uk/government/publications/are-you-ready-good-practice-in-school-readiness (accessed 22/6/16).

Observations of how differently the concept of school readiness is viewed and prepared for through practicing settings achieving good and outstanding inspections.

2

THE HISTORY AND DEVELOPMENT OF SCHOOL READINESS

THIS CHAPTER WILL

- look at the history of British childcare as a background to the concept of school readiness
- consider the current legislation affecting the concept of 'school readiness'
- provide practitioners with a broader discourse of what it really means to be 'ready for school'.

In order to understand school readiness we must understand how it has evolved as a concept. This chapter will provide a background to the history of early years in the UK and the key developments of the 20th century together with a breakdown of the four curricula that currently guide practice throughout England, Wales, Scotland and Northern Ireland. It will also look at testing, assessment and inspection within the early years to offer context to the current practices and highlight the important role of confident, informed adults within children's lives in securing appropriate foundations for our children.

History and current research demonstrates the importance of ensuring that children are on the right path long before school begins. To see them brimming with confidence, social awareness, imagination and intuition throughout their schooling, children must be equipped with meaningful experiences ready to recognise, embrace and optimise opportunities as they arise. Research and flagship programmes have provided the evidence to encourage targeted government attention into the profession, including the integration of education and social work services, reformation of regulations, standards and training, the creation of a Children's Commissioner and a 10-year strategy for childcare. However, good intentions will fall short without complete understanding and appreciation of what is needed to enhance positive trajectories of children, and will be incomplete until public understanding, recognition and equality of status for the early years are satisfactorily addressed. Only then can we begin to prepare children from all backgrounds for an effective lifetime of learning.

History of childcare

Views of childhood have changed dramatically over the last 150 years, despite the needs of the child fundamentally remaining constant.

Experiences of children throughout history have been, and for many still are, governed chiefly by the societal and political needs of the time. With the British statutory school entry age of five decided in 1870, long before the child study movement when little was known about child development, it had no rational basis in educational theory (Bertram and Pascal, 2002). Before 1870, children as young as two would typically be cared for in churches and secular schools, especially when mothers were required to work. As the industrialisation of 19th century England proceeded more work was found outside the home and a practical need for 'infant schools' and 'babies' classes' was soon identified and filled (Brooker, 2008), with the first 'school for mothers' opening in St Pancras in 1907. There was also a raft of legislation to address the perceived nation-building threat posed by inadequate mothering (Read, 2015) despite the belief that, except in the case of the poorest families, young children should be at home with their mother (Board of Education 1908).

In 1905, before under-five's provision was recognised within policy agenda, five women HMIs investigated conditions in infant provision in England and Wales and condemned the large class sizes, insufficient physical exercise or changes of posture, air and scene, and teachers' repression of originality in individual children through instructional teaching, causing strain to muscles and nerves (Board of Education, 1905). Recognising the impact of physical conditions on children's abilities to learn and develop and the role of early provision in the ability of schools to fulfil their function, the Froebelian nursery school pioneer Margaret McMillan aimed to provide an alternative to 'the forbidding, heavy wall of prison-like schools and its hard asphalt, shadeless space and iron gates!' with 'schools in the garden' that were to 'ring with laughter and the tripping of little feet' (McMillan,1923: 4, cited in Read, 2015). With bright airy rooms allowing access to the garden, children would grow plants and model in wet sand, sing, play with balls and blocks, thread reeds and beads and share nursery rhymes, story-telling and story-acting. With no inspections, examinations, rigid timetables or formal lessons children were provided opportunities for movement, games and free play, in the open air for as much as half the day (Read, 2015).

During the 1940s many state nurseries were opened to release mothers for war work before closing soon after the end of the war, making way for men to return to their civilian employment with little account taken of the needs or most favourable environments for children. The 1960s was famed for its child-centred philosophies and the emergence of English primary education (Pluckrose, 1987). Whilst childcare provision reflecting healthy programmes of singing, stories and free-play both in and out of doors was available (Brooker, 2008), it was however uncommon for children to access more than a few hours of preschool per week. For the majority of children, the years from birth to five were spent at home, with occasional afternoons at mother-and-baby groups set up by mothers (Brooker, 2008).

REFLECTION

Ask your parents and colleagues to consider the most influential memories from their early childhood and do the same for your own – what was enjoyed and what experiences have most vividly remained?

By the 1990s most children were starting in reception classes soon after their fourth birthday, despite an official school start date a year later (Woodhead, 1989; Dowling, 1995), but it wasn't until 1994 with the publishing of the Start Right report (Ball, 1994) when substantive recommendations were made for a systematic approach by government to consider early childhood education and care (Grauberg, 2014). The review of the evidence suggested that high-quality early education combined with family support would lead to lasting cognitive and social benefits in children. Recommendations followed for compulsory part-time nursery education from age three with parents learning alongside their children, guided by fully trained nursery school teachers offering wide-ranging support.

This was followed in 1996 with the Desirable Outcomes for Children's Learning, a predecessor to the 'learning goals'. With a move away from the holistic practices previously recognised, this documented a formidable set of 'goals for learning for children by the time they enter compulsory education' (SCAA, 1996), emphasising early literacy and numeracy and the development of personal and social skills. With clear links to the national curriculum there was barely a mention of play (Miller, 2010). Baseline assessment at five years followed in 1997, together with National Literacy and Numeracy Strategies (DfEE, 1998a, 1998b) bringing over-fives under increasing central control (Miller, 2010). By the end of the Conservative government in 1997, a range of early years provision was available; however, there was still little consistency of quality (Brooker, 2008) or any definition as to what a quality early years' experience meant.

REFLECTION

What effect do you think these initiatives would have on the experiences of young children?

The National Childcare Strategy (DfEE, 1998c) afforded a more relaxed approach to childcare. Focusing on choice, flexibility, availability and affordability, it also promoted the concept of quality. In July 1998 the government-backed Sure Start programme was announced, an area-based early intervention programme working with disadvantaged families to offer evidence-based services (DfE and DH, 2011) integrating local childcare, education and health services (House of Commons Education Committee, 2013). With the 'core purpose' of enhancing overall developmental competence ready for school (All Party Parliamentary Sure Start Group, 2013) the programme was designed to tackle disadvantage among young children (HM Treasury, 1998); however, it attracted criticism from Ofsted when it came to children's preparedness for school (House of Commons Education Committee, 2013: 7) and its ability to target those most in need.

The Effective Provision of Preschool Education (EPPE) research in 2004 and the subsequent Effective Preschool Primary and Secondary Education project (EPPSE) in 2014 clearly demonstrated the importance of quality within early year settings for 3–5-year-olds, drawing attention to the effect of *horizontal* and *vertical transitions* (Brooker, 2008) and underpinned the work of the Sure Start programmes and Children's Centres in targeting areas of high social disadvantage (Sylva et al., 2004). Attempting to improve outcomes and reduce inequality, Labour launched the Ten Year Childcare Strategy (2004), brought into force by the Childcare Act 2006, to focus again on giving parents choice of available, affordable, high-quality care with plans to expand the '*free entitlement*' to most disadvantaged 2-year-olds. A new *Ofsted Childcare Register* was established, a new training and qualifications structure announced, and commitment expressed for all full day-care settings to be led by graduate early years professionals. The Birth to Three Matters (DfES, 2002), the Foundation Years Learning Goals (QCA, 2000) and the Minimum Standards for Under Eights (SureStart, 2003) were also brought together to form an integrated quality framework encompassing the full 0–5 age range, subsequently known as the Early Years Foundation Stage (EYFS) (HM Treasury, 2004). Focus on quality and investment into the early years continued in 2009 with the Next Steps document (DfCSF, 2009c), which considered the legal requirement for graduate leaders and for all staff to hold a full and relevant Level 3. Growing evidence of the importance of communication in early childhood saw an expansion of the Every Child a Talker programme and an extension of the pilot-free entitlement for disadvantaged 2-year-olds (DfCSF, 2009a).

Throughout the UK, early years provision became a focus of development, with targeted curriculum focusing on the specific needs of the formative years introduced throughout England, Wales, Scotland and Northern Ireland. During this time a number of influential reports were published; the Field review (2010) and the Allen review (2011) highlighting the effect of foundations established in early childhood on success in later life and the Tickell review (2011) recommending a simplified English early years framework, streamlining the initial 69 learning goals and dividing the six areas of learning into four *Prime Areas* and three *Specific Areas* (DfE and DH, 2011). All these reviews emphasised the importance of the home environment and the role of parents and carers as partners in their children's learning.

Whilst differences were seen, such as the drawing together of Birth to Three Matters (DfES, 2002) and the Foundation Stage curriculum for 3–4-year-olds (QCA, 2000) to incorporate the full 0-5 age range within the English framework, all aimed to recognise the importance of child-initiated approaches and allow the

Table 2.1 Comparisons of the English, Welsh, Scottish and Northern Ireland early years curricula

	England	Wales	Scotland	Northern Ireland
Name	Early Years Foundation Stage (EYFS)	Early Years Foundation Phase (EYFP)	Curriculum for Excellence (CfE)	Foundation Phase within the Enriched Curriculum
Areas of Learning	**Three Prime Areas** (focus under two) • Communication and language • Physical development • Personal, social and emotional development **Four Specific Areas** • Literacy • Mathematics • Understanding the world • Expressive arts and design	**Seven Areas** • Personal and social development, well-being and cultural diversity • Language, literacy and communication skills • Mathematical development • Welsh language development • Knowledge and understanding of the world • Physical development • Creative development	**Three core subject areas** • Health and well-being • Literacy • Numeracy **Eight Curriculum Areas** • Expressive arts • Health and well-being • Languages • Mathematics • Religious and moral education • Sciences • Social sciences	**Seven Areas** • Language and literacy • Mathematics and numeracy • The arts • The world around us • Personal development and mutual understanding • Physical development and movement • Religious education
Date introduced	2012 (previous format, 2008)	2008	2010	2007
Notable change	Care and learning now integrated	Addressed concerns of young children introduced to formal reading and writing too early, sitting too long at desks with insufficient creative and linguistic opportunities or cultural awareness	Aim for a more developmentally appropriate curriculum	Aim for a less formal and more developmentally appropriate, play-based curriculum in the first two years of primary education

(Continued)

Table 2.1 (Continued)

	England	Wales	Scotland	Northern Ireland
Age range	0–5	3–7	3–18	5–7
Expectations	17 Early Learning Goals (ELGs) to be achieved by the end of reception year	17 Early Learning Goals (ELGs) to be achieved by the end of EYFP (age 7).	Children progress through levels when they are ready. Although not determined by age, the early level is intended for preschool and first year of primary	Attainment throughout the seven areas of learning
Attitude to play	To be planned and purposeful	Central to delivery	Central to delivery with active learning	Self-initiated play is central to delivery
Delivery	Mix of adult-led and child-initiated activities	First-hand experiences through experimentation, risk and problem solving	Holistic delivery of the core subject areas through lessons in the curriculum areas, presenting a joined-up curriculum	Less formal play-based and child-led challenging activities
Assessment	Progress check at age two; assessment of achievement in the prime areas. EYFS Profile (EYFSP); assessment of achievement in the 17 ELGs at end of reception	Short narrative at end of EYFP to assess progress in 17 ELGs and describe the child's learning characteristics	Report cards and parent–teacher consultations at end of first year of primary	Ongoing assessment is based on teacher observations with a pupil profile at the end of each year

key principles of play to be embraced, moving away from formal approaches within the early years (see Table 2.1).

Continuing their focus on early years, the new Coalition government (2010–2015) extended free childcare to more disadvantaged 2-year-olds with the publication 'Supporting Families in the Foundation Years' (DfE and DH, 2011). Following a consultation on a revised EYFS and a review of early years qualifications in England, new proposals were put forward and included a developmental review for 2-year-olds to be linked to the *Healthy Child Programme*. The revised EYFS of 2012 offered a universal framework for integrated, play-based learning and care from birth to five with its now seven areas of learning emphasising prime skills within the first two years. The Nutbrown qualifications review followed in June 2012. Supporting the goal of graduate leadership throughout England, Nutbrown proposed entry requirements into the profession including GCSE English and Mathematics; with minimum standards of Level 3 for the workforce by 2022, it recommended an early years specialist qualification with *Qualified Teacher Status* (now defunct) (Nutbrown, 2012). The government's response, 'More Great Childcare' (DfE, 2013), accepted the GCSE requirements, proposed a new Level 3 Early Years Educator and a new Early Years Teacher status. With the same entry requirements as school teachers, this status would not contain Qualified Teacher Status and as such would not attract equal benefits. These moves, together with encouraging younger children into school nursery classes, fuelled concerns in the profession that policies were being rushed into without proper consideration, resulting in short-term and disparate government policy in the area of early years (House of Commons Education Committee, 2013).

With a strong early years focus over recent years much has been achieved, and demanded; however, much is becoming lost as emphasis centres on preparing children for formal education. With Sure Start outcomes in England criticised and their value to children and families questioned on the strength of Foundation Stage profile testing (House of Commons Education Committee, 2013), a wider view of children's achievements must be sought and celebrated beyond measured performance with pre-established criteria. Whilst early development of social, physical and intellectual abilities are fundamental, they must not become tailored preparation for first days of school but rather wide-reaching foundations for a lifetime of achievement (see Table 2.2).

REFLECTION

Look back at the development of childcare. How would you define people's perceptions of early years provision? Do you think the early years are afforded the same importance as later stages of school life? Why do you think this?

Testing and assessment

Lack of achievement in our young children and concerns regarding abilities at the point of school entry seem to be a consistent feature of government debate.

Table 2.2 Key developments in early childhood since the late 20th century

Date	Findings	Recommendations	Consequence
1994	Start Right Report	Systematic approach by government to consider early childhood education and care	Compulsory part-time nursery education from age three
1996	Desirable Outcomes for Children's Learning	Goals for children's learning by the time they enter compulsory education	Emphasis on early literacy and numeracy with little mention of play
1997	Early Years Development and Childcare Partnerships (EYDCPs)	Attempts to clarify policy	Local Authorities given the responsibility to audit, monitor and regulate their own under-five provision
1997	Concept of Baseline Assessment at school entry introduced	To inform schools of the progress children are making, helping identify those needing additional help	Largely unwelcome by parents and teachers fearing potential 'schoolification' of early years. 2014: Baseline Assessments confirmed for all children starting primary school to replace EYFS profile testing from 2016. Concerns regarding unfamiliar tasks, low levels of concentration and lack of resulting comparability possible were voiced by the profession. April 2016: Following the Reception Baseline Comparability Study (STA, 2016) concluding that results between trial schools were not comparable, this plan was scrapped. Schools encouraged to assess children's 'baseline', but no current plans to use results to measure school accountability.
1997	National Literacy and Numeracy Strategies	Strategy to improve standards, addressing concerns regarding developing literacy and numeracy skills	Whilst individual successes were documented, when viewed against national targets improvements in standards and progress were considered too slow
1998	National Childcare Strategy	Focus on choice, flexibility, availability and affordability within quality care	Childcare tax credit and 'free entitlement'

Date	Findings	Recommendations	Consequence
1998	Sure Start Programme	Government-backed, area-based early intervention programme	Early Years and Health working together with families to address needs
1999	Inception of the Foundation Stage	Detailed statutory guidance focusing on six areas of learning	Considered children from age three to the end of the reception year as a distinct phase in education
2001	Ofsted takes over regulation	National Standards introduced	Attempts to standardise and raise quality
2002	'Birth to Three Matters'	Focus on the interrelationship between growth, learning, development and the environment for under-three's	Considered provision for the under-three's
2002	New Foundation Stage Curriculum for 3- and 4-year-olds	Focus on the interrelationship between growth, learning and development for the 3–4 age group	Considered provision for the over-three's
2004	The Effective Provision of Pre-school Education (EPPE) research published	Demonstrated the importance of quality within early years settings	Emphasised need for consistent quality, especially pronounced in areas of deprivation
2004	Ten Year Childcare Strategy	Improve outcomes and reduce inequality	Expanded the 'free entitlement' to most disadvantaged 2-year-olds
2006	Childcare Act 2006	Improve the well-being of children through secure sufficient childcare, raising qualifications and reforming and simplifying regulation and inspection	Aimed to reduce inequalities throughout the five Every Child Matters outcomes, offered better parental information and introduced an integrated education and care quality framework and Ofsted Childcare Register
2009	Next Steps document	Recognition and promotion of quality within early years	Considered the requirement for graduate-led practice with minimum Level 3 for all staff
2009	Expansion of the 'Every Child a Talker' programme	Recognition of importance of communication in children's early childhood	Help for practitioners and parents to create appropriate, supportive and stimulating environments for children to enjoy experimenting with and learning language

(Continued)

Table 2.2 (Continued)

Date	Findings	Recommendations	Consequence
2010	Field Review	Address child poverty, recognising that children's life chances are most heavily predicted by their development in the first five years of life	An independent review on poverty and life chances. Established a foundation stage to now cover the period from womb to five. Recommended Life Chance Indicators
2010	Supporting Families in the Foundation Years	Continued focus on early years	Extension of free childcare
2011	Allen Review	Recognise the importance of early intervention in children's life chances	Focus on quality within settings and assessments within the early years designed to detect and address emotional and social difficulties
2011	Tickell Review	Simplified and coherent EYFS	Streamlining of early learning goals and splitting of the areas of learning
2012	Revised EYFS	Looked to offer a universal framework for integrated, play-based learning and care from birth to five	Now with seven areas of learning incorporating prime and specific areas and 17 early learning goals
2012	Nutbrown Review	Audit of qualifications and their importance throughout the sector	Supported the goal of graduate leadership, minimum Level 3 throughout the workforce and a specialist Qualified Teacher Status qualification
2013	More Great Childcare	New Level 3 Early Years Educator qualification announced	Early Years Teacher Status would not attract Qualified Teacher Status
2014	The Effective Pre-school, Primary and Secondary Education (EPPSE) research published	Early investment in children's lives through quality provision and attention to home has significant effects on learning pathways and life trajectories	Credible longitudinal research evidencing the long-term legacy of preschool

In recent years attempts to examine and track this trend in England have been introduced through *pupil profiles* and summative assessment of the early learning goals at the end of the Foundation Stage.

From September 2016, *baseline* national testing for reception-aged children in England aimed to assess children's development, from beginning formal schooling to the end of Key Stage 2 (age 11). Administered by three approved providers, a 'pass/fail' for each scoring item would be given and condensed to a single result, individual children's baseline score would then be compared with their end of Key Stage 2 result (a format that also saw revisions in summer 2016 as national curriculum levels were replaced with performance descriptors detailing what pupils were expected to know and be able to do to demonstrate expected standards). Children's progress between their two outcomes were to be 'calculated' and compared as schools were measured and 'held to account' by the average progress of their pupils (DfE, 2015).

Similar to the approach introduced by the Labour government in England in 1997 and abandoned as an 'ineffective and damaging policy' (Nutbrown, 2015) in 2002 and Wales in 2011 (withdrawn in 2012 as 'time consuming, ill-thought through and denied children and teachers essential teaching time' – ATL, 2015), tensions remained within the profession with such formal assessments at an early age (Tickell, 2011), considered inappropriate by most other countries (Hurst, 1997). More formal than the now optional EYFS Pupil Profiles that aimed to look holistically at children's development over a longer period of time, the baseline tests were to take place within six weeks of children starting school, during a period of transition that for most children will be experienced before they turn five.

Following the conclusion of the Reception Baseline Comparability Study (STA, 2016) that results between trial schools were not comparable, the plan to use baseline assessment in measuring primary school accountability was scrapped. Whilst schools are still encouraged to assess children's 'baseline', the government (at the time of writing) does not currently plan on using these as a school accountability measure (STA, 2016).

By looking at abilities such as counting and number and letter recognition, the plan had been for these tests to give teachers a clearer picture of children's initial skills, enabling higher standards by focusing attention where it is needed most and providing a quantifiable measure of the progress children are making. However, concerns remain that rather than formatively assisting teachers to support and encourage individual children's development (Sylva et al., 2004), such testing only adds the pressure of exam performance (Claxton, 2008b), emphasising trivial aspects of subjects and encouraging disconnected teaching by rote (Bruner, 1977).

School cultures emphasising technique, where performance rather than learning is the applauded attribute, will drive pedagogy further towards teacher-directed learning (Nutbrown, 1998), losing children's current developmental needs in the process (Broadhead, 2001). The result of this, Hargreaves (2010) suggests, is a future of competitive elites trained in specific, streamed skills – far from ready to embrace the unique features of a world yet unknown, armed with the skills needed to adapt and achieve.

REFLECTION

Whilst testing of children upon entering reception may lead to improvements in primary school accountability, how do you think this will impact on children's short-term and long-term outcomes?

Performance and displays of learning at this young age are highly personal, yet numerical league tables demanding quantifiable, consistent data puts the focus on standardised testing (Hurst, 1997) lacking in context (Bjorklund et al., 2014) and unsympathetic to cultural differences. Limitations of language and materials impact on the assessment of children's ability to think and process (Deák and Wiseheart, 2015) as the diversity of early childhood experiences and achievements are undervalued, pushing children to demonstrate low-level, discrete skills and bite-size facts at the expense of thoughtful learning.

REFLECTION

In a rapidly changing world, how can we begin to presume what specialist skills our adults of the future will require?

That is not to say that assessment does not have its place, but it must be viewed as a combination of *summative*, diagnostic and *formative* procedures that form a picture of achievement, identify areas of weakness and highlight future direction (Hurst, 1997). To assess quality and the merits of early year's provision, accurately evaluating the benefits of rich early childhood experiences, a far wider lens is required. Children's deeper thinking (e.g. looking for patterns, finding strategies and designing their own actions) must be recognised and celebrated within opportunities to embed these skills during the years preceding school – opportunities that must be followed through into Key Stage 1 if we are to continue to offer children effective practice and aid their transitions (Tickell, 2011).

REFLECTION

In order to decide the timing, content and purpose of assessment, decisions must be made on which attributes of the child should be measured. As a practitioner, what do you think are reasonable assessments to make of a child in their early years? How can this demonstrate quantifiable progress for all children?

The cumulative experiences gained during these formative years is vast, the impact of which resonates further into the future than any form of baseline testing can hope to quantify. Every new experience encountered during the years to come will sit on top of those that have come before, continuously guided and shaped by them. Therefore any attempts at judging the early years' experience must be done so with deep knowledge and understanding of that which is being viewed, including how it nurtures and holistically promotes the features of learning, such as the development of self-esteem, emotional well-being, confidence and motivation of children in ways that will form the bedrock for later success.

REFLECTION

As a practitioner, how can you ensure that you are safeguarding against the effects of children's differing backgrounds and experiences, 'late bloomers' or simply an 'off day' adversely affecting the child for what could be many years to come?

If standardised testing remains as a measure of children's progress, how can you as a practitioner ensure that it captures the areas of real importance and demonstrates all abilities of the children in your care?

Inspection

Pursuit of quality whilst grappling with the seemingly uncomplimentary demands of regulation and legislation within everyday practice generates much strain within the profession. With tensions intensified by the perceived expectations of parents, demands of management and, more importantly to many, inspections, behaviours of practitioners will be influenced not just by how they are judged but also by how they believe they are being judged (Munro, 2011), with the direct and indirect influence of these key stakeholders standing to greatly affect day-to-day practice. With inspection outcomes influencing where children are placed, these realities inevitably influence and direct the priorities of settings and therefore the foundations that children are receiving in their early years. Whilst regulating for consistent quality within the early years is essential to driving practice forward, it must be based on a deep understanding of the sector equipped to capture that which is important. Inspectors must instil trust from the profession by possessing the knowledge and experience to identify and evaluate quality in its varied presentations by focusing on the actions and dispositions of the children.

REFLECTION

Needing to account for the quality of care delivered in settings will always be a reality – how could you ensure that it is focused on the areas of your practice that you consider important?

Despite the push for higher qualifications in a sector increasingly looking to the professionalism of its staff to raise quality of practice (DfE and Gyimah, 2015), confidences are lacking, with practitioners openly acknowledging limited understanding for the possibilities of developing early literacy and numeracy through play-based, experiential approaches. Rather than developing the enduring features of Lifelong Learning, processes and rote practices can become the primary feature (Miller, 2010). Adaptable frameworks permitting diverse experiences that embrace the learning features of all children within child-centred processes must be used skilfully by practitioners and recognised by an inspectorate with the skills to consistently guide settings towards improved practice, including those previously judged as good or outstanding if a culture of complacency is to be avoided. Without these skills in its inspectors we are in danger of focusing on indirect measures of performance that overlook key features, and this essential time in a child's life of implanting and embedding the roots essential to healthy growth in the future will be squandered.

CHAPTER SUMMARY

This chapter has considered both the historical implications of school readiness and the current legislation that frames our early years, inviting debate around the demands these place upon settings. It has explored the potential detriment of allowing formal testing and snapshot inspections to affect the long-term success of our children.

This chapter has proposed that, in order to judge the success of school readiness, we must look beyond the immediate performance abilities of individual children as they begin school and consider instead the longer-term holistic successes of children as they progress through primary school and beyond with the abilities and characteristics required to succeed.

Ten Key Concepts

1. To set children on the right path for life we must start with the right level of understanding in the early years. (Nutbrown, 2012)
2. We must make sure that our focus in the early years is based on children's needs rather than any adult driven agendas. (Noel and Lord, 2014)
3. As focus and investment in the early years grows, the importance of quality, play-based experiences becomes more pronounced. (Allen, 2011)
4. Links with families and the development of effective home learning environments are key. (Sylva et al., 2014)
5. Children's early preparations must be for a lifetime of learning, not simply the first day of school. (Whitbread and Bingham, 2012)
6. The early years must be recognised as laying the foundations required, determining how strong all future learning can be. (Sylva et al., 2014)
7. Careful consideration must be given to the use of formal testing at an early age if we are to avoid over-emphasis on testable qualities and lose the potential of open-ended thoughtful learning and deep thinking. (Claxton, 2008b)
8. Focus must be centred on rich experiences that will provide the foundations of future learning. (Tickell, 2011)

9 Experiences are more important in every way than known facts or achieved skills. (Samuelsson and Carlsson, 2008)

10 Allow inspections to recognise and celebrate good practice rather than becoming the driver or perceived determinant of it. (Munro, 2011)

IDEAS FOR PRACTICE

Practical Project

Carry out a set of practice observations with the focus of identifying common, consistent approaches and routines that are being used with the children in the setting.

Future Activities

For each of these common practices consider how these develop the long-term learning needs of the children. This may require you to reflect on the purpose or style of some and adapt them in light of what you have learnt through this chapter.

Work-based Tasks

Design a leaflet or blog to be accessible to all parents and staff that identifies the key practices being used and their long-term benefits, linking these to the developmental needs of children.

FURTHER READING

http://www.younglives.org.uk/publications/WP/early-childhood-transitions-research/bvlf-ecd-wp48-vogler-early-childhood-transitions

A look at the effects of key vertical and horizontal transitions within early childhood. Part of the National Strategies Every Child A Talker (ECAT) range of materials, this booklet aims to support the work of Early Language consultants and Early Language lead practitioners by sharing examples of practice.

Merrell, C. and Tymms, P. (2007) 'What children know and can do when they start school and how this varies between countries', *Journal of Early Childhood Research*, 5 (2).

This study based in Scotland looked at the apparent abilities of children starting school following baseline testing, compared with those of other countries. The results are reflected on through the effect of early years provision and the limitations of baseline testing.

(Continued)

(Continued)

Read, J. (2015) 'Transformation and regulation: a century of continuity in nursery school and welfare policy rhetoric', *Journal of Education Policy*, 30 (1): 39–61.

A fascinating account of the ideals and beliefs fuelling nursery provision over the last century, reflections of which are recognised but not necessarily appreciated within today's agendas.

3

ENSURING THE BEST START IN LIFE

THIS CHAPTER WILL

- look at the effect of children's early experiences on their future development
- look at the effect of transitions on children and consider the impact of quality care on their well-being
- offer practitioners practical advice on delivering quality practices
- suggest a new way of thinking that considers not being 'school ready' but being a Lifelong Learner.

Given the enduring effects of early experiences on children's lives it is essential that questions are asked regarding the nature and long-term effectiveness of provision offered, mindful of the lenses that responses are viewed through, if we are to ensure the holistic needs of childhood are safeguarded. To this end this chapter explores not simply what is required to prepare children for their first day of school, but also that which will nurture and promote the features of Lifelong Learning. This begins by understanding the intrinsic and behavioural qualities that enable enduring approaches to thinking and learning and recognising how the foundations of these are set securely in the experiences afforded within the early years.

Early intervention

To offer enriched, enduring experiences to children we must take into account the holistic nature of their need for care and long-term nurturing. Children are more than the sum of their skills and it is a keen attention to this 'more' that allows us to look at interactions and planned pursuits in refreshing and productive ways. Foundations laid throughout children's early life have staggering direct effects on their future development (Sylva et al., 2014), but they also fundamentally establish how children respond to experiences, opportunities and situations yet to come. Positive effects on long-term outcomes will likely be derailed if this time is not nurtured and valued. Recent moves encouraging schools to offer provision for younger children have included publication of the 'Two year olds in schools baseline survey' (www.gov.uk/government/uploads/system/uploads/attachment_data/file/307281/RR348_-_Two_year_olds_in_schools_baseline_survey.pdf) and Ofsted-led debates regarding judgments based on the extent settings 'prepare children for school' (Ofsted 2014a). With formal testing at ever younger ages it is vital that focus be drawn to essential early childhood experiences, supported by investment into children's futures where it is most effective.

It is imperative that children are afforded quality experiences from birth underpinned by an understanding of their needs within nurturing and supportive places of safety. Unfortunately not all children are lucky enough to experience this. Opportunities and influences during this time are massively diverse, affecting the nature of abilities attained and determining dispositions towards learning. Economic disadvantage and social isolation with their effect on parenting and interactions result in poor cognitive and social development with substantial effect on children's language acquisition, self-regulation, behaviour and confidence (Dearing et al., 2006). As these factors go on to affect children's readiness for formal classrooms and ultimately their success within it, inequalities must be addressed and trajectories reset at the earliest possible opportunity. In order to effectively close an attainment gap one must begin where the gap starts forming with an early years steeped in supportive, evidence-based practice, where the experiences and observations of well-informed, experienced early years professionals and supporting multi-professionals are valued.

Foundations are laid in such profoundly enduring ways during the early years that attempts to tackle problems displayed later on invariably fail. Government-commissioned reviews independently looking into the effectiveness of early intervention demonstrate that preventative measures within early childhood far out-perform reactive attempts (Field, 2010; Allen, 2011; Tickell, 2011) and strengthen the case for an early years steeped in professionalism and high esteem, underpinned by strong developmental knowledge of children.

REFLECTION

What do you consider to be the most effective involvement you have during children's early years?

Importance of quality in the early years

The impact of quality experiences on a child's life chances and ultimate achievements wherever they occur are the most significant influence to children's life-long prospects (Sylva et al., 2014). If children are to realise their full potential, positive trajectories must be followed from birth. Where this occurs in the home, parents must be well informed and supported to ensure that their seemingly *insignificant practices* are appreciated and utilised, which greatly impact the development of their child. Where this occurs outside the home (family care, nursery, preschool or childminders), good quality care has the potential to provide children even in difficult circumstances with an intervention that could redirect otherwise negative trajectories.

Qualifications and ongoing support are intrinsic to the quality of early years provision, informing delivery of holistic care, education and social development, particularly when held by those leading practice (Nutbrown, 2012). But this in itself is not enough to determine quality. Quality comes from the daily experiences afforded to children and the style in which they are delivered.

SUGGESTIONS FOR EVERYDAY GOOD PRACTICE

Promote enquiry: provide children with free access to environments encompassing natural materials and open manipulation of resources.

Promote investigation: invite exploration, wonder and enquiry with measured risks and challenges as commonplace.

Engage: ensure that all children's interactions are consistently and effectively promoted, observing where pondering has become disengagement.

Sympathetic to needs: ensure that children are given continual opportunity for total emersion in their own enquiries. Routines must support children, not restrict or derail their play.

Knowledgeable: comprehensive understanding must underpin learning and development, sensitively promoting pace and depth that is both challenging and rewarding.

Emotionally available: freely interact within warm, collaborative relationships that confidently offer the care and nurturing required.

As early years settings respond to government initiatives offering extended child-care of 30 free hours to increasingly younger children (HM Government, 2016), the need to focus on the nature of this care becomes more pronounced. Formative, quality experiences can have great impact on children's self-esteem, attitudes and behaviours determining everything from socio-emotional outcomes to vocabulary (Baker et al., 2008), mathematics and reading (Sylva et al., 2014; Melhuish, 2003; Melhuish, 2004a, 2004b). As children within quality early years provision access experiences and opportunities they may otherwise have been denied, they are provided with a better introduction to the dispositions of Lifelong Learning. Alternatively, within poor quality provision of little substance children's social and development behaviours will suffer (Tickell, 2011). A criminal waste of opportunity, this sees precious and unrepeatable formative years squandered at a time when *windows of developmental opportunity* are closing and children are less able to direct their own opportunities. Whichever path is taken, the purpose and impact of the early years must be valued and viewed very clearly as it fundamentally sets the scene for future learning.

Preparing to transition to 'big school'

An important part of the process of a child preparing for 'big school' is the prospect of facing another transition. Through changing work and social circumstances, children often begin school having experienced many transitions; *horizontal transitions* between environments and *vertical transitions* as they progress between rooms and settings. Whilst forming a very real part of growing up and worthy of celebration, transitional experiences are fundamentally linked to a child's well-being. Informing attitudes and emotions towards their new start requires appropriate respect, sensitive handling and the right kinds of preparation to meet the needs of the child, especially where there are additional considerations. If previously not handled well, careful, sensitive nurturing will be required in preparation for the move to school.

REFLECTION

How could you ensure that all your transitioning procedures are designed around the needs of the child rather than the needs of your setting or the parents?

Transition to reception should be eased through the continuing early years curriculum blending learning through play and playful learning. However, experiences of reception can be very different from that of preschool. Regardless of where children are transitioning from this will involve different relationships, roles and identities as children learn to relate to new staff. As new learning styles are embraced, unfamiliar demands, customs and expectations of new environments must be learnt. The more opportunity children have to form strong attachments, the more transferable skills will have developed and the easier this transition is likely to be. Parental attitudes to preparation will vary from downplaying to visibly excited, although contrasting views regarding the purpose of play-based preschools to that of learning and teaching school environments is usually very clear and must be born in mind.

Children afforded appropriate early years experiences will be ready and eager to embrace the social and emotional challenges they are about to face and formal learning can be embraced. If instead preparations have focused on attaining prescribed levels, learning pre-determined actions or performing specific skills, children find themselves with a difficult challenge, unprepared to navigate this alien environment.

REFLECTION

How do you think schools can ensure that they are aware of the diversity of the children joining them and develop individualised approaches as the school becomes 'child ready'?

During transition children experience many emotions, anticipations and anxieties that must be managed sensitively. Fuelled in part by parental expectations, practitioners must be aware of cultural issues, equity, social justice and the rights of the child. Handled appropriately these have the potential to aid relationship-building through a shared sense of experience. With new layers of family, home, school, community and the wider society adding to children's experiences, each with their different demands and expectations informing the expectations of the next, we can see how difficult this time could be. Ineffective handling can lead to feelings of isolation, affecting the expectations and feelings towards their new school. In a system where success at each level depends greatly on the achievements of the last, children must be given every opportunity to make the smoothest transition into formal schooling to enable the most industrious start.

REFLECTION

What impressions do you give to children of what school and future learning will be like?

Quality experiences

Whether solving a problem or following an enquiry, freedom of experimentation and repetition interspersed with periods of reflection must be offered within a play-based environment. Self-motivating and intrinsically rewarding children will promote inventiveness, ingenuity and enthusiasm. The acquisition of specific knowledge will naturally be gained during the process, but in ways meaningful to the child. With no single right answer, processes accessed through play are adaptable by the children and powerfully driven through their interests, abilities and the tangents their minds seek to follow.

Katz (2010) suggests that for such practices to be an effective approach to learning they must focus on the equal and simultaneous delivery of four goals: to develop children's knowledge and understanding; to develop achievements of key skills; to foster specific dispositions; and to promote positive feelings within children (Katz, 2010 in Smidt, 2010: 5). However, due to assessment-driven focus on the product of the school-ready child, these practices tend not to be delivered as Katz recommended, either in their balance or areas of focus. Whilst the demonstration of discrete practices such as cutting, drawing, counting or problem solving do display measurable skills, knowledge and understanding tend to have a surface-level focus of naming rather than understanding underlying concepts, customs or constructions. And the long-term building of character-forming dispositions, referred by Katz (2010) as 'Habits of mind', and feelings of self-esteem or confidence are largely overlooked.

The EYFS in England aimed to raise standards and improve access to positive experiences for all children, in all types of provision by simultaneously addressing welfare, learning and development requirements and acknowledging children's sense of security whilst aiming to develop positive attitudes to learning. The role of play in early learning is recognised, emphasising experiences and opportunities within a learner-centred curriculum; there is even a focus on the characteristics of effective learning. However, with an emphasis on 17 prescribed early learning goals to be assessed, measured and used to inform the baselines of the receiving primary school, good intentions of these learning characteristics of engagement, motivation and thinking can become overlooked, undervalued or misunderstood. This balance needs to be redressed. See Table 2.1 for comparisons with Scottish, Welsh and Northern Ireland curricula.

Early Learning Goals within the EYFS

The seven interconnected areas of learning and development shaping the EYFS are intended to be of equal importance. The three prime areas are the expected focus for the youngest children, forming the basis of future learning. Then as abilities within these grow, a more equal balance across all seven areas is intended for children to develop and learn effectively. The 17 Early Learning Goals (such as listening and attention, moving and handling) can be found within these seven areas of learning as set out in Table 3.1.

Table 3.1 Statutory framework for the EYFS (DfE, 2014)

	The prime areas		
Communication and language	Listening and attention	Understanding	Speaking
Physical development	Moving and handling	Health and self-care	
Personal, social and emotional development	Self-confidence and self-awareness	Managing feelings and behaviour	Making relationships
	The specific areas		
Literacy	Reading	Writing	
Mathematics	Numbers	Shape, space and measures	
Understanding the world	People and communities	The world	Technology
Expressive arts and design	Exploring and using media and materials	Being imaginative	

The features of a Lifelong Learner

So a monumental journey is travelled by a child during these few short years as neural pathways driven by every experience offered to these young developing minds are laid down. Structures deep inside the brain are forming and reinforcing, determining how children will see and interact with their world, the relationships they will make and the ways they will grasp or bypass every opportunity presented. Bodies are growing, core muscles are developing and systems of balance and *proprioception* are fine-tuning as children become acutely aware of the world and their place within it, hopefully as nurtured, valued and loved individuals.

With these years acting as precursor to more rigid and prescribed formal schooling, responses to learning experiences formed during this time are clearly fundamental to successful transitions, enjoyment and later achievements, demonstrating the overwhelming responsibilities of any individual privileged enough to share this journey or effect the planning of it. We must not become driven by the grasping of testable skills or discrete items of knowledge – far more important are the underlying attitudes, characteristics and dispositions that are forming. Once these are established and secure and being routinely and instinctively demonstrated, all other learning will naturally follow. Rather than creating children with some arbitrarily defined label of 'school ready' earned by the sum of discrete skills demonstrated on demand, we will instead have established within children the foundations, dispositions and values required to become Lifelong Learners.

The Lifelong Learner

Through informed and effective learning experiences, children can develop the underlying attitudes, characteristics and dispositions of the Lifelong Learner that will permit and promote deep-level learning in any encountered situation. Encompassing intrinsic attributes, behavioural traits, ways of thinking and approaches to understanding new experiences, the features present within the Lifelong Learner as represented in Figure 3.1 provide familiar and effective approaches to learning. Enhanced through permitted, repeated experiences and practiced techniques, these holistic features are readily adapted to any given situation – features so strong that their successful attainment continues to benefit throughout adult life as is demonstrated in Table 3.2.

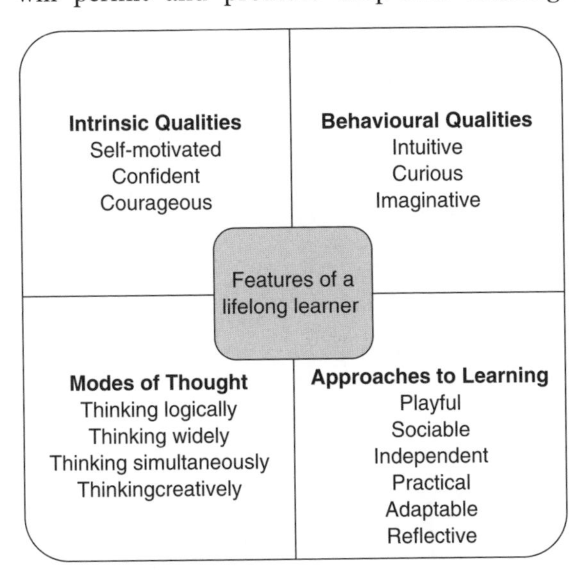

Figure 3.1 Features of a Lifelong Learner

Table 3.2 The features of the Lifelong Learner as reflected in the child and the adult

Intrinsic qualities	Reflected in adult life
Courageous Comfortable to be uncertain in complex situations, they will have experienced pleasurably intrinsic rewards of pushing perceived limits and stretching abilities, mentally and physically, to safely achieve goals. Not afraid to take measured risks, they are keen to seek challenges and eager to test boundaries rather than being content to remain within comfortable familiarity.	***Courageous*** Courageous adults are life's go-getters, unlikely to become stuck in a job or relationship that is unfulfilling, too scared to make the move. Not put off by fear of the unknown or feelings of personal inadequacy, they are ambitious and keen to get the most out of life through work and personal endeavours.
Self-motivated Self-motivated children display enthusiasm and self-esteem born from experiencing satisfying, rewarding proficiency that comes from persistence with tasks. Keen to embrace challenges for their own gratification, unperturbed by the absence of praise or reward, they will persist with tasks for the time required to succeed through various approaches untroubled by initial setbacks, mistakes or distractions. Unhampered by fear of failure, resilience and sense of investment will see them value the extra effort required to achieve.	***Self-motivated*** Pursuit of long-term goals such as academic qualifications, promotion, or when mastery is gradual such as learning to drive, martial arts or playing a musical instrument requires self-motivation to persist through delayed gratification, un-reliant on external praise or recognition even when setbacks or difficulties arise.
Confident Confident children develop self-assurance in the belief of their endeavours and appreciation for their developing abilities and qualities. This competent self-esteem originates from feelings of security and emotional well-being that allows them to embrace challenge, happy to request assistance when they require it.	***Confident*** Confident adults have self-belief that allows them to strive for what they want and succeed with it. Without appearing conceited they are assured of their own worth with the practiced confidence to demonstrate this to others, able to seek the support and guidance required to develop into a complete all-rounder.

Behavioural qualities	Reflected in adult life
Behavioural qualities	***Behavioural qualities***
Imaginative	***Imaginative***
Able to initiate activities, or new directions within them, imaginative children inquisitively try new approaches just to see what will happen, able to mentally rehearse situations in order to explore their possibilities, uncovering new potential along the way as their proficiency develops. Not unnecessarily tethered to perceived or expected outcomes, they use their inventiveness and ingenuity to approach situations from new directions.	In a rapidly changing world it is imaginative adults that are able to embrace the challenges this brings. Without the need to follow well-trodden paths they can look at problems in new and exciting ways. With the ability to mentally process ideas, they can run through multiple scenarios before selecting the right one. With good imagination they are less likely to become bored with a world of new possibilities open to them.
Intuitive	***Intuitive***
Informed by all previous practical experiences, intuitive children are able to make logical judgements and reasoned predictions given new situations or sets of resources with a level of understanding to begin further enquiries and predict potential outcomes with a starting place to test those predictions.	When we encounter problems in adult life they are rarely exactly the same as problems we have encountered before, or provide all the information we would like. Intuitive adults can take the information given and together with previous experiences use instinct to draw conclusions without needing immediate proof. These are skills used by doctors during diagnosis or police officers understanding a crime scene.
Curious	***Curious***
Seeking out opportunities to indulge a wonderment about objects, events and people, children with curiosity will be fascinated, wanting to go deeper in their understanding, enthusiastically questioning that which is presented. With an appetite for knowledge and an insatiably enquiring mind, they probe with healthy scepticism, driven to investigate, experiment and play with ideas.	Curious adults are not content to take things at face value, wanting to know more, to really understand how a thing operates. It is curious adults that will invent new solutions to future problems and succeed in academic study; medical researchers, designers of new technologies, innovative architects and anyone seeking refreshingly new solutions will require a curious nature.

(Continued)

Table 3.2 (Continued)

Approaches to learning	Reflected in adult life
Approaches to learning	***Approaches to learning***
Playful	***Playful***
Able to approach problems and situations in a playful way, children use past experiences and observations of others to trial ideas within safe environments as they play, able to experiment and rehearse without commitment, experiencing complete emersion in satisfying learning experiences, independently and with others.	As an important source of relaxation and stimulation, being playful has the ability to enhance creativity and fuel imagination as well as having positive effects on emotional well-being. Playing around with ideas in unstructured, creative ways enhances problem-solving abilities, allowing new ideas to emerge. Unafraid of getting something wrong, variations can be trialled and experimented without commitment when the focus of experience is play, not accomplishing preconceived goals.
Sociable	***Sociable***
With the ability to interact and engage in active learning with others, sociable children balance a level of diplomacy, self-promotion, assertion and self-regulation, allowing them to benefit from collaborative and cooperative learning within group dynamics. Utilising emerging acquisition of language and the social nature of learning, they communicate and share ideas with others for feedback, promoting new ideas and taking on others' perspectives with empathy and understanding.	Being able to interact and engage well with individuals, exchanging ideas and communicating through multiple means leads to the friendships and mutually beneficial relationships essential to adult life. The ability to convey ideas or points of view whilst listening and taking on board that of others are invaluable skills necessary to effective working with others, benefiting from collective knowledge and skills. Adult life will invariably involve interacting with people, working within teams and communicating ideas; understanding how to interact with others is key to good personal and career relations.
Independence	***Independence***
When understanding has been the result of their own discoveries the learning is significantly more powerful and able to drive the next discovery with an autonomous self-motivation. Through this ease within their own abilities and sense of mind, independent learners become aware of the power of their own thoughts, ideas and opinions and will not have a reliance on following others within a group, instead taking responsibility for their own endeavours.	In order to achieve success there are times that we need to be self-reliant. Whether it is finishing an assignment, a project at work or one within the home, adults need to draw on personal qualities to know the direction to take. Fuelled by previous feelings of satisfaction from having completed a personal endeavour, and with the qualities to determine their own progression and access what they need, the motivation and capabilities to succeed are secured within themselves.

Approaches to learning	Reflected in adult life
Practical	***Practical***
Through many practical experiences where they have played with concepts such as trial and improvement and cause and effect, practical learners will have ideas on how to approach a problem. They are able to mentally plan and reactively adjust their thinking as they encounter unforeseen difficulties, unafraid to change direction, appreciating successes, even when the end result is different from the original objective.	When contemplating how to approach a situation, previously gathered information is invaluable. The experiences of a practical adult will supply a real-world dimension to this. When looking at a ton of soil that needs moving they will know the effort, time and resources required and realise how dark clouds overhead may need to adapt the approach. When considering catering for a party of 20 they will have some idea of how and where to start, even if informed the night before that a vegan is amongst the guest list. Through previous hands-on experiences the practical adult will be well equipped to proceed with any new endeavour.
Adaptable	***Adaptable***
Having experienced possibilities arising from being open-minded to a situation and the successes that come from open-ended, evolving approaches, adaptable children are not overly concerned with rigid precision where specific end products are not the main goal. Instead they are able to remain flexible in their approach, reacting to circumstances and resources, evolving their ideas as needed.	Adaptable adults are flexible as things change, open to new people, ideas and concepts; they can work independently or as part of a team, able to carry out multiple tasks, projects or assignments, setting priorities and adapting to changing conditions as they arise. Adults who are experienced in adapting their thinking and embracing an evolving approach are able to take developments in their stride and arrive at an end point that has benefited from the diversities of the journey.
Reflective	***Reflective***
Following an experience, reflective children will consider what has happened and consider alternative approaches when repeating the experience without losing confidence or even being aware that this process is taking place. Able to hold a thought, an idea or an unsolved challenge in their head, they can ponder a problem then come back to it to trial a different approach.	Reflective adults are able to naturally and instinctively look back and assess prior actions and thoughts, using them to inform personal learning and self-development. By allowing this process to inform future understanding, they gain insights from past endeavours that can be used to inform and improve current and future actions.

(Continued)

Table 3.2 (Continued)

Ability to ...	Reflected in adult life
Ability to ...	***Ability to ...***
Think simultaneously	***Think simultaneously***
Intuitively gaining and processing information from multiple sources, not limiting experiences to what their eyes are telling them, children are able to simultaneously process information from a variety of sources, using their *peripheries* while focusing on specific detail as required.	When dealing with many issues in adult life we need to process information from a variety of sources to fully understand the situation. Only by combining what we see, hear and feel together with what our previous experiences intuitively adds can we fully assess the issues involved.
Think creatively	***Think creatively***
Able to look at things in fresh and unique ways, creative thinkers embrace new ideas knowing how to ask questions, have ideas and seek their own answers. They are able to react in innovative ways even when limited information is given or an unexpected situation arises.	Within adult life, personal and work events will often necessitate the need to think creatively. The ability to 'think outside the box' in new and refreshing ways when combined with qualities of curiosity and imagination allows new opportunities to become possible in a constantly changing world. Not put off by setbacks or changing circumstances, creative thinkers can find innovative ways around potential obstacles, producing new creative solutions.
Think Logically	***Think Logically***
Able to find the familiar within unknown situations, logical thinkers can see patterns and notice commonalities with previous experiences, constructing links within their own understanding. Given a new problem or an unfamiliar set of circumstances, they are able to draw on methods of sequencing, grouping and categorisation within what they already know to direct them towards a common ground.	Coming into unknown situations, adults with the ability to think logically can rationalise information presented, noticing or extracting understanding and forming logical conclusions based on previous experiences or trusted sequential steps. They are able to consider the realities of a situation as well as being able to explain observed events through concepts such as probability and chance. Looking at any number of potential solutions to a problem they can test the merit of each, using any negative results to inform and arrive at a preferred course of action.
Think widely	***Think widely***
Unafraid of mistakes, children able to think widely, are happy to embrace open-ended activities and resources, evaluating and considering the potential of all the opportunities on offer. With an investigative nature they are keen to explore without needing to be told what to do, or made uncomfortable when there is a lack of adult direction. They are comfortable in trying new directions and think laterally rather than jump to conclusions or preconceived end results.	The ability to think widely is utilised in adult life whenever we need to consider a number of different variables or employ a number of different techniques. By not limiting our approach or our actions many possibilities become available to us and biased views can be avoided.

CHAPTER SUMMARY

By reflecting on transitional childhood experiences and the potential impact of the adults within them, this chapter has considered what it means to offer children the best start in life, not just for starting school but as preparation for all the years to come.

This chapter suggests that young children must be seen as more than school children in waiting and instead recognise them as the Lifelong Learners they are. It suggests that by offering the experiences and opportunities to develop fundamental qualities, approaches to learning and ways of thinking, children can be given the best opportunity to succeed not just in their academic journeys but throughout life.

Ten Key Concepts

1 Children are so much more than the sum of their skills. (Bruce, 2011b)

2 Children's early experiences have a staggering effect on both their future development as well as the ways in which they will respond to experiences, opportunities and situations yet to come. (Tickell, 2011)

3 Enriched and informed experiences within early childhood delivered by those with a strong developmental knowledge of children do more to effect the life trajectories of children than any measure of reactionary actions later on. (Field, 2010)

4 Quality-sensitive experiences are imperative in developing children's future life chances, whether these come from the home or another setting. (Sylva et al., 2014)

5 A successful transition to school will hinge upon previous experiences of transitions and will be supported by the attachments the child has in place. (Fisher, 2011)

6 Preparations for school must not be limited to short-term, discrete skills but look to develop a foundation for all future learning. (Biggs, 1996)

7 Intrinsic qualities must be nurtured and developed within children to enable them to become confident, courageous and self-motivated learners. (Wong, 2008)

8 We must support children's imaginations through their naturally intuitive and curious behaviours. (Hurst, 1997)

9 Children's approaches to learning must be developed and extended through a range of experiences that allow them to be playful, social, independent, practical, adaptive and reflective. (Oers and Hännikäinen, 2001)

(Continued)

(Continued)

10 Through solving their own problems and driving their own investigations, children must be given the opportunity to develop their approaches to thinking logically and creatively whilst simultaneously considering wide-ranging variables. (Faust, 2010)

IDEAS FOR PRACTICE

Practical Project

Consider the characteristics of a Lifelong Learner and identify examples within your practice where you actively nurture these.

Future Activities

With a focus on the characteristics of the Lifelong Learner, ask your parents which of these features they would choose for their child to possess as an adult.

Work-based Tasks

Establish methods of delivery within your practice to enable these characteristics to flourish. Then, whilst being mindful of improvements you may put in place in Chapter 4, communicate these to your parents.

FURTHER READING

Department for Education and Standards and Testing Agency (2014) *Early Years Foundation Stage Profile: Exemplification Materials*. London: DfES. Available at www.gov.uk/government/publications/eyfs-profile-exemplication-materials (accessed 22/6/16).

A series of materials that practitioners are expected to use to demonstrate whether a child is developing as expected throughout the EYFS early learning goals.

Krogh, S.L. and Morehouse, P. (2014) *The Early Childhood Curriculum: Inquiry Learning Through Integration*, 2nd edn. London: Routledge.

Fully referenced with current research and early childhood theory, this book considers the advantages of integrating inquiry-based learning into curricula for children in primary as well as early years. Through holistic methods of delivery it suggests that academic standards can be exceeded once the skills are in place to move beyond following stipulated curricula.

Smidt, S. (Ed.) (2010) *Key Issues in Early Years Education*. London: Routledge.
This book offers chapters from a range of voices as it explores the concept of seeing the child as central to learning and development.

Whitbread, D. and Bingham, S. (2012) *School Readiness: A Critical Review of Perspectives and Evidence*. London: TACTYC Association for the Professional Development of Early Years Educators.
This article looks at what it means to be school ready and the dangers of concentrating on the wrong skills.

4

HOW CHILDREN LEARN

THIS CHAPTER WILL

- supply a theoretical basis for how children gain dispositions for a lifetime of learning
- look at the development of children's neurology during the early years and the importance of experiential learning
- consider the need for social interactions and effective environments within quality early experiences.

If we are to prepare children for meeting all the demands of their future we need to understand how children learn, where and when this process takes place and how we can best facilitate these processes for all children. By understanding the unique nature of children's individual learning journeys and the importance of social interactions, this chapter will consider the environments essential to developing children within their early learning and the mindsets that need to operate within them.

Acquiring the features needed for Lifelong Learning

The process of learning is far more complex and important than simply bestowing information; concepts need to be understood, rather than discrete facts to be simply known. The ability to learn, a skill like any other, needs capturing as early as possible and rehearsing throughout a life spent in an ever challenging and adapting world, something children instinctively practice from the moment they are born.

A multifaceted process, learning is a highly personal affair combining cognitive, linguistic, perceptual and motor skills in a multitude of formal and informal ways as children combine newly acquired and continuously perfecting skills to arrive at answers meaningful to them. Developing from before birth, abilities are built up over time in *hierarchical* and *cyclical* ways as children revisit, adapt, improve and perfect their skills as the dispositions for and attitudes towards all future learning are established.

Within powerful learners, key dispositions will have been formed during previous experiences of learning. Reflected on in the *characteristics of effective learning*

(DfE, 2014), these have been termed 'habits of mind' by Katz (2010). These dispositions or features of the Lifelong Learner must be identified, celebrated, protected and strengthened throughout children's early development through opportunities offering more than prescribed delivery so that they may reside in all children. Nurturing and developing appropriate opportunities through self-motivated, diverse, accessible, practical experiences and real-life problem-solving activities explored through their own timescales during early childhood prepares our children for school and a lifetime of enjoyable, successful learning more than any amount of formal testing, numeracy or literacy development could do.

Understanding the importance of early brain development

The early years are a critical and highly sensitive period of development and rapid growth. This is nowhere more pronounced than within the infant brain. As we look to secure the most auspicious beginnings it is important that a basic understanding of how this incredible organ grows and develops is present in the minds of all who care for children during this highly sensitive period.

Experiences afforded to us during the early years are fundamental in forming the person we are destined to become: sensitive relationships offer attachments; the language surrounding us fine-tune our ability to hear the nuances of speech; and physical development stimulates the body and mind. As the roots of these core processes are laid down they are supported and underpinned by more executive functions of cognitive flexibility, working memory and inhibition ready for complex functions of problem solving, reasoning and planning to follow (Whitbread and Bingham, 2012). This is demonstrated by children's growing abilities to self-regulate, their ease of remaining flexible as situational demands fluctuate, and self-control, all of which will be crucial within the school environment and beyond (Diamond & Lee, 2011).

Clearly a great deal smaller than an adults, the brain of a new-born baby will already contain the majority of its brain cells along with a number of functioning processes essential to early survival. What is not yet present are the vast majority of connections or *synapses* between the cells that will map out the structure and workings of the developed brain. Ready to react and develop through the experiences afforded it, this largely unmapped structure allows for initial *plasticity*, enabling adaptation to environments and specific circumstances children find themselves confronted with. Of enormous benefit to the survival of the child, this also demonstrates the huge vulnerability of the infant and their dependence on the actions of those around them. During the early years sensitive windows of time for a number of processes close, long before children reach school age, as structure formed through the highly personal evolving banks of experiences and unique opportunities afforded to the child become locked into place during these irreplaceable years.

As active and independent thinkers, children do not learn all they need about their world through *rote delivery* and adult-led objectives, but through every experience afforded to them. Through personal choices and social contacts, their relationship with the world and other minds around them enhance as knowledge develops in highly personal ways, internally driven through emotional and intellectual motivations generated through experiences, relationships and contexts unique to that child.

During the first three years of life, 80 per cent of the basic architecture and social and emotional structures of the brain will be laid down for life (Allen, 2011) through experiences that were traditionally automatic; everyday routines, walks to the shops, play with older siblings and family friends, and intimate times of cuddles and play full of rich, sensory experiences unconcerned with learning goals or downward pressures to succeed. With connections increasing in number from around 10 trillion to around 200 trillion at three years of age (Katz, 2010), acquiring this volume of brain growth is a massive undertaking, yet children are born with the motivations to grasp all opportunities for learning.

The process of establishing and mapping out these connections can be likened to a stroll through a field of corn: as we take that first unmapped walk through the untrodden growth, we etch out our unique path. Whilst the path is trodden and the corn flattened by our actions, this will have little effect if we never take the route again, as the corn will soon recover and it will be as though we never passed through. However, if this shortcut proves to be enjoyable or beneficial and we repeat it, the path we take will become more pronounced and defined until such time as its permanence no longer needs us to repeat our journey, because the formed path will always remain. Within the infant brain, every time an experience is had the synapses fire, making the connections in the brain stronger and more permanent, which demonstrates the need for children to access and repeat the experiences they need within their own timeframes. As areas processing the senses rapidly develop, every sight, smell, taste, sound and touch causes the synapses to fire and so the process of adding growth, of constructing and fine-tuning this amazing organ will continue.

The quality of the relationships and the attachment that develops between a baby and their carer in these early months are significantly linked to the child's social skills, *self-efficacy*, behaviour, and mental and physical health, and by extension their future learning and educational attainment (DfE and DH, 2011), not just as they prepare for transition to formal schooling but throughout the rest of their life. If early relationship experiences have not been positive, this will negatively influence how future events are responded to, determining the child's ability to empathise with others. This in turn will deeply affect the quality of experience for not just that child but all those within the school classroom.

As neuroscience confirms the importance of an emotional engagement in learning (Hall, 2005; Frith et al., 2011), we can clearly see the need for children to learn in environments free from adverse stresses, such as pressures to conform or an imposed sense of failure. If instead children are provided with creative environments and tangible experiences, their intrinsic motivation, interest, confidence and self-regulation will be able to bloom as the diverse thinking and reflection required for symbolic and abstract thought has an opportunity to flourish.

To build stability, children's emotional needs must be tuned into from day one, ensuring that they feel cared for, valued and understood. Healthily attached babies who have grown with empathy and love, who have had appropriate and managed experiences of stress, will learn to regulate their emotions as they grow (Allen, 2011). With emotional, social and motivational domains emerging in early childhood and developing well in to primary, the importance of stimulation and interactions offered by primary care givers through these years and the support needed by rapidly adjusting families becomes clear.

REFLECTION

How can the profession help to support families facing all the challenges of raising children during their early years?

The unique and highly personal way children view the world must be understood and respected if we are to facilitate their learning in ways they can relate and respond to. Only when we do this can we recognise and develop the deeper levels of cognitive, perceptual, linguistic and motor skills needed to aid children to grasp meaningful levels of understanding that goes beyond surface knowledge (Feinstein and Duckworth, 2006).

How to acquire meaningful experiences through play

To apply their learning in a range of situations, children need to develop concepts of knowledge acquisition from their earliest years through deep, first-hand, spontaneous experiences that offer opportunities to practice and rehearse both autonomously and in shared situations. The acquisition of knowledge and understanding also requires perseverance, curiosity and the ability to think in creative and logical ways. Luckily there is a multifaceted and immensely powerful mechanism for this that is intrinsically motivating, deeply rewarding and accessible to all children: play.

SOME OF THE MANY BENEFITS OF PLAY

- Through creative play children have the opportunity to trial new and unique experiences.
- Through whole-body physical movement children develop muscle recall, balance and *proprioception*.
- Through play involving real objects and materials comparisons can be drawn to that which is familiar, establishing links in thinking and using greater levels of purposeful, multidimensional vocabulary.

(Continued)

(Continued)

- Water, sand or mud kitchen play explores cause and effect, establishing relationships between actions and consequences.
- Using generalised symbols within their play, ideas are represented and relationships between language and symbol are formed.
- Experimentation, trial and error, inventiveness and risk-taking where there is no wrong answer establishes resilience, persistence and curiosity within safe boundaries.
- Misconceptions are demonstrated, enabling responses to be tactfully guided.
- Through age-appropriate and tempting play children are encouraged into new areas of knowledge and challenge.
- Opportunities to reflect on pertinent ideas, to think, consider, ponder and come back to as they need, offers children a way of autonomously and seamlessly experimenting with ideas before committing them as fact.

Play, when taking full advantage of interlocking supported environments both inside and out, is young children's most powerful mechanism for understanding the world (Rinaldi, 2005), allowing children to 'try the world on for size', manipulating ideas through hypothetical 'as if' or 'what if it were' (Guha, 1994) scenarios, thereby developing highly personal understandings in order to make sense of the world and work out their responses. So powerful that when it is overlooked children will automatically inject it, engaging a common spirit through 'silly' or 'playful' words when set more constructed activities (Oers and Hännikäinen, 2001), seemingly not distinguishing between learning and play as both occur simultaneously, feeding off each other at all times. Requiring opportunities grounded in experiences of 'real life' relevance rather than artificial scenarios (Hurst, 1997), instruction woven through the context of playful activities (Wasik et al., 2011) ensures the purpose is clear (Faust, 2010) as play, unlike 'learning activities', is freely initiated by children regardless of potential limiting factors such as resources, time, language or other external demands.

REFLECTION

If playing and learning are so intrinsically linked, why do you think they become separated once children enter formal schooling?

Deep learning of a meaningful quality is highly personal and achieved by repeated explorations of ideas rather than through sequences of steps identical for every child (Bronfenbrenner, 2005). This cyclical or spiral process must be accessed as and when individual children need to, and this can only be known by them as they acquire the next piece of their learning puzzle. As young children gain understanding through their play they use this as building blocks for more sophisticated patterns of learning to follow. Through these playful experiences of improvisation, interaction and listening to one another, children relate to their surroundings, explore ideas and concepts and understand how the world works and their place within it.

Unlike surface knowledge, meaningful understanding of a process, its underlying concepts and how it relates to other experienced ideas requires opportunities to structure patterns within individual understanding (Feinstein and Duckworth, 2006). Take for example concepts of weight and mass: experiencing a jug of water weighing less as it empties provides ideas that can be applied to other materials, such as sand or feathers being transported and poured from different vessels. Playing with these principles allow children to apply new concepts to familiar situations, instilling deeper awareness that will in future allow them to know things without needing to experience it, skills that will inform visualisation and reflection. The importance of experiential learning within young children's pursuits, especially as the demands of more formal classrooms replace the early years environment more naturally drenched in play, must be recognised if this powerful learning medium and the deeper understanding available through it is not to be lost.

Social learning

An important feature of play is the opportunity for social interactions. As social learners children develop their thinking, extending what they know whilst supporting their sense of belonging and well-being through interactions and observations when afforded opportunities to connect with a diverse mix of people within relevant, contextual and interesting environments (Katz, 2010). Children's narratives and opportunities to express opinions, tell stories or share perspectives is dependent on these relationships. As contact with others within cooperative situations promotes an emotional togetherness within activities (Hicks, 1996), concepts are more clearly and deeply understood. Language-based narratives develop within imaginative discussions as individual memories become shared experiences (Samuelsson, 2004), promoting social behaviours and togetherness.

Children also need to experience situations and actions of others in a group with the opportunity to discuss and argue with their peers, exploring their own thinking and that of others (Johansson and Pramling Samuelsson, 2006) as they become aware of thinking as a process (Dunn, 1988). Even misunderstandings and eventual conflict are integral to building relationships and children must be allowed the freedom to explore them, practicing retaining control of a situation through altercations, understanding what it takes to develop friendships alongside exchanges of ideas (Broadhead, 2001). With motivational and emotional support, children need to learn to manage these situations and keep going despite them. This needs time and space without well-meaning adult interference, and encouragement through activities that develop self-confidence, independence and the ability to cooperate with others (Maynard and Waters, 2007).

REFLECTION

In your experience of working with children and families, how do you think children's gender or cultural backgrounds affect the personal choices that are encouraged for them, and how does this impact on the experiences they receive? How do you manage this within a preschool class of 30 children?

To realise and benefit from rich, social methods of learning, children need to arrive at school full of self-esteem, happy to explore, experiment and have a go, even when this means making mistakes. Positive experiences of these practices must therefore have been embodied throughout their childhood, and care must now be taken to not undervalued or overlook these with teachers' (or other adults' in the child's life) expectations or practices. Taking risks is a part of this process, and removing obstacles physically and mentally is grossly misguided. Children want and need suitably risky challenges to learn how to manage them and themselves, developing confidence, experiencing new learning paths and learning how to keep themselves safe (Moyles, 2010; Maynard and Waters, 2007), thus experiencing satisfactions of success and persisting through setbacks so that future challenges are embraced. Risk exposure involves careful judgement, balancing possible harms against potential benefit and outcomes and often uses social discussion and cooperation. This is easily managed through sensible assessments, taking realistic views of actual risks and benefits involved through risk–benefit analysis. Given opportunities, those most able to do this are the children involved – the only person to know how these variables relate to them. Children do not seek out risks they are not yet ready for, uninclined to put themselves in unnecessary or unmanageable danger. Trusted, they will stop climbing a tree when it feels too high or branches seem unstable, but only when given opportunities establish an inner perception of risk and ability.

REFLECTION

How risky is it to allow children of all ages to play together in the outside space? What have you seen to be the risks involved? How could these be managed?

Importance of child's use of language

Throughout our lives we express our meaning, reasoning and thinking in increasingly sophisticated ways, learning to appropriately give voice to feelings, vocalising ideas and experiences as we listen and respond to the thoughts and feelings of others through socially conforming reactions. Confident language abilities of competent speakers, even at two years old, offer strong indications of successful transition to school (Roulstone et al., 2011).

With research unsurprisingly demonstrating inevitable links between a child's level of communication and their relationships with others (Sommer, 2003), the inability to converse suggests social incompetences that may present as introverted or extroverted behaviours as feelings of frustration and potential isolation develop. Associated with lower rates of cooperation and conformity, disruption or disobedience within classrooms may follow as lower cognitive development scores become confused with lower ability (Sylva et al., 2004). If we imagine the experiences of these children facing the realities of the school classroom compared to the head-start experienced by confident speakers (Roulstone et al., 2011), the resulting outcomes and class dynamics are clear.

Determined more by limited communications within the home than social backgrounds and more pronounced in children whose first language, and therefore the language surrounding them from birth, is not English, inhibited communication and language affects many children. For future *social mobility* (Blanden, 2006) emerging from successful school experiences to be an achievable reality for all children, language and communication development must be a keen focus of early childhood.

REFLECTION

How can you support all children to participate and express their feelings in a class where there may be many children with different languages?

Staging an environment for play

If new learning is to be effectively experienced it needs to be motivated and owned by the learner, at levels achievable for their stage of development and embedded within the scope of previous experiences. Motivated to please themselves or others or to achieve an objective, the strongest motivations will always come from within the child but will be dependent on many variables – current interests, previous experiences and what happened that morning all play a role, so cannot be second guessed or planned well in advance. Instead children must be trusted with the freedoms to pursue their motivations, freely initiating and combining new experiences so that intellectual processes can be accessed, practiced and explored. With time to explore new insights and consolidate what they know, new ideas can incubate, persistence is encouraged and attentions become focused for prolonged periods of time as deeper understanding develops along with a love of the learning process.

Children given free choice are able to access the areas they need to make sense of, practicing and using multiple approaches. Permitting spontaneous exploration of activities promotes choice and imagination, creativity and the trying out of roles. Able to initiate and manipulate well-considered experiences offers opportunities to investigate and make decisions, persisting in ways needed to make sense of their world (Samuelsson and Carlsson, 2008). In order to simultaneously cater to these needs with multiple children requires well planned environments inside and out, preferably with free and instantaneous movement between them as independent thought is facilitated and gratified.

The quality environment

Boys and girls struggle in their own ways with cooperation, conformity, peer sociability and confidence. When opportunities are given to develop skills within appropriately encouraging environments, these issues need not embed future gender differences but instead supply experiences that remain with children throughout their future learning experiences. But enriched environments need careful consideration, viewed as a central element of the process rather than simply a container for learning.

SUGGESTIONS FOR AN AUTHENTIC ENVIRONMENT

Realistic, familiar and relevant to all children: Children can embrace their own culture and relate to previous experiences within the home provided this is not done in tokenistic ways, with opportunities to explore their own identity and other people.

Experiences within it need to be tangible: To make connections children need to touch and manipulate objects, experimenting with ideas as they explore new concepts.

Experiences must be interesting and satisfying, related to what children know and what they want to know: Familiarity in songs, rhymes and books brought to life with genuine objects. Experiencing growing, shopping, preparing and eating food during real events such as picnics and celebrations. Planning expeditions involving walking, public transport and new and familiar locations, all steeped in natural experiences of nature.

Embedded in everyday practice: Seeing something real come of something they have talked about will enhance connections and add personal relevance, allowing for increased motivation in future discussions.

When offered in ways that are stimulating, well established and appropriately managed, the environment has the ability to engage children, to challenge thinking, to promote social exchanges and fuel all features of Lifelong Learning. But certain aspects must be carefully considered when creating an engaging, quality environment.

Play-based learning

Children have no hesitancy in freely initiating or valuing the learning potential of play. Allowing central themes of open-ended and self-motivated activity to flourish, access to a multitude of natural resources within environments owned by the children will encourage natural exploration of pattern and problem solving when given the freedom to combine, transport, adapt and use freely within their play, unconstrained by predetermined objectives or expected actions.

Appropriately managed learning

Early childhood curricula focus on how children learn, allowing experience of success to secure confidence and strength to meet and succeed within future challenges, to make self-initiated and sustained choices through challenging, active learning opportunities where perseverance is rewarded. However, these ideals can become misguided through assessment or goal-driven practices, denying capable children the chance of advanced displays of learning that would flourish within purposeful, pleasurable activity (Dombey, 2010). To offer appropriate learning environments they must be managed unobtrusively:

- Children must be given opportunity for appropriate challenge and risk.
- Open-ended and natural resources naturally support enquiry provided children can access and manipulate as needed.
- Resources that dominate or limit alternative pursuits should be actively managed (e.g. bikes, IT equipment).
- Whilst being on hand to promote inquiries and aid children in the management of their own disputes, adults should not be too quick to intervene.
- Active learning environments should offer sufficient space for both social opportunities and quiet reflection.
- Children should be permitted to move around freely, revisiting and embedding concepts with developing self-sufficiency.
- Children's needs should drive spontaneous and directed activity.
- Children should be involved in the care, upkeep, organisation and stocking of their environment, facilitating access to all they need.

Awareness of routine

Whilst important for children's stability and natural rhythms of the day, routines must not be detrimental or invasive to children's experiences. Interruptions such as snack times can offer wonderful opportunities for communication, self-expression and engagement when these occur naturally rather than as enforced breaks from enquiries about to be solved.

Awareness of timing

Children are not driven by long-term goals but rather questions occurring to them in the here and now. As such they need freedom to respond to whatever drives the moment, with decisive time restrictions kept at a minimum. With a limit to how much assimilated information they can keep in mind (Bruner, 1977) and the need to allow ideas to germinate, timescales must follow children's observed needs rather than second-guessed, with the opportunity to return to assumedly abandoned pursuits.

Social learning

Experiencing the joint motivation of achieving a shared learning experience promotes social learning, cementing the social group and adding a personal sense of involvement (Oers and Hännikäinen, 2001). Children are also helped to make sense of their experiences, views and those of others, but resources must be sufficient in number and the environment designed to facilitate.

Resources

Suitably selected resources should be offered with the time, space and freedom for the rich learning opportunities available to germinate, free from excessive noise, distractions and management. Resources should be:

- fresh, interesting and stimulating, to generate discussion and challenge thinking
- plentiful, so that sharing issues do not derail experiences and all can play
- able to collectively anchor the children's attention
- sufficiently thought-provoking so that companionable discussions and enquiries are prompted
- diverse so that all have an opportunity to be the 'expert'
- open-ended rather than manufactured for an immediate purpose.

Practitioners

Practitioners emotionally connected and in tune with children's needs are mindful of where interactions are required, and those that would be intrusive or detrimental to engagement levels previously attained. While learning needs a sense of structure, this is present within the child's mind and as such is highly personal as connections are made between that known and the new information gained. Second-guessing where these connections are required can result in deeply unfulfilling and frustrating learning experiences. Whilst we must observe and sensitively offer tools required for building these structures, we cannot be the architect of them as only the child is privy to the brief.

Literacy

Often misguided within early years, it is important to understand the developments appropriate at this time for future literacy skills. More important than the ability to read for these very young children is familiarity and affection for print as a medium and the development of core muscles. The concept of print literacy embraces the wide-ranging purpose of being literate and promotes the ease and pleasure with which it is engaged. Great emphasis will be put on the use of print once children begin school, so preparing children through ease and familiarity within all print will aid their success and promote a love of reading (Purcell-Gates, 2001). If viewed as a set of skills to be mastered (Lynch, 2009), we are in danger of losing the social significance and joy of reading and it is then that children struggle greatly.

Mathematics

Mathematics in very early childhood is often thought of as an *oxymoron*, but far from calculus and trigonometry, mathematics with its problem solving, spatial awareness and pattern is how young children begin to make sense of their world. Rather than a 'maths table', mathematical concepts suitable for the age and stage of children must be embedded throughout the environment within authentic situations that children can relate to and adapt with their own ideas and contexts. Opportunity must be given for practical uses of:

- classifying sequences and sorting
- noticing patterns and shape
- measuring length, capacity and time
- problem solving in many contexts
- playing with counting and number representation
- mimicking practical use of numbers
- representing features of play graphically.

CHAPTER SUMMARY

This chapter has explored how children learn and develop during early childhood. With discussion of children's neurology during the early years the chapter looks at the importance of quality, sensory experiences and offers suggestions for how these can be offered.

With discussion around key variables effecting quality experiences, the chapter invites reflection on the importance of authenticity and freedom for children to access areas required in order that they may combine and connect their learning as required.

Ten Key Concepts

1. Nurturing curiosity and a motivation in children to know and understand is more important than the ability to perform any discrete skill. (Claxton, 2008b)
2. Children are active and independent thinkers, learning through combinations of many processes that must be allowed to flourish. (Faust, 2010)
3. Children's brains grow and develop through every experience afforded them. (Rinaldi, 2005)
4. Children must be allowed to access the repeated experiences they need, when they need them and how they need them. (Hurst, 1997)
5. Sheltered from excessive pressures or sense of failure, children will thrive in environments that promote self-expression and recognise their own motivations and interests. (Allen, 2011)

(Continued)

(Continued)

6. The best way to ensure that children have access to all the experiences their developing brains and body require is to offer an environment of free play. (Moyles, 2005)
7. Social interactions with peers where discussion and collaboration is encouraged are fundamental to the learning process. (Samuelsson, 2004)
8. Mistakes, risk and challenge are an inevitable part of the learning journey and must not be avoided. (Maynard and Waters, 2007)
9. Children's grasp of language is fundamental to their participation in the learning process and must be supported. (Roulstone et al., 2011)
10. Environments must be owned by the children, freely accessed and manipulated and full of the resources that offer familiar and genuine experiences to the child. (Samuelsson and Carlsson, 2008)

IDEAS FOR PRACTICE

Practical Project

Perform a 'sensory audit' on different age groups of children to identify ways in which their experiences are being informed through their senses. By observing each child every five minutes, record which of their senses they are using.

Future Activities

How free are children to access the experiences they need? Can they explore new ideas and discoveries through different environments, combining different resources and concepts? Observe one child for a day with these questions in mind.

Work-based Tasks

Identify ways that resources and activities can be enhanced through considering children's senses. For example, exchanging plastic fruits and vegetables with real ones or exchanging paints for chocolate spread and yogurt.

FURTHER READING

Early Years Interboard Panel (no date) *Learning Through Play in the Early Years.* Belfast: CCEA. Available at www.nicurriculum.org.uk/docs/foundation_stage/learning_through_play_ey.pdf (accessed 21/6/16).

This booklet offers guidelines on provision and progression in play within the foundation stage, underpinned by 10 common principles of early years education that are echoed throughout this book.

Gehris, J., Gooze, R. and Whitaker, R. (2015) 'Teachers' perceptions about children's movement and learning in early childhood education programmes', *Child: Care, Health and Development*, 41 (1): 122–31.
This article looks at promoting learning and school readiness through movement, identifying key themes demonstrating young children's innate need to move and the benefits in teaching academic concepts.

MacBlain, S. (2014) *How Children Learn*. London: Sage.
This book considers what effective learning looks like and how this can be facilitated.

5

THE ESSENTIAL ROLE OF THE PRACTITIONER

THIS CHAPTER WILL

- explore what it means to work effectively with children during their preparation for formal schooling
- consider the pivotal roles of the practitioner and teacher working within the early years
- invite practitioners to consider the range and scope of their role through suggestions and debate.

To secure in children features of Lifelong Learning capable of effecting long-term achievement and optimal life chances requires highly specialised practices and behaviours. Informed, confident and equipped to facilitate and enable the experiences required, early years practitioners must recognise opportunities for learning whilst challenging misguided and inappropriate practices and requests. This chapter will explore the mindset and actions of the practitioner as their actions naturally guide children towards every future learning experience. This chapter will also consider the essential role of the practitioner within multi-professional practice and the importance of communicating these messages to families

The early years profession

Early childhood is developmentally the most important time in a person's life (UNESCO, 2011). With clear evidence demonstrating differences made to outcomes for young children through quality early years provision (Tickell, 2011; Grauberg, 2014; Mathers and Smees, 2014), we must look now to the practices of those delivering it. Ensuring that children's natural learning abilities are identified, expanded and celebrated during this finite period requires skills of effective, well-qualified and supported early year's practitioners delivering quality experiences within carefully considered roles.

It is of vital importance that the profession is recognised for the important role it plays in shaping lives, challenging the perception that these precious years can be left in the hands of a low-skilled, low-paid, low-status sector. However, with the largest gap in salaries between those working in nurseries and those in schools of any country in Western Europe (House of Commons Education Committee, 2013), this does nothing to counteract this view. In order to offer children high-quality provision the sector must be adequately recognised and supported, consisting of an aspirational workforce attracted by the rewards of working in a highly esteemed and valued profession, credited with the deep and long-lasting effects of their practice. It must feature tailored career progression and specialised professional development supporting, challenging and inspiring professionals with new ways of thinking, generating well evidenced practices designed to support those new to the field, as well as progressing skills of experienced practitioners. To be attractive to highly skilled and qualified candidates, salaries and career structures deserving of the level of study of early years teachers must be in place if we are to develop resources for the future and look towards a day when every early childhood playroom is staffed with these highly specialised roles (Sylva et al., 2014; Finnegan, 2016).

REFLECTION

Why do you think the profession has historically been seen as having low status, attracting little career progression, recognition or pay?

The qualities of an early year's practitioner are varied and extensive, on the surface simultaneously nurturing developmental needs of all children, delivering child-centred practices and focusing on individual requirements. But this is just part of the role.

REQUIREMENTS OF THE EARLY YEARS PRACTITIONER

The early years practitioner must be:

- *a role model*, able to relate and model concepts with understanding and appreciation for their importance
- *an informed professional*, not allowing themselves to become swayed by agendas they may feel compelled to comply with, instead having the confidence and knowledge to demonstrate professional judgement within perceptive practices
- *reflective*, whilst remaining secure in the role, be challenged by new ideas, developing and enhancing practice

(Continued)

(Continued)

- *the multi-professional*, taking their place as enthusiastic and respected members of a multi-professional sector where their opinion is heard
- *a parental support*, often the only source of information or support frequently encountered guidance through every nuance of early childhood may be sought, so an understanding of effective parenting must also be present
- *a Lifelong Learner*, incorporating all of the above whilst continuously developing and displaying themselves as Lifelong Learners.

Role models

International evidence frequently celebrates the importance of an experienced, well-trained and supported workforce in the immediate and ongoing well-being and development of young children (Peisner-Feinberg and Burchinal, 1997; Peisner-Feinberg et al., 2001; Melhuish et al., 2000a. 2000b; Nutbrown, 2012), in fact anything else would be detrimental. However, quality practice takes more than credentials. Engrained within practice of practitioners and teachers are their personal pedagogies: their vision of childhood; how they believe children learn; their interpretations of frameworks and guidance; and ultimately their belief in their role within the process of children's learning.

REFLECTION

How do you ensure that your practices are rooted in the long-term needs of children rather than short-term goals driven by adult agendas?

Despite overwhelming evidence demonstrating the importance of developing children holistically from birth rather than rushing them into formal practices of literacy and numeracy (Whitebread, 2012; O'Connor & Angus, 2014; Ellyatt, 2015), misguided practice still sees formal learning starting earlier and earlier. The focus on measurable abilities is at the expense of basic cognitive and emotional needs essential to long-term well-being and success, and this can intensify as children transition to school. When progressing to formal schooling *self-initiated, free-flow* experiences of early childhood can undergo quite a change. Whilst many teachers will strongly believe in play, subject-based curricula can be at odds with this, introducing pressures to structure play, environments and opportunities focused on delivering content-driven goals. Previous open explorations of creative and imaginary enquiry and self-motivated pursuits of knowledge can become threatened in favour of acquiring and demonstrating surface-level learning and attained discrete skills as thinking becomes less imaginative or diverse.

Focusing on heavily pre-planned experiences within targeted objectives suggests a future of children taught to rely on guidance and specifically phrased problems, only able to apply set logic to given situations. To overcome problems in an unknown world requires understanding on a deeper level. To capture and develop features of thinking, children's achievements must be recognised in all their formats; in effect following the grain of children's thinking rather than trying to teach against it (Drummand, 2010). The pivotal role of practitioners and teachers within this process is *multifaceted*, changing daily with every child, but needs to embrace certain qualities.

QUALITIES REQUIRED FOR BEING A QUALITY PRACTITIONER

Here are some suggestions for demonstrating quality practice:

- *Demonstrate yourself as a continual learner and thinker*: With a personal sense of wonderment and discovery, visibly enjoy the process of new experiences within unplanned areas without having all the answers.
- *Extend children's understanding*: Draw attention to new ideas, introducing and using key vocabulary to progress learning.
- *Offer carefully considered resources*: Consider the optimum sensory potential, modelling uses where required then stage and leave available for children to practice and explore as they link and process their learning.
- *Act as a scaffolder*: Model techniques and skills to demonstrate new ideas enable children to immediately have a go, actively learning through repeated practice and free-reign over their experience.
- *Communicate freely with children*: Include timely, encouraging, interested questions that seek open-ended responses and two-way engagements, avoiding interrupting or dominating their play.
- *Enhance children's communication*: Model opportunities for children of different ages to express themselves and listen to each other. Offer alternative methods to match ages and abilities, making thinking visible such as post boxes, message walls or creating objects.
- *Encourage children's attempts*: Give feedback and offer targeted praise without creating a culture of one right answer; pre-empt misconceptions and be ready to alleviate anticipated issues in sensitive ways so that children are not afraid to try for fear of getting things wrong.
- *Understand the motivations of children*: Know intuitively what is right for a child's age, developmental stage and interest allowing their deep levels of motivation to draw them in, supporting the skills they need at that moment, recognising them as the only ones they care about.

(Continued)

(Continued)

- *Provide both stimulating and challenging environments*: Children can only interact with resources and guidance offered, so make sure these are diverse and rich, stimulating all senses whilst promoting cognitive development, discovery and choice.
- *Children don't know what they don't know*: Our knowledge needs to provide the links taking them to the next level, holistically extending and supporting their thinking.
- *Make use of the whole day and every experience within it*: Nappy changes, feeding, walks to the park must all be appreciated for the learning potential within, harnessing the opportunities.
- *Put quite simply – promote all the features of Lifelong Learning*: To be a quality practitioner you must see yourself as a Lifelong Learner, embracing and demonstrating all the features of Lifelong Learning outlined in Chapter 3.

By engaging in ideas not as the holder of all the answers but as a fellow Lifelong Learner on this journey of discovery, deeper questions can be prompted and mistakes can be made as new ideas are discovered and explored together. During this collaborative learning process adults need to make themselves available, immersed in children's physical and *metaphysical* environments, inviting genuine conversation and open discussion that encourages peer interactions, relaying messages whilst being careful to prompt interested dialogue, enquiring without interrupting play or derailing engagement. By working alongside children, taking account of social and emotional aspects of learning, adults are able to demonstrate the features of Lifelong Learning as a genuine and powerful reality, giving opportunities to progress all aspects of knowledge, all within a focus of play.

REFLECTION

Within your practice, when do you think it is right to engage with children at play, and when do you feel that well-meaning dialogue or questions are disruptive to children's investigations?

When developing and encouraging social learners we need to model skills of communication. To engage with children requires active listening if their messages and attempts at communication are not to be missed. It is easy to become blinkered and assume we know what they need, or become swept up in the procedures of the day. Children convey meaning in many ways and we must develop effective listening techniques if we are to understand their underlying messages and develop levels of confidence and trust that enable children to feel comfortable enough to share.

Open opportunities for mutual interactions within wide-ranging experiences incorporating all methods of communication will achieve this.

REFLECTION

How do you hear children's messages? What if they are pre-verbal or non-English speaking? How do you encourage the skills required to listen to others?

Supporting experiential learning

Children are born ready and eager to learn. Continual learners, they constantly absorb information from every ongoing, diverse experience throughout their body and senses. With the vast array of knowledge they will need to embrace over the coming years this requires powerful methods of learning and children are equipped with these; however, they need opportunities to utilise them. As children encounter new situations through play, their brain actively searches its knowledge banks for similar past experiences, looking for the 'best' rather than the 'right' answer to the problems they encounter (Ebbeck, 1996). Looking for familiar patterns to categorise and classify the experience, they constantly and subconsciously fine-tune, constructing ideas, testing hypotheses and reinforcing or adjusting existing ideas and ways of thinking, effectively refining and reinforcing understanding. But for this process to work effectively, past experiences must be present to underpin and accommodate the new.

As children move from understanding concrete concepts to more abstract, operational phases, where objects or symbols are manipulated in their mind, the importance of these existing experiences becomes clear. Without sufficient genuine experiences within multitudes of situations of personal relevance, unpicking these abstract ideas in the mind will be an arduous task. We can consider this within our own learning if we were to contemplate attempting a new language. Without familiar words or genuine resources to supply familiarity, we would have nothing to pin the new learning to and conversational vocabularies would remain impenetrable.

With an immense capacity to process highly complex and difficult ideas when presented in interesting ways, children will use these methods provided they offer a context rooted in personal meaning. However, learning will be limited and expectations fundamentally undervalued if opportunities are not familiar or real to the child. Their capacity to express themselves and their meaning will be skewed where relevant experiences are missing, and it may be this rather than any personal failing that accounts for apparent lack of ability. Recognising what this means to each child and being able to simultaneously offer it to many takes knowledge of child development, knowledge of every child and a willingness to consistently understand and connect at more than surface levels (Browne, 1998 in Miller, 2010).

Links between presenting new learning within meaningful and *tangible* early years experiences and developing features of learning that secure success throughout school are well documented (Fisher and Frey, 2009; Hirsch, 2003; Marzano, 2004).

Shown to be the biggest indicator of how readily new knowledge can be acquired in reading (Neuman, 2010), maths and science (Grissmer et al., 2010), relevant experiences provide a medium that allows for deep engagement with profound and lasting effects (Wasik et al., 2011; Laevers et al., 2011). Conscientious preparation for formal education must then secure in children wide-ranging, genuine experiences ready for all the diversities of future learning to be pinned to.

REFLECTION

What experiences do you think children need to fully understand concepts of weights and measure?

But effective practice requires deep-rooted conviction for long-term beliefs to be effected. As early years moves into reception, teachers without specific early years training can feel uncomfortable working within reactive, play-based and child-led curricula that involve greater freedoms both in and outdoors. Significant research suggests that when this understanding is missing, confidence and competence to practice in ways that open up a world of knowledge to children is lacking, and instead prescribed activities delivering expected outcomes are relied upon (Fleer, 2009). For children to believe in the value and relevance of tasks they are pursuing, adults around them must appreciate and value them too. Reflected in the time and resources offered, encouragement and support to explore and the attitudes displayed by key professionals, confidences must be supported to avoid the lack of challenge and diet of instruction that can exist (Lynch, 2009). Worries about covering required criteria need to be assuaged by understanding the purpose of informal, real practices such as baking and gardening to teach maths and science. Once the child moves to school, connections with parents and families, compared to that enjoyed in early years' settings, can also decrease and with it knowledge of children's communities and the background realities that once supported the evidence base that directed genuine experiences.

SUGGESTIONS FOR DELIVERING QUALITY PRACTICE

- ***Enable***: Children must be given diverse opportunities with freedom of choice and movement necessary to access what is meaningful to them at every moment, exploring throughout their body and senses.
- ***Motivate***: To access intrinsic features of learning children must be motivated to do so through meaningful, enticing experiences pitched at a level to both support and challenge.

- ***Empower active learning***: Learning goals must be translated into activities that see children as active learners, thinking things through for themselves, reflecting on their decisions and developing their own mastery as learning strategies become more refined.
- ***Scaffold***: Knowing where enquiries could go next, stretch children's minds and investigations within opportunities substantially more significant than any end product, participating only when children's reactions require it to access learning that would be missed if left alone.
- ***Freedom of enquiry***: Through self-initiated play, experiences empower independent discovery, in as far as possible, free from over-prescribed routines, preconceived agendas or time constraints.
- ***Help children to discover their own passions***: Through accessible and exciting investigations offer discrete guidance and nurturing rather than directives.
- ***Encourage autonomy, creativity and reflection of meaningful experiences***: Allow discoveries and explorations to follow children's directions and be revisited so that conceptual understanding has real experience to pin to.

High-quality reflective practice

To provide a level of practice informed by those it impacts upon and rooted in the needs of children, adults must understand how children learn and develop whilst remaining realistic and reflective within their own practice. Naturally influenced by the actions and expectations of those around them, practices followed without conscious knowledge of underpinning principles may lead to assumptions, misunderstandings or underappreciated adaptions. To secure effective delivery of *explicit* curriculum and policy as well as *implicit* procedure requires regular, *multidisciplinary* and effective training, complete with follow-up supervision. Dissemination to teams that identify and consolidate learning will strengthen cumulative knowledge and skills, providing opportunity to check understanding and retain consistency. Without such investment, internal practices, often behind closed doors, could be misguided for some time.

Peer observations are an immediate way of obtaining constructive, targeted and highly relevant feedback on practice. Following rare opportunities to simply stand back and observe practice, peer observations are invaluable in offering practitioners opportunity to reflect on the practices of others and receive targeted feedback themselves. By observing practice, we can ensure that children are not underestimated or their potential limited by practitioners failing to appreciate achievements. It can identify practice unconsciously swayed by cultural expectations or misunderstandings, overlooking depths of thinking by focusing on surface displays of *discrete abilities*.

To question the strength of every element of practice we can start by asking 'Why am I doing this? Is it because it is right for the child, or because it is right for the parent/management/inspectors or government?'. If our environment, actions, routines or practices are driven by the needs of anyone other than the child, we need to think again.

Measures of quality can be difficult to define; values and expectations can differ greatly between professionals, populations can vary considerably bringing with them a mix of cultural expectations. Changing government initiatives can offer polarised directives. Far from static, the understanding of what makes high-quality practice within the field is continuously evolving and enhancing with every piece of research. Practitioners must be reflective within their own practice, open to new ideas, redefining and evaluating actions within the context they are operating, taking care to avoid passive approaches because 'that is how it has always been done'. Adaptation and progression must be a realised feature of every setting supported with the understanding that improvement requires long-term, ongoing progress felt deeper than an acquired qualification or inspection judgement. Where 'practitioner researcher' techniques including disseminated training and peer observations that allow staff to reflect on the impact of their work is a productive experience for all involved, practice is enriched and reflective, and professional skills are developed (Oberhuemer, 2005; Cameron and Moss, 2007; Peeters, 2008; and Urban, 2008 in Pirard, 2011; Allen, 2011).

The multi-professional

Multi-agency working refers to the range of professionals working together in integrated ways to promote positive outcomes for children and young people (DfES, 2005). This may include mental health services, speech and language and other therapists, social workers, teachers, early years practitioners, child health practitioners, doctors, liaison officers and police. Across all sectors this can take many forms but rather than separating focalised specialisms the approach aims to place children, families and communities at the centre (Gasper, 2010), to be fully involved in discussions about their child, listened to, respected and supported by the specialists they require (DfE and DfH, 2011).

By working together to solve families' problems more effective, focused and holistic approaches should result, with speedier and more appropriate referrals that allow greater focus on prevention and early intervention. By establishing professional relationships between agencies with a shared purpose the intention is that understanding, support and trust will develop. However, this requires effective communication and information sharing supported by adequate resourcing, in terms of funding, staffing and time, and professional identities that are respected (Atkinson et al., 2007).

Within any multi-professional framework, every element is relied upon to safeguard the needs of children in what are often highly complex cases. There must then exist a high degree of professional trust throughout every link of these coordinated and integrated chains. Close working relationships must be established between adequately trained and skilled key players, underpinned by excellent communication and the utmost professional respect. The astute practices of all key individuals are fundamental in safeguarding against mistakes, uncommunicated messages or undervalued opinions and recognition of the early years practitioner is essential to ensure an equality of status that allows for recognition of their unique views and understanding. Practices must permit a blending of professional boundaries, cross-pollination of ideas and exchanges of respected knowledge essential in producing a complete picture of the issues at hand. When the inexcusably high price paid is for children to slip through the net, this must be prevented at all costs.

Addressing the concerns of parents

Part of the role of the early years practitioner and teacher is to form and sustain effective partnerships with the families of children. Sometimes this involves delicate management of misconceptions. One of the most pronounced issues practitioners face when discussing children's preparation for school with parents is the visible proof of literacy readiness, demonstrated through their reading and writing abilities. There is a pronounced drive for children to be literate at increasingly early ages, fuelled by media, government and present in the minds of most parents, however there is much evidence to suggest that this is in fact detrimental (Drummand, 1997; Mills and Mills, 1998). It is staggering to realise that in the 10 years following the introduction of the National Literary Strategy, while reading ability rose, reading enjoyment declined (Clarkson and Sainsbury, 2007 quoted in Claxton, 2008b). As a fundamental part of everyday life it is important that a person can read. But literacy is richer than the ability to decode. It is essential that engagement and enjoyment of reading and a belief in its value and purpose is understood so that children grow up not only as adults who can read, but as adults who *do* read. The preparation of this is most assuredly placed deep within the early years.

However, research shows a remaining uncertainty in the minds of practitioners regarding how and when young children should learn to read and write, with concern regarding their role within literacy development and how they can make this process more informed, motivating and fun. Staff need appropriate knowledge to support its development and to create conditions for early literacy learning, supported through informed and shared practice both with other settings and parents (Lynch, 2009). To promote the desired literary practices of the future, words and languages must be an enjoyable feature throughout a child's early life both in the setting and in the home.

SUGGESTIONS FOR PROMOTING EARLY LITERACY

- *Learning through play*: Avoid seeing literacy instruction as something different to play.
- *Playful learning*: Play with language through meaningful, creative and theatrical play-based experiences where literacy has a purpose. By encouraging fun manipulations of language (e.g. discovering new words for 'squelchy') the social implications of communication can be appreciated.

(Continued)

(Continued)

- *Show the purpose*: Meaningful, practical relevance together with the demonstrated importance and function of print must be seen throughout the lives and thinking of all the people around the child.
- *Utilise the written word*: Demonstrate the many purposes in the child's environment, leave notes and messages, instructions and information, all of which can be rehearsed by children in their play.
- *Displayed and represented in all its forms*: Ensure that environments are rich in print of many fonts, colours and sizes (e.g. display signs, favourite book covers, labels, instructions and directions).
- *Make the connections*: Make links between spoken language and the use of written and read formats – take notes of conversations or when plans are being made and refer back to them.

Children are expected to grapple with many new words, experiencing them on their tongue as they hear different sounds in preparation for deeper understanding of their use. As we approach the promotion of language development in the early years it is important that we focus on sensitive, accessible yet stimulating opportunities for children that acknowledge a sense of autonomy, discovery and fun. This requires teaching and learning experiences full of appropriate and safe spaces for speech rehearsal and play. Through playful games, tasks such as spelling and finding meaning will become more accessible. Sensitively timed responses should be used to add content without intrusion, taking care to make the language culturally and intellectually suitable. Features can then be added to offer depth and aid children's understanding through experiences familiar to them.

CHAPTER SUMMARY

This chapter has explored what it means to work effectively with children through their early years, nurturing and enabling the development of key characteristics. With suggestions that look at methods for delivering effective quality practice, it considered how experiential learning in tune to the needs of individual children can be delivered by practitioners equipped with the underpinning knowledge and convictions.

With consideration of key roles this chapter has invited practitioners to take a reflective look at their own practice, examining and questioning the reason why things are done in certain ways. With consideration of the potential impact on children's future learning this chapter also offers discourse on working within the demands of parents and a multi-professional arena.

Ten Key Concepts

1. Children's level of success at school is secured long before they start. (Edwards et al., 2016).
2. To identify, enhance and celebrate children's natural learning abilities requires the skills of an effective, knowledgeable and supported early year's workforce delivering considered, quality experiences. (Smidt, 2010)
3. The role of the early year's practitioner is multifaceted. Whilst nurturing the developmental needs of all children in their care they are often the most influential source of support for young families, acting as role model and reflective multi-professional whist themselves remaining a lifelong learner. (Hurst, 1997)
4. Quality practice takes more than qualifications and experience, it also hinges on the day-to-day conscious practice of passionate, informed staff. (Kalliala, 2011)
5. Practitioners must be confident and suitably informed within their practice to be able to deliver the holistic play-based enquiry and investigation essential to developing the skills children need throughout life. (Maynard and Waters, 2007)
6. Practitioners must appear to children as Lifelong Learners themselves, ready and eager to explore the possibilities of problems rather than simply being the holder of all the answers. (Pramling Samuelsson, 2005)
7. Mindful of children's depths of engagement, practitioners must be careful not to interrupt children's play where this will have the effect of derailing it rather than promoting further learning. (Rayna and Laevers, (2014)
8. Practitioners must embrace all the potential of learning through play, allowing children to self-direct their enquiries into areas meaningful to them within their own timescales. (Hamre et al., 2014)
9. Quality practice must be reflective practice, questioning how our actions and procedures directly impact the development and well-being of children. (Pirard, 2011)
10. Practitioners must be confident enough within their own practice to conduct themselves effectively when dealing with parents and other professionals. (DfE and DH, 2011; Home Office, 2015; HM Government, 2015)

(Continued)

(Continued)

IDEAS FOR PRACTICE

Practical Project

Look again at the suggestions for being a quality practitioner and share these with those you work with. Do you all agree with all of them? How well do you think these are demonstrated within day-to-day practice?

Future Activities

Focus on a key aspect that you can all agree on and establish a system of peer observations so that you can all observe the delivery of these qualities in practice. At the end, share examples of best practice around the team.

Work-based Tasks

As a team identify how these methods of practice are essential for developing children as Lifelong Learners. Create a visible reminder for all staff and parents that demonstrates the importance of embracing these methods when working with children.

FURTHER READING

Bain, J., James, D. and Harrison, M. (2015) 'Supporting communication development in the early years: a practitioner's perspective', *Child Language Teaching & Therapy*, 31 (3): 325–36.
This research study explores the practitioner's role in promoting communication development in early years' classrooms.

Brooker, L. (2002) *Starting School: Young Children Learning Culture.* Buckingham: Open University Press.
Case studies of children starting school in urban Britain analysing how parents, children and teachers strive to cross the cultural and linguistic boundaries to come to a common understanding of 'school'.

Haller, E. (2013) *The Reflective Early Years Practitioner.* London: Sage.
Looking at the role of the practitioner, this book offers research and case studies to help develop reflective practice for students and practitioners at all levels.

Swaminathan, S., Byrd, S., Humphrey, C., Heinsch, M. and Mitchell, M. (2014) 'Winning beginnings learning circles: outcomes from a three-year school readiness pilot', *Early Childhood Education Journal*, 42 (4): 261–9.
This article looks at school readiness outcomes following staff participation in professional workshops in child development, social-emotional health and parent engagement, highlighting the potential of professional development programmes and the importance of teacher quality in promoting positive outcomes for preschool children.

6

FAMILIES AND PRACTITIONERS WORKING IN PARTNERSHIP

THIS CHAPTER WILL

- explore the importance of the family unit and the home environment on children's well-being
- look at the role of the parent at home and as a key member of the effective parental partnership with the setting
- offer practitioners practical advice for working with all parents both in the setting and beyond.

Deeply engrained within children's potential for healthy growth and development is their level of well-being and this must be firmly established before learning within the school classroom can be optimised. To facilitate healthy levels of well-being during early childhood it is fundamental that practitioners establish affective relationships of mutual respect and understanding with all families, creating effective parental partnerships that provide mutual support and encouragement. Dependent on secure attachments to all adults in their lives, by establishing an informed appreciation for the nature of learning during early childhood and an understanding of their role within it, families can be empowered to make a real difference to their children's life chances.

The importance of developing secure relationships

Parents and carers as well as grandparents and extended family are the first and most significant influence on the lifelong prospects of children. Warm, supportive parenting is shown to have deep effect on the confident, autonomous and empathetic behaviours of 5-year-olds, both now and throughout their future (The Millennium Cohort Study referenced by the DfE and DH, 2011; see also CLS, 2015). Through consistent, caring and stimulating responses received from these influential adults, children develop bonds of empathy and trust. Feeling supported, valued and treasured, children develop a sense of security and well-being that enables them to venture out from familiar, trusted situations to explore new territory. As school beckons it is this security that allows children to engage head on with the challenges ahead. But this does not happen automatically for all families, and sensitive, astute support may be required as we work together effectively.

The importance of strong primary attachments on children's cognitive and social development in early childhood did raise questions regarding the suitability of external childcare for very young children. Research showing this depending largely on how well attached children are to key figures already in their lives and how securely relationships were forming within care settings (Clarke-Stewart, 1992; Lamb et al., 1992; Thompson, 1991), targeted early intervention programmes such as the Family Nurse Partnership (FNP) which focuses strongly on relationships formed around the child at home and elsewhere (Allen, 2011), and *key worker* systems were actively imbedded into early years practice.

Through these relationships, levels of trust can establish, nurturing children's well-being while enabling productive and supportive learning environments to become tuned into children's specific needs. But as social mixing on a global scale becomes a way of life, practitioners must be mindful of the variety of experiences children encounter and avoid misunderstanding cultural differences, or view them with unsuitable expectations. Understanding individual effects on dispositions, hopes and fears, essential to developing secure relationships, requires an appreciation of the backgrounds and experiences of families. Considerations may include:

Cultural diversity or bilingualism (Sims and Ellis, 2015):

- Families may be struggling to achieve a sense of belonging.
- Many languages may be spoken by the families in the setting.
- Some families (or family members) may have no English at all.
- Differing views may exist regarding the language/s parents wish their children to speak.
- Many different, culturally intrinsic, views may be held on childcare, discipline and education.
- Parents may be seeking a competitive advantage for their children in the future.

Sociological and historical backgrounds of the family and community (Shildrick and Rucell, 2015):

- Some families will feel uncomfortable approaching or engaging with the setting.
- Social inequalities may be felt with regards to income, rights or education.
- Historic events could have seen a dramatic change to feelings of social equality or economic stability causing far-reaching problems that may include family conflict and depression.

Disadvantage including level of well-being of key family members (Mensah and Kiernan, 2011):

- Maternal anxieties or post-natal effects may affect engagement and care.
- Regular attendance at the setting may be a struggle.
- Expectations on families (such as 'Home Link' books, dressing-up days, providing items from home) may be an impossibility and further source of anxiety.

Experiences children may have been exposed to (Tang and Adams, 2010):

- Children may be used to demonstrating very low or very high levels of independence, or appear resilient to extreme dangers.
- Experiences of migrant children, both of their home and journey, may compound feelings of loss and insecurity.
- The loss of a family member may have deeply affected the family's ability to function.
- Children may have seen or experienced abuse, warfare or great hardship, drawing on personal reserves that leave them hardened. Whether experienced by the child or by close family members, it will have far-reaching effects.

Family's experiences and views of childcare and childhood (König and Van der Aalsvoort, 2009):

- In some cultures child care is a female dominated or collective affair involving extended families and communities that may now be lost.
- Attitudes towards the 'unique child' may differ. Where we celebrate individual success, in some cultures being singled out is dreadfully uncomfortable. Children and their families may resist eye contact or seem reluctant to acknowledge individual praise.
- Pressures and expectations may exist towards more formal learning at the expense of play.

REFLECTION

How do you consider and account for the variety of children's backgrounds and experiences within your day-to-day practice?

Family well-being

As well as educational ambitions and aspirations of the family we must also be mindful of the well-being of the family unit. How well a parent can meet the needs of their child is often determined by the extent to which their own needs have been and are being met and naturally impact the well-being, self-esteem and development of their child. Numbers of siblings, family income and educational background of the mother (Sylva et al., 2004, 2014), social class, deprivation, ill health and single-parent status (Desforges and Abouchaar, 2003) can all potentially create a despondent home environment with low expectations lacking in interactions capable of stimulating young minds. The quality of home learning environments are more important for children's social, intellectual, cognitive and non-cognitive development than parental income or education, occupations (Sylva et al., 2004) or even the role played by the school (Thomas, 2014; Allen, 2011). Whilst income poverty may not be turned around overnight, supporting families offers a chance for *intergenerational* cycles to be broken.

Empathetic parental involvement, effective encouragement and quality experiences are indispensable to young children, but this takes understanding, a good knowledge of children's needs and appropriate levels of parental well-being. Effective parent–child interactions that recognise and respond to their baby's cries, react appropriately to toddler demands or secure effective transitional preparations for children during monumental periods of adjustment are an impossible task for many without the care and support of professional networks. Being surrounded by low self-esteem, with their needs for affection and continuity misinterpreted or not met at all, informs children's understanding of relationships. If this coincides with individual urbanisation away from extended families, such difficulties may be experienced without previously relied upon family support, further promoting feelings of isolation. Before needs become too great, varied external support from well-informed, professional contacts must be offered, ranging from information to emotional and physical assistance (Margetts, 2013).

Building relationships and guiding families towards needed help can create positive and nurturing home-learning environments that establish trajectories long before school can have an effect on children's prospects for life. As we work in partnership to nurture, guide and support families, the effect these relationships can have on the quality of parenting must be valued and recognised. Parents tend to be more motivated to learn and receptive to advice during pregnancy and through the first years of their child's life (Tickell, 2011), offering key opportunities to nurture relationships appreciating the role families play. Only by working together, considering not how families can best support agendas of academic preparation but how children's experiences can be extended and nurtured in the home, will the needs of every child be realised.

SUGGESTIONS FOR WORKING WITH PARENTS IN THE SETTING

- *Ensure all parents are offered a safe and secure environment to discuss their needs*: At different times families need opportunities to seek advice or help with sensitive concerns. Raising children is a complex and often bewildering task, so with community support often lacking, alternative networks are essential.

- *Find or establish networks for different groups of families*: Especially important for hard to reach families, bringing families together with similar needs or backgrounds enables targeted help by those who can associate, support and understand.
- *Be aware of outward signs that families need help*: Parents are not always comfortable asking for help. Offer various, discrete methods of support including printed information in key languages, contacts for parenting groups, multi-professional help in the community and visual support such as podcasts or film.
- *Take the time to get to know your families*: Consider what it means to be Polish or to live in the Polish community. Find out what support networks are targeted to vulnerable families as you take time to understand the realities facing them.
- *Do not assume that parents unable to stop and chat are disinterested*: Many parents are unable to discuss concerns at pick-up times. Be sensitive to individual needs and find alternative ways to make contact.

The role of parents in the home

Early childhood is a time for amassing the plethora of physical, linguistic and social experiences enabling natural, healthy growth and development, and much of this will come from home. Attitudes and environments offered here are of great significance to children's future aptitudes and attitudes towards learning, especially when delivered by the most revered figures and enduring influences on children's lives. With every event laying pathways for future learning, parents need to be confident and secure in their approach, appreciating how the experiences they provide offer the foundations their child needs, seeing their child not in levels of achievement with expected milestones of development such as reading by the age of five (Maynard and Waters, 2007) but as holistic rather than solely linear learners.

Higher parental involvement in, for example, reading during these early years promotes higher scores on 'pre-reading', 'language' and 'early number' attainment (Sammons et al., 2007). Practices of early language and literacy skills can mitigate effects of disadvantaged backgrounds (DfE and DH, 2011), with research showing that children read to on a daily basis by parents who are interested in their education were less likely to be living in poverty at age 30 (Blanden, 2006).

Parents, influenced by popular media, are often quick to use behavioural strategies that include time out ('naughty steps'), reprimands and punishments and explanations beyond the child's level of understanding. Far more effective and in keeping with young children's scope of understanding is positive behaviour techniques including praise and encouragement, positive reinforcement (rewards) and the modelling of desired behaviours. Such positive behaviour techniques may need guiding with effective suggestions (Thomas, 2014) if a good understanding of suitable expectations for children's developmental stages are to be established that ensure specific or *cultural expectations* and demands (Wang et al., 2002) or messages from parents' own academic journeys do not detrimentally influence their actions. Through communication, consistent practices between home and setting can be established and parents supported to think of their children within realistic scopes of understanding (Dunlop et al., 2008).

Of special consideration and often overlooked is the involvement of fathers in children's lives. Increasing steadily since the 1970s (O'Brien and Shemilt, 2003), the father's relationship is distinct and independent from that of the mother. Whilst depending on behaviours of the family, it has the potential to significantly impact young children's lives, especially in the case of sons (Flouri, 2006), influencing developing attitudes and behaviours that affect later educational outcomes (Asmussen and Weizel, 2010). As with all family relationships, the quality of paternal involvement is more important than length of time spent with their child (Goldman, 2005), however, in studies nearly 70 per cent of fathers suggested that they are not as involved with their children as they would like (Peters et al., 2008) with many fathers reporting no daily direct interaction at all (Fisher et al., 1999). As the potential bridge there is much we can do to encourage fathers' involvement, providing we appeal to the areas they would feel most comfortable with and do not exclude them through inappropriate timing or activity choices. Outdoor and physical activities are often popular, but must be organised when fathers have greater chance of attending. Fathers may feel uncomfortable in a room full of mothers or having to sit on tiny chairs for prolonged periods, so be mindful of their sense of ease within the activities.

SUGGESTIONS FOR ADVISING PARENTS IN THE HOME

Be happy to play with your child:

- Free of expectations, be happy to make mistakes, showing yourself as a Lifelong Learner, confident to explore with a contagious sense of adventure.
- Allow play to take any number of twists and turns, where children need dissuading from a particular course of action, do so graciously.
- Be open-minded and inquisitive, suggesting interesting directions to extend play.
- Have a two-way debate about how play should develop, listening respectfully to your child's suggestions, avoiding being too quick to offer solutions.

Set safe clear boundaries and routines that offer structure without becoming restrictive:

- Establish a safe environment then allow your child to explore ideas and investigations freely.
- Set aside opportunities to explore within their own timeframes unimpeded by agendas.

- Allow children to lose themselves in activities enabling deeper engagement and more involved learning. Stopping prematurely limits experiences and sets precedents that such pursuits are frustrating and unrewarding.

Offer an abundance of interesting challenges free to the child's imagination:

- Give your child safe, open-ended resources without expectations.
- Without heavily designed toys, children play freely, encouraged to find their own challenges and seek their own solutions – both deeply valuable learning experiences.
- Offering toys with set tasks or expected outcomes becomes deeply tedious, unsatisfying and uninspiring.

Establish a language-rich environment full of two-way communication from birth:

- Engage with your child at every opportunity, connecting with smiles and facial expressions.
- Focus on them free of distracting music or noise so that rhythms of language and *nuances of speech* can become familiar.
- Resist the use of dummies so that vocabulary is emulated and speech encouraged.

Ensure a wide range of available opportunities:

- Allow your child to find adventure within every experience, building memory banks and enhancing understanding to inform future experiences.
- By avoiding the large-scale distractions of television, music, tablets or gaming consoles, higher quality experiences are discovered.
- Make use of book and toy libraries to offer new experiences.
- Even household objects such as pots, pans, jugs or wooden spoons together with some water, earth or a bag of flour can make for the most enjoyable afternoon.

Make books a constant feature within your home:

- Regularly share intimate, positive experiences of books, even before birth.
- Involve your child in the closeness of the experience.
- Together, engage in rhythmically turning brightly illustrated pages, experiencing the organisation, rhythm and dependency of a well-loved story.
- Through exclamations, voices and excitement you can convey the purpose and motivation of reading like a gift that will stay with your child for life.
- To the less competent reader, books can contain little or no words, where imagination tells the story.

(Continued)

(Continued)

Be considerate of children's multi-sensory approach to learning:

- Avoid your child becoming overwhelmed by brightly coloured toys, flashing lights, sounds and actions.
- Consider instead how they can use their senses within natural experiences, such as exploring vegetables for tea.

Develop secure attachments

- Through your dedicated time and attention at key points throughout the day, during intimate care, sharing meals and becoming actively involved in their play, you will develop the secure attachments essential to your child's well-being.

Supporting positive parenting

Supporting children effectively in the home through positive experiences involving appropriate boundaries and routines whilst being responsive to children's needs have demonstratively positive impacts on children and their future life chances. Whilst most parents want to do the very best to support their child they may lack the understanding, opportunities or motivations to do so; for some their own child may be the first experience of children they have had, for others expectations may be misguided. To support children's development during early childhood it is important to encourage families to become actively involved, demonstrating the impact this has on young children's development and the importance of the little things they can do that will make a massive difference to their child's lives.

In order to offer guidance to parents, deep levels of trust and mutual respect must be established. Through blended approaches of support this must begin from the very first contact, embed during transition procedures and continue throughout the child's time at the setting. It is all too easy to concentrate on new parents yet it is often when a family has been at the setting for a period of time that the need of this relationship will be tested. As parents may be experiencing practical as well as emotional barriers to participation within the setting, suitable guidance must be offered in a range of formats.

SUGGESTIONS FOR OFFERING THE SUPPORT FAMILIES NEED

- *Offer opportunities for family members to volunteer and get involved*: Parent forums, stay and plays, workshops and social events in and away from the setting can be arranged at times when various members of the family can attend. Be sure to publicise events well ahead of time in a variety of ways without targeting specific families.

- *Offer parental support for current key issues:* Effective behaviour management techniques, routines to help children sleep through the night, toilet training and methods to encourage healthy eating will all be reoccurring needs.
- *Offer support during difficult phases*: Frustrations can be experienced when children are expected to behave in ways they are not emotionally or physically ready for. Children's emotions need understanding and viewing in context of their age and stage of development. For example, whilst an environment of security and dependable boundaries will benefit a child's sense of well-being, harsh parenting can be seen as the most robust predictor of children's behaviour problems (Snyder et al., 2005; Bradley and Corwyn, 2007).
- *Offer programmes of support that develop confidence and enhance skills*: By offering strategies for play, parents can learn to experience the joy of spending time with their developing child. Share games and activities to try at home, such as those involving turn taking and problem solving to develop children's listening skills whilst carefully demonstrating that they are being listened to. Invite parents to share story times that demonstrate bringing stories to life through voices, props and music.
- *Develop understanding of key practices*: Verbal and physical engagement with children from birth stimulates the infant brain, modelling rich vocabularies and developing core muscles. Help parents understand that engaging with children throughout the day during play, routines and household chores enhances children's language, physicality and creativity.
- *Offer information in a variety of formats*: Offer resource packs and leaflets to guide and support suggested activities, give ideas for open questions and offer prompts for interactions, free of jargon and acronyms and written in a variety of languages. Support further through recorded verbal direction or filmed demonstrations showing children at play in familiar environments so that guidance is viewed in contexts representing all cultures.

Role of parents in settings

Whilst many parents are often keen to become involved in the classroom very few parents actually volunteer to do so, despite the extensive positive effects (Child Trends DataBank, 2013). For some cultures the idea of partnership working will be an alien concept, especially for anyone other than the mother. For some parents time, language or simple geography may prevent their involvement being a simple affair. Given demanding home and work schedules and potential lack of awareness for the importance of links between experiences in the home and setting, many parents struggle to prioritise involvement. Lone parents or those with heavy demands on their time, non-resident parents, ethnic groups where English is not the first language or where their own experiences of school were not positive, are all unlikely to feel involved in their children's education and may lack confidence or opportunity to approach the school or talk to teachers. However, the parental relationship establishes a fundamental bridge into the child's home, culture, development and well-being, and needs careful encouragement with an understanding of these issues in order to overcome potential barriers.

Parental involvement remains equally valid as children get older; however, parental support tends to drop off further (Peters et al., 2008), becoming focused on homework and reading at the expense of the rich engagements of early childhood. As parents become swept up in the end product that homework often demands, focus can become centred on output and corrections. However, this approach leads to lower achievements by children than had their autonomy been supported (Sharp et al., 2001) or deeper attributes of learning been the focus. By allowing parents first-hand opportunities to spend time in the setting, they can see how to engage with their child and better support their learning. Through these approaches significant sustained improvements in reading, writing and numeracy are reported with improved classroom behaviour, motivation and achievement as parents become more confident both helping their child at home and communicating with the teacher at school (Brookes et al., 1997).

REFLECTION

Every setting has its 'hard to reach families'. What is it that makes your parents hard to reach? Given that they have the same need for contact and support as any other family, what are their specific barriers? How can these be overcome?

SUGGESTIONS FOR ENCOURAGING PARENTS INTO THE SETTING

- *Make sure all parents are made to feel welcome*: This can be a greater issue for schools but is vital for building good relationships. Unfamiliarity with the environment can add psychological barriers and must be actively prevented.
- *Make sure all parents are able to become involved*: Time restraints of the school day can cause problems, so arrange activities at different times and days where possible.
- *Make sure all parents are made to feel comfortable*: Limited understanding of the curriculum, its content or intentions may hold some parents back from becoming involved. Producing guidance for the intentions of activities or an idea of what they will experience will help.
- *Help parents to help each other*: Especially helpful for lone parents or those new to the area, establish buddy systems for parents to help overcome lack of confidence in approaching the school, talking to teachers or the discomfort felt over perceived lack of skills or knowledge.
- *Establish support for non-resident parents*: Where possible ensure that all parents are able to feel involved in the development of their child.

Parents and family as the first educator

Large proportions of issues experienced in adult life, including adult mental health, are thought to have origins in early childhood (DfE and DH, 2011). If children begin negative trajectories during early childhood it becomes increasingly difficult to undo the disadvantages put in motion (Field, 2010). Unsupported through the right opportunities or if social expectations are low, early abilities, even when advanced, do not continue into later schooling, with lack of support acting as a barrier to later success (Feinstein Duckworth, 2006). As the divide between secure early childhoods and those of disadvantage become more pronounced the longer they go unchecked, it is essential that relationships tuned into children's needs are established with all families. Otherwise the question emerges: are we celebrating the achievements of certain children when what we really mean is that they had the good fortune to grow up in families where the right dispositions for learning were a realised part of their early years?

Simply being interested in their education allows parents to raise their children's life chances considerably, with a move out of poverty as much as 25 per cent more likely (Blanden, 2006). Ensuring that all children are offered enriched early cognitive development, especially when they happen to have been born in families of low socio-economic status, where the education of girls is not valued, where expectations are unrealistic or experiences have been very different, is of crucial importance in aiding social mobility. These areas of inequality can be vastly improved if we support the adults in these children's lives with opportunities to play, learn and socialise in environments responsive to their needs. We must support parents' natural wish to give their child any advantage, especially in an environment where they may feel the odds are stacked against them through perhaps language barriers, their lack of relatable experience, their capability to support the child themselves or where they feel concern for their child's ability. We must be mindful of cultural backgrounds, experiences and expectations both of their children and the British education system as we sensitively support families and address misconceptions. For example, families where English is not the primary language will often request their child has complete emersion in it to maximise their child's understanding. However, skills learnt in the home language provide the bridge into learning English both verbally and in supporting pre-literacy skills. Research shows that to deny them this rather than seeing bilingualism and diverse experiences as an asset and resource to be built upon does the child a massive disservice (Shin, 2010).

REFLECTION

How do you understand the diverse hopes, fears and expectations of all families you work with when this often includes parents without English, those with very different experiences of their own childhood or those unable to stop and chat?

To many families the holistic learning through play approach of the EYFS as a pedagogical strategy appears as an alien concept when expectations are for their child to 'listen to the teacher and study hard' from a very young age (All Saints' study in Brooker, 2002). The value of its approach in supporting ongoing learning dispositions must be communicated with care and understanding. The value of play as a foundation to all learning must be communicated and sensitively demonstrated so that its rightful place can be taken in the consciousness of all parenting. As we support children's development in the home, the nature of the parental role and the manifestation of the educational ambitions and aspirations held for the child become key. As growing evidence demonstrates how long-term goals of parents drive greater involvement in children's academic progress and ultimately affect prosperity and success (Gutman and Akerman, 2008; Field, 2010; Margetts, 2013), it is essential that these are informed and realistic. Set at an appropriate level, parental involvement has the potential to mitigate even effects of social and economic disadvantage (Pilling, 1990; Hurst, 1997; DfCSF, 2003; Field, 2010). However, excessive expectations and demands or misguided bearings can be equally detrimental, with strong influence felt throughout adolescence and adulthood.

REFLECTION

If good achievement is a result of cultivating the right dispositions, is this possible for all children?

SUGGESTIONS FOR SHARING GOOD PRACTICE

- *Encourage parents to develop a love of books with their child*: Develop story sacks featuring different cultures and multi-sensory resources and props such as recordings of the story in key languages.
- *Share the intrinsic value of activities done within the setting*: Create recipe cards to take home for activities such as playdough or cornflour play that detail the benefits across all areas of learning.
- *Explore the importance of shared experiences*: Demonstrate the discussions and explorations possible when a walk to the shops is allowed to take the time it needs examining every leaf and crack in the pavement rather than being seen for its end goal.

CHAPTER SUMMARY

This chapter has explored the important role of the family within effective support of the well-being of children in the home and setting. By recognising the importance of secure attachments, this chapter offers suggestions to establish and promote effective partnerships with all families, proactively encouraging their involvement in the setting.

By understanding the diverse backgrounds and needs of families, this chapter has offered practical advice to assist practitioners and families. Recognising where concerns, misconceptions and difficulties may arise, this chapter considers the sensitive support required to address difficult issues.

Ten Key Concepts

1. Children's attachments and well-being must be secure before optimum levels of learning can be considered. (DfE and DfH, 2011)
2. Sensitive consideration of family backgrounds, experiences and expectations must be taken in mind. (Brooker, 2002)
3. The well-being of the family unit must be nurtured and cared for if the same is to be offered to the child. (Sylva et al., 2014)
4. The role of the family in the home is vital and parents must be helped to understand and optimise the difference they make. (Thomas, 2014)
5. Parents must be aware of realistic expectations and behaviours for the age and stage of their child. (Wang et al., 2002)
6. The importance of shared books, discussion and time within sensitive environments free of distraction must be communicated to families, where the quality of time spent with children is more important than the length of time. (Goldman, 2005)
7. With understanding of potential barriers, families should be encouraged to become involved in their child's setting and school, guiding and informing the support they can offer their children. (Sharpe et al., 2001)
8. Systems and relationships must be in place to know when things have the potential to go wrong and observe the early signs. (Field, 2010)
9. Parents must be offered support, guidance and knowledge needed in a variety of formats to support them in every aspect of childcare and development. (Feinstein and Duckworth, 2006)
10. Families must be recognised for the deeply important role that they play and the effect that this has on children's lives. (Evangelou et al., 2009)

IDEAS FOR PRACTICE

Practical Project

By looking at all families you work with, who are the most difficult to communicate with? Consider the methods that could be used, the help that could be available and the various formats of information that could be utilised so that all parents can receive the information and guidance they need.

(Continued)

(Continued)

Future Activities

With specific attention to an area of communication that is problematic, identify the reasons why.

Work-based Tasks

Seek out the support you need to overcome the issue you have identified. This may be an interpreter, literature in other formats or an accessibility issue that needs to be addressed.

FURTHER READING

Degioia, K. (2009) 'Parent and staff expectations for continuity of home practices in the child care setting for families with diverse cultural backgrounds', *Australasian Journal of Early Childhood*, 34 (3): 9–17.

This Australian article investigated the expectations for cultural continuity of care between home and early childhood settings, showing that staff with the same cultural background as families are pivotal in understanding expectations, communicating and responding to their own macro-cultural beliefs.

Department for Children, Schools and Families (2003) *The Impact of Parental Involvement on Children's Education*. London: DfCSF. Available at http://webarchive.nationalarchives.gov.uk/20130401151715/www.education.gov.uk/publications/eOrderingDownload/DCSF-Parental_Involvement.pdf (accessed 15/7/15).

A look at the role of the parent, its benefits and barriers, with a focus on ethnic diversity.

Harris, Y.R. and Schroeder, V.M. (2012) 'What the Berenstain bears can tell us about school readiness: maternal story grammar style and preschool narrative recall', *Journal of Early Childhood Research*, 10 (2).

This article looks at the link between maternal story-telling and narrative-rich environments and children's abilities to relate to these within their school experience. As preparation for school, the provision of narrative-rich learning tools for parents is also discussed.

Hibel, J. (2009) 'Roots of assimilation: generational status differentials in ethnic minority children's school readiness', *Journal of Early Childhood Research*, 7 (2).

This American study looks at the effect of racial, ethnic and national origin differences on children's readiness for school and the effects of family context and background as it considers the need for equality within early educational experiences.

Kiernan, G., Axford, N., Little, M., Murphy, C., Greene, S. and Gormley, M., (2008) 'The school readiness of children living in a disadvantaged area in Ireland', *Journal of Early Childhood Research*, 6 (2).

This study looked at the effects of children's health and the context of their home and communities on readiness for school within an urban, disadvantaged area of Ireland. Despite promising beginnings, regression analysis demonstrated children's characteristics, home and school environments, and parenting skills caused difficulties that influenced socio-emotional and cognitive progress within the first year.

Lipscomb, S., Pratt, M., Schmitt, S., Pears, K. and Kim, H. (2013) 'School readiness in children living in non-parental care: impacts of head start', *Journal of Applied Developmental Psychology*, 34 (1) 28–37.

This article looks at the effects of Head Start on the development of school readiness outcomes for children living in non-parental care. The sample included 253 children living in non-parental care and revealed modest direct short-term and indirect longer-term impacts of Head Start on school readiness outcomes.

Schaub, M. (2015) 'Is there a home advantage in school readiness for young children? Trends in parent engagement in cognitive activities with young children, 1991–2001', *Journal of Early Childhood Research*, 13 (1).

This article looks at the effects of parental involvement in cognitive activities with their children during the early years, introducing children to the culture and practices of school.

7

THE IMPORTANCE OF PLAY

THIS CHAPTER WILL

- explore the importance of play as a natural process, intrinsic within the actions and pursuits of children gaining positive, contextual, whole-body experiences that lay the groundwork for ongoing development
- explore the potential of play as a doorway to all areas of development, allowing the features of Lifelong Learning to flourish
- provide practitioners with a broader discourse of the purpose and structure of play and their varying role within it, appreciating its purpose and considering key features such as when and how to engage and the essential nature of outdoor play.

As children move to school from an early years that advocates play as an essential element in promoting effective development across all areas of learning, this chapter will look at the enduring importance and purpose of play. Delivered effectively by adults who openly acknowledge its importance in their actions and support and embrace it within their approaches, play has the potential to develop all the features of Lifelong Learning. Unlocking methods of understanding and enquiry that can deeply effect children's perception of the learning process, their motivations and their belief in their own capabilities, play has the potential to affect academic trajectories and future life chances.

The importance of play

Freely chosen child-initiated play, when combined with opportunities for adults to extend children's thinking, is becoming more recognised for its powerful capacity to generate deep learning in children (Sylva et al., 2014). With its many styles, stages and characteristics it becomes difficult to define play in any universally accepted and all-encompassing way, and often this lack of definition to highlight its construction or identify the powerful learning opportunities within it can lead practitioners to undervalue play, seeing it is something different to the 'proper learning' going on elsewhere. Practitioners must do all they can to recognise its potential, delivering it in ways that do not represent play as inferior to more teacher-lead or organised activities.

REFLECTION

Play is intrinsically motivating and deeply absorbing, allowing children to display abilities they may not demonstrate in other situations. What have you observed children doing when absorbed in play that you did not realise they were able to do?

When children engage in self-motivated pursuits, becoming deeply involved in their own investigations independently and with their peers, they do not consciously divide their time between learning actions and playing actions. Instead they become absorbed in the rich tapestry of experiences motivating their activities, propelling experiences and fuelling curiosities. Environments children find themselves in and the people within them offer constantly evolving and adapting playing fields of discovery for children to understand through processes that seamlessly entwine learning opportunities in their play and playful learning. In fact labels such as 'lesson time' and 'play time' only become relevant when adults create divides between important pursuits of the former whose successful completion may be rewarded with the latter. Persistence through difficult concepts often requires freely alternating periods of joyful play and serious consideration. To try to pigeon hole these approaches instigates a disservice to children's intrinsic, natural abilities to learn.

REFLECTION

What do you think children are aware of when they are playing? What evidence do you have from your practice that leads you to think this?

As children develop, the forms or 'stages of play' they engage in change and mature alongside emerging physical, social and cognitive skills and developing physicality. These are represented in Figure 7.1 with an indication of the age at which

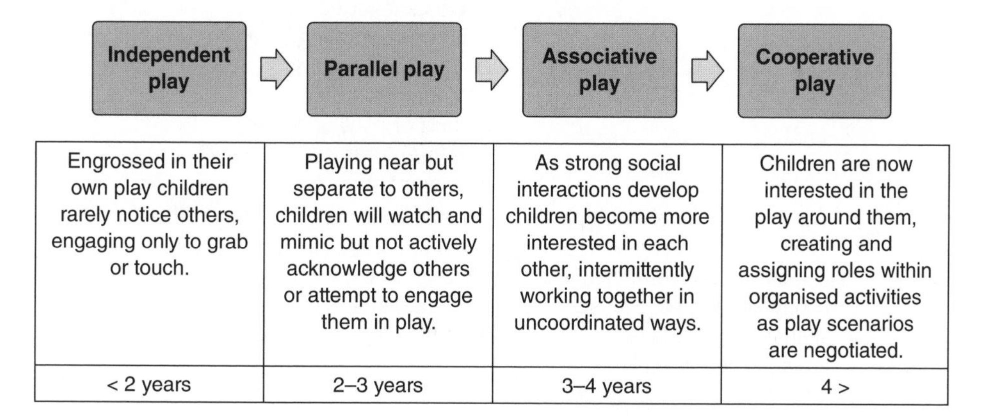

Independent play	Parallel play	Associative play	Cooperative play
Engrossed in their own play children rarely notice others, engaging only to grab or touch.	Playing near but separate to others, children will watch and mimic but not actively acknowledge others or attempt to engage them in play.	As strong social interactions develop children become more interested in each other, intermittently working together in uncoordinated ways.	Children are now interested in the play around them, creating and assigning roles within organised activities as play scenarios are negotiated.
< 2 years	2–3 years	3–4 years	4 >

Figure 7.1 Stages of children's play

children's play will begin to include them. As maturity develops, children's scope and range of play grows and with it the demands for cognitive and social skills such as language, discussion and increasingly developed intellect (Broadhead, 2001). Whilst children will often return to previously enjoyed styles of play, growing maturity allows for greater depths of involvement in them as children move along this developmental continuum. Table 7.1 provides an overview of theorists advocating these ideas.

REFLECTION

In what stages of play characterised by the younger children in the setting do you frequently see older children you work with revisit?

Table 7.1 Theorists throughout history (1)

Connected names	Theory	Current application	Further reading
John Comenius (1592–1670)	Learning is holistic and should be experienced through all senses from early childhood and continue throughout life.	Free-flowing sensory play with natural objects.	See the Comenius Foundation (www.comeniusfoundation.org)
Maria Montessori (1870–1952)	Learning from birth is most effective when children are interested and motivated. When adults act as observers, abstract concepts can be understood through real experiences.	Uninterrupted, child-initiated play using authentic resources and determined by children's interests.	Montessori (1996)
Jean Piaget (1962–1980)	Children's intellectual development occurs in naturally sequenced stages, reconstructing their reality as more complex concepts are experienced.	Active, hands-on experimentation where children are exposed to knowledge and ideas they are developmentally ready for. Individual interests followed by children controlling their own learning within long, uninterrupted periods of play, observed to inform future development.	Lindon and Brodie (2016)
Howard Gardner (b. 1943)	The importance of 'multiple intelligences' spanning linguistic, logical-mathematical, bodily-kinaesthetic, musical, spatial and naturalist intelligence, drawing on previous methods of thinking and exploring as more abstract thinking develops.	Holistic learning environments allowing children to extend their investigations in multiple ways.	Gardner (2011)

Practices such as talking aloud or 'self-talk' (Verba, 1994) allow children to explore more advanced ideas in their play, effectively creating a bridge for themselves towards greater mastery. Before they have developed skills of running things through in their mind, such techniques allow children to develop the processes of their thinking and help to invite interaction with children around them. As play becomes more vocalised, phrases such as 'Let's pretend that ...' and 'I know, you can be ...' are heard as adventures are planned and complex social relationships of marriage, family and alliances are acted out and explored in ways children can begin to make sense of. These vital explorations are a vehicle for children to understand and gain some sense of ownership over the highly complex issues affecting them, providing experiences of negotiation, empathy and understanding that allow engagement and practice within their highly social world. Vygotsky strongly advocated social learning: Table 7.2 provides some prompts for futher inquiry.

Table 7.2 Theorists throughout history (2)

Connected name	Theory	Current application	Further reading
Lev Vygotsky (1896–1934)	Language develops abstract thought and is fundamental in understanding. Self-talk helps regulate actions, aiding understanding of tricky concepts. Discussing familiar experiences and assigning labels supports problem solving alongside physical and visual stimuli.	Social learning. Giving children time to discuss and plan their own experiences.	Neaum (2016)

REFLECTION

When engaged in play that requires turn-taking, the assigning of roles or an involved story line, what skills are children demonstrating? How are their abilities within these skills demonstrated as you watch the play unfold?

The purpose of play

Play is a deeply rewarding intrinsic method of learning from first-hand experiences that children are born with. Recognised within early years frameworks as developing all areas of learning and essential in developing confidence and social abilities, the importance of play is reflected and highlighted in the English EYFS (DfE, 2014) within the characteristics of effective teaching. Not requiring expensive resources or extensive planning, children will find play in any place with anything and with anyone. Overcoming social, language and ability barriers with ease, play allows children the independence to experience the world in their own terms, relating to their own levels of understanding. By adding genuine, open-ended, child-initiated and well-resourced opportunities in unrushed, creative and adaptive ways, children's experiences grow along with the learning and development which is based on them, deepening their understanding (Marton & Booth, 1997; Samuelsson and Carlsson, 2008) as they actively create knowledge as they play (Dau, 1999; Levin, 1996). Whilst attempts have been made to measure the benefits of play (Smith, 1988) and the effect it has on children (Hurst, 1997), the scope of this learning medium is far from fully understood.

Supported through timely, sensitive interactions and appropriate methods of delivery, play helps children develop confidence and flexibility of thought as they come to understand and cultivate their views (Tickell, 2011), in essence developing the skills required to become good learners. When play is denied or overly managed children are deprived learning of the deepest kind, limiting opportunities now and effecting perceptions and attitudes towards learning opportunities of the future. It is this future that must be considered when evaluating the purpose of play as we look beyond abilities measurable at the time of school entry, towards the deeper potential play offers, developing features of Lifelong Learning that have a dramatic impact on the trajectories of children's lives. See Table 7.3 to further explore theorists advocating experimental, playful approaches to learning.

Table 7.3 Theorists throughout history (3)

Connected names	Theory	Current application	Further reading
Jean Jacques Rousseau (1712–1778)	Advocated merits and importance of play within a revered childhood free of restriction.	Understanding children through observations of naturally occurring play.	Boone (no date)
Robert Owen (1771–1858)	Every child has potential for greatness, depending on their experiences, so appropriate nurturing is fundamental.	The unique child, treated with respect and equality.	Davis and O'Hagan (2014)
John Dewey (1859–1952)	Children learn through doing within real-life situations, experimentation and independent thought.	Authentic opportunities to develop own interests within engaging, relevant experiences.	Pound (2008)
Margaret Donaldson (b. 1926)	Children need to make 'human sense' of concepts so tasks must be set within familiar contexts.	Authentic experiences presented from children's points of view, mindful of previous experiences. Avoiding unfamiliarity of context, especially within assessment requiring disembodied or abstract thinking.	Donaldson (2004)

REFLECTION

What do you think are the barriers to play becoming fully embraced within practice? Are some environments better able to deliver play-based curricula than others?

The role of play in developing the features of Lifelong Learning

The powerful medium of play threads its way throughout all aspects of learning, supporting and encouraging the development of each feature. Without pressures to succeed or expected outcomes to conform to, play enables children's natural emersion in a world of endless riches. From the explorations of the very young to the enquiries and investigations of older children, we shall look first to the intrinsic ways play promotes every feature of Lifelong Learning (see Table 7.4) before focusing on how these features can be promoted within practice that looks at babies, under-threes and under-fives over the next three chapters.

Table 7.4 Core attributes of Lifelong Learning

Feature	Purpose
Courageous	Within play there are no wrong answers. Given this cushion from the stress of expectation children are less likely to hold back, afraid of making mistakes. Instead they freely try new ideas in unique ways, stretching their limits, taking risks and pushing beyond familiar or perceived boundaries as they experience the joy of succeeding in areas they were not aware they could.
Self-motivated	Intrinsically rewarding, play offers emotional motivations that enhance children's persistence in trialling new techniques, practising and revising approaches until they achieve mastery. With a limited chance of losing confidence, play motivates emergent making of marks and symbols and the gratification of perseverance is felt. As play is often carried out in the absence of adults, children do not learn to rely on the motivation of praise or reward.
Confident	Within play children are given the opportunity and safety to assume, explore and trial many roles and behaviours, opportunities and actions. Through play children find an ownership of their learning, demonstrating many talents as their unique abilities are given the opportunity to shine. As level playing fields that have little to do with background, class, race or social status establish, children develop emotional well-being and their self-confidence can bloom.
Imaginative	Within play children experience many changing situations as new children join, ideas are offered and resources embraced. This allows children to continuously and spontaneously develop their imagination, adapting their course of action and solving new problems in situations that are not pre-subscribed. Granted the freedoms that play is rich in, children imaginatively initiate and trial new ideas, using resources to represent imagined realities.

(Continued)

Table 7.4 (Continued)

Feature	Purpose
Intuitive	Without set agendas, in play children are able to approach situations from their own vantage point. Trialling ideas repeatedly, they are informed by all the rapid successes and failures they experience to develop an intuitive approach to new situations.
Curious	Through play children are given permission to be inquisitive, gaining new experiences and sensations first hand. With deep levels of involvement they can investigate whatever draws their interest for the time their curiosity needs.
Playful	In a playful environment children are given opportunities to act out things they have seen and experienced in ways they can make sense of, for example through fairytale play. Possibly coming to terms with difficult concepts in their own lives, play offers children a safe place to experience uncertainty, to immerse themselves in other worlds and trial ideas without having to commit.
Sociable	As children become aware of others' perspectives, the emergence of social play sees groupings form, disband and reform freely as the nature of the game or wishes of children dictate playing needs. Social skills of sharing, communication and negotiation as well as conflict resolution and self-regulation are rehearsed to meet the needs of the play as the specific skills of each child finds a platform, encouraging new social links to form. Self-control and tolerance are rehearsed as play involving mixed abilities and cooperative turn-taking allows being in control then handing it to another to be safely experienced.
Independence	Found anywhere with anything, children are able to create play freely without the guidance or direction of adults. Able to carry out imagined actions to see where they may go with no expectations of specific end results, play allows children freedom of direction to follow their enquiries. Because play can be enjoyed alone, children also experience ease within their own company, developing the abilities to not rely on others.
Practical	Play offers children hands-on opportunities to engage in practical investigations where the end product is not important; instead, practical elements of the journey can be freely enjoyed and explored for their intrinsic interest. Whilst a practical paint mixing or ingredient weighing may never result in the colours imagined or the correct recipe followed, the experience comes in the freedom to adapt plans and trial practical techniques as play takes many different tangents.
Adaptable	Play continually adapts and changes with new ideas and as children join or leave the activity. Through these experiences children will adapt their thinking and actions, accommodating thoughts and opinions of others, managing limitations of environment and resources as well as unexpected opportunities that present themselves. Within the open arena of play there is no rigid path to follow and children experience first-hand that adaptability is both useful and successful.

Feature	Purpose
Reflective	Because play can be freely joined, left and come back to, children are given opportunities to ponder ideas and approaches. With no requirement to achieve given outcomes children can attempt something for as long as they are motivated to do so, returning to it once new perspectives have been considered. Opportunity to reflect will renew motivation and encourage fresh ideas, promoting a reflective approach to learning.
Think simultaneously	As play develops it demands an ability to consider multiple variables simultaneously – characters involved in a game, how storylines are evolving and what objects are being used to represent – all the while playing a seamless role, communicating in character and offering plotlines to meet their own agenda whilst understanding the possibilities and limitations of the environment.
Think creatively	Within play children's creative tendencies can be enhanced, demonstrated and valued. Taking any form or direction, children's inventiveness and resourceful use of props add new dimensions while setbacks allow for creative solutions. With the ability to react creatively, no problem need derail the fun as these traits are recognised and celebrated.
Think logically	Play allows children to continuously encounter contextual experiences. Through motivated and rapidly changing circumstances children develop skills to quickly pull on previous experiences, recognising similarities, informed by previous actions and solutions. Freely initiated and governed by its participants, this often follows familiar patterns as interests of those involved drive repetition of required experiences, allowing practice of familiar patterns, problem solving and exploring links to the real world and their experiences within it.
Think widely	With infinite possibilities of play children direct their learning of every concept in directions they need. Able to combine thoughts and actions, explore motivations and seek out the understanding they need, they gain knowledge in ways that hold meaning for them.

The delivery of play

Managing the development of children through their early childhood requires considerable understanding. To play with a child, however, requires a skill of a different kind; a 'letting go', a relaxing into the world of childhood that children gladly guide you into, provided they are ready for visitors. To adults with their own childhoods often far behind them, stepping into this world of imagination can be a struggle. Fortunately, paired with a child we have the best guides into this world of make-believe, if we are prepared to be guided. With thoughts of objectives, routines and demands put aside, down at child level simply enjoying spending time together play should naturally follow.

REFLECTION

What training do you have available that combines an awareness of the importance of play with the often not instinctive skills to play? Is this available to parents?

As we have seen, children are multisensory, active learners gaining knowledge from experiences afforded throughout childhood. As they grow and mature, they become exposed to more highly developed concepts and ideas and will continue to need repeated practice and free opportunities to play with ideas, imitating behaviours they see around them and processing the effects of their endeavours. The need for play continues, it does not diminish. As children begin school, experiencing shifting focus towards more traditional methods of learning, they remain aware of their need for play in processing their learning and do not easily relinquish it. It may become 'invisible' (National Research Council, 2001) and lose favour with adults (Samuelsson and Carlsson, 2008), but despite its lack of appearance in curricula wording children continue to be irresistibly drawn towards this method of learning, and if we want to do well by them we need to catch up.

Despite wide acknowledgement of its importance, play is still seen as something that happens when work stops rather than recognised as where all the real work of childhood takes place. Whilst children happily generate their own play, opportunities are heavily affected by the adults governing them; the pedagogy of the setting, the passions of the adults, the respect that play is afforded and the degree of trust that children know what they need, all have ongoing and deeply felt effects. When observing the process and the journey of learning rather than any preconceived end destination, we can begin to understand and appreciate this highly enjoyable yet fiercely powerful learning medium provided it is offered in well resourced, accessible and meaningful ways that refrain from being tokenistic. Table 7.5 provides an overview of some key theorists to further support your exploration of these ideas.

Table 7.5 Theorists throughout history (4)

Connected names	Theory	Current application	Further reading
Susan Isaacs (1885–1948)	Play following children's interests and curiosities within authentic experiences acts as a bridge into children's emotional and intellectual development when not overly governed by curricula or rules. Children should embrace emotions, regulating their own behaviours within environments free of punishment.	Understanding behaviours, interactions and expectations through discussion, behaviour modelling and activities.	Isaacs (2013)

Connected names	Theory	Current application	Further reading
Burrhus Skinner (1904–1990)	Behaviour is shaped through the reactions of others. By rewarding small, achievable tasks, counterproductive punishment is avoided.	Role modelling positive behaviours, repeating babies' recognisable words, reward policies.	Pound (2013)
Jerome Bruner (1915-	Through play children experience perception, thought, language, creativity, intuition, motivations and personality. Informing knowledge of all things, preparing for experiences to come.	Active exploration of ideas and experiences through play; creating art, building structures, expressing ideas verbally and symbolically through marks.	Lindon (2012)
Chris Athey (1924–2011)	Applied schema theory to understand young children's acquiring of knowledge. Observing children making sense of environments and people through classifying and categorising understanding through their actions.	Patterns in children's observed behaviours used to understand/ inform and resource planning that supports children's development.	Nutbrown (2011)
Paulo Freire (1921–1997)	Children must be enabled to think for themselves, forming opinions that contribute to a fair society.	Through practitioners engaging in learning alongside children, ideas are shared and respected.	Irwin (2012)

To harness the intrinsic learning potential that is the right of the playing child, a variety of opportunities must be continuously available and offered in ways that can adapt to children's needs.

HARNESSING PLAYS INTRINSIC LEARNING POTENTIAL

Play should be:

- responsive to the initiations and motivations of the children involved
- owned by the children, not planned by adults who have an end goal in sight
- open-ended and evolving, directed only towards destinations of the children's imagining
- offered alongside the companionship of fellow players

(Continued)

(Continued)

- set within real situations that children can relate to
- encouraged by offering appropriate opportunities and resources at opportune moments
- free from constraints of time and space in as much as is possible.

When play is offered in ways that children can own and freely respond to it has the potential to:

- adapt to the evolving needs of all children involved
- respond to children's individual thoughts, feelings, imaginings and curiosities
- nurture developing minds and bodies
- establish its own challenges and risks within safe environments
- offer a highly motivational bridge between children's current understanding and progression towards the next step.

As we watch play unfold we must be careful not to intrude with well-meaning intentions. As children develop and mature into more advanced styles of cooperative play, adult interactions are not always required, in fact interjected at inopportune moments these can derail both the depth of engagement enjoyed and the flow of their investigations. Left alone, deeper levels of cooperative and social play can develop as children display more involved commitment to the processes they are engaged in. Advanced problem solving and communication can develop as more adventurous challenges are explored, which by definition become more rewarding. Within these shared experiences of untethered play, greater levels of trust develop between children, alliances are formed and disbanded and very real issues are explored and considered, all through the emotional outlet that play provides.

Unfortunately children's natural instincts are not always trusted. Developments demonstrated through play are often seen as less valid than those acquired within traditional learning formats and practices demonstrated become separated from the 'real' business of learning focused on knowledge, understanding and accumulated assessable skills (Moyles, 2010). Far from limiting learning experiences, when concepts are approached in ways children manage for themselves, more advanced learning can be introduced at earlier ages, providing foundations for later understanding to pin to. With mythical, magical and metaphorical dimensions (Wood, 2008), play allows children to experience complex adult behaviours of love, anger and betrayal through scenarios they can begin to understand, free of expectations or fear of doing things wrong. If we resist preoccupations with evidencing learning and instead step back and observe children naturally engaging in play, we are offered wonderful demonstrations of highly motivated, inter-connected learning goals fuelled to greater levels of achievement. Viewed as a 'key to unlock the minds of others' (Harris, 1990: 18–19), insight into children's plans, hopes and fears are

Table 7.6 Theorists throughout history (5)

Connected names	Theory	Current application	Further reading
Johann Pestalozzi (1746–1827)	Play with purpose is fundamental, investigating and understanding nature and the spiritual and material worlds.	Offering tangible challenges within interesting environments.	Frost (2009)
Sigmund Freud (1856–1939)	Repeated trials within play allow children to experience and reconcile negative emotions, inner anxieties and instinctive urges, expressing difficult feelings safely within rules of society.	Supporting children to work through disputes and conflicts, using role play and creative outlets.	Ingleby (2012)
Rudolf Steiner (1861–1925)	Children must set their own learning pace within carefully structured environments, balancing experiences of thinking, feeling and willing. Premature pressure to succeed will destroy children's motivation to learn.	Holistic, playful, imaginative experiences within environments promoting creativity and adaption, avoiding objective-based subject learning.	Bruce (2011b)
John Bowlby (1907–1990)	Children need and seek out attachments to key adults from birth and the security and safety that these relationships bring. Most sensitive within the first two years, levels of secured attachments influence all ongoing relationships.	Strong links between home and setting, key worker systems and settling and transition policies that respect children's key relationships.	Lindon and Brodie (2016)

granted, offering opportunities to nurture and support their developments if we understand what we are looking at and are equipped to handle them sensitively. See Table 7.6 for an overview of theorists exploring some of these ideas.

REFLECTION

Children overwhelmingly agree that play is what they like to do best (Samuelsson and Carlsson, 2008). How can we harness this level of motivation and offer maximum learning potential? Are there any concepts that cannot be explored through play?

The unique potential of outdoor play

Children remain physical learners long beyond the time they are expected to sit at desks or on the carpet for prolonged periods of focused activity. To deny children their need for activity, especially as their first impressions of class learning, is in effect setting them up to fail. If we consider that children's average attention span in minutes roughly equates to their age in years, that puts the majority of reception children understandably fidgety after around four minutes, firmly implanting impressions not of the lesson's objectives, but of their lack of ability to achieve them. It is no wonder then that class management is listed as a primary concern of new teachers. With improvements in class and pupil behaviour management, engagement and motivation to learn (Sijthoff, 2014) and mental functions such as memory, perception and attention (Bilton, 2002) all demonstrated by incorporating physical movement into playful learning approaches, the importance of getting children actively involved in their learning is clear.

Outdoor play naturally offers increased potential for active learning, but the benefits continue. Beyond the obvious increase in physical activity the potential available outdoors, even when environments vary greatly, sees increased achievement across many areas, especially in boys (Pelligrini, 2005; Sylva et al., 2014), as children's personal and social development, problem solving and teamwork are promoted through more authentic tasks such as den building.

REFLECTION

What areas of learning would be used by children lifting a bucket of sand to a platform using rope?

Interactions between children and adults become more supportive outdoors rather than the directing and monitoring familiar inside, with more open questions and greater promotion of sustained shared thinking. Unnecessary intrusions and periods of directed learning also naturally happen less when play moves outside as adults are more relaxed and less likely to govern or direct children's actions, allowing for independent investigation (Maynard and Waters, 2007). When inside children are often expected to sit still and listen, whereas outside expectations are that children will run around and make increased noise through actions described as 'blowing off steam' or 'uncorking a pressurised bottle' when in reality they are accessing the physicality they need.

BENEFITS OF OUTDOOR PLAY

- Outdoor space offers great potential for promoting children's health, motor fitness, balance and coordination.
- Rich, sensory filled environments offer opportunity for free movement and louder, faster, messier play with permissions to push the boundaries of who they are and what they can do.

- With less fear of repercussions or doing wrong, greater risks are embraced and bigger challenges attempted with resulting success and escalated confidences.
- More relaxed attitudes to routines and set tasks allow for time to explore and seek out areas of interest rather than given objectives or directed focus.
- Freedom to initiate investigations allows opportunity for more complete absorption in them.
- Additional space permits greater freedoms: throwing and catching, running games and the ability to move away from frustrations and confrontations.
- Constructions can be embraced on bigger scales requiring cooperation and verbal negotiations.
- Wild spaces with growing, evolving landscapes supply opportunity for nature to be embraced first hand, stimulating climbing, balancing, creating imaginary landscapes and building shelters.
- Changing seasons offer experiences connected with weather, colour, light and shadow, growth and the effects of temperature.
- Environmental education can create in children an appreciation for its care.

REFLECTION

With so many unique benefits to outdoor play, why do you think children are not offered continual access to outdoor learning?

However, access alone is not enough, environments need managing in unobtrusive ways for these benefits to be realised. Like all quality experiences, sensitive, inconspicuous organisation must ensure that provision is free of hazards, resourced appropriately and ready to offer children continual, unique experiences. This 'behind the scenes' attention to detail allows for the confidence to stand back and let child-initiated investigations take place. Opportunities for children to follow their own investigations provides the chance to use and enhance knowledge across a range of areas of learning, identifying their own next steps and uncovering misconceptions, when authentic activities are offered in ways to be purposeful and real. To be granted extended opportunities to play freely without direction or intended outcome, children can immerse themselves in their experiences, learning from each other without the need to conform, where anything is possible. Table 7.7 provides details of some key theorists to further develop your understanding of historical attitudes towards play.

Table 7.7 Theorists throughout history (6)

Connected names	Theory	Current application	Further reading
Friedrich Froebel (1782–1852),	Self-expression and play (especially outdoors) pitched at children's current level of development is fundamental to developing the individual, fostering emotional well-being and mutual respect.	Sensory, experiential learning valuing children's current stage rather focusing on future goal preparations.	Veale (2013)
Margaret McMillan (1860–1931)	The importance of giving children time and space to play in fresh air.	Unrestricted outdoor play, experienced through every part of the body.	Tovey (2007)
Loris Malaguzzi (1920–1994)	Believing in the potential of all children, learning is seen as a holistic process involving families, the environment and all resources within it. Educators open to all messages of children (verbal and non-verbal) learn together, with parents as partners and children recognised for their ability to think and act for themselves.	Children given opportunity to express themselves, representing and viewing ideas in many inter-related formats: projected, seen through coloured glass, mirrors, video.	Edwards et al. (2011)

REFLECTION

Can you specify any barriers to offering outdoor play continuously within your practice? What can you do to overcome these?

- Can children be taken out in smaller groups to alleviate the difficulties of getting many children ready altogether and having to wait around?
- If free access is not possible, are children of all ages able to indicate when they wish to go outside? Can they put their image on a picture of the garden? Do you react to them standing by the door?
- Can coats and boots be stored in a way that children can access and put on for themselves?
- Can you help parents to understand the vital and unique importance of outdoor play through invitations to play, leaflets or parent evenings?
- Can you promote the use of 'messy clothes for messy play'? Encourage parents to dress children in clothes they are free to play and explore in, emphasising children's need to do so.

- Fear of catching a cold or becoming unwell is often given as a reason for not wanting to go outside. Help parents see the benefits of fresh air, away from environments that keep coughs and sneezes sealed in.
- Most of all practitioners must be enthusiastic and keen to embrace outdoor play:
  - appropriately dressed for the weather, welly boots and a warm coat should be seen as essential equipment for doing the job
  - play, investigation and enquiry must be embraced as practitioners recognise the deep, unique learning occurring
  - appropriate attitudes to risk and challenge need embracing so that children's enquiries are facilitated appropriately
  - outdoor environments must never be viewed as simply a place to huddle and chat.

CHAPTER SUMMARY

This chapter has explored the importance of play as a highly motivated method of gaining the experiences required for learning, a method so powerful that it is a natural part of all things children do. It highlights how every feature of Lifelong Learning is offered, developed and enhanced through play and has specifically explored the additional benefits afforded through outdoor play.

This chapter has provided practitioners with a broader discourse of the purpose and structure of play, exploring their varying role within it and the effects this can have on the developments and attitudes of children towards their learning.

Ten Key Concepts

1. Play is the most powerful vehicle for long-lasting and effective learning. (Moyles, 2010)
2. Play allows for safe exploration of complex themes. (Hurst, 1997)
3. Play is a universal construct available to anyone, overcoming barriers of language, ability and background it can be found anywhere in anything. (Broadhead, 2001)
4. Every feature of the Lifelong Learner can be explored and enhanced through play. (Brown and Patte, 2013)
5. To play effectively with children requires skills of a different kind that do not always come easily to adults. (Harris, 1990)

(Continued)

(Continued)

6 The best way to learn how to play as an adult is to enjoy unhurried, unscripted time with children. (Roberts, 2011)

7 Children remain aware of their need for play in their learning long after it has lost favour within curricula. (Miller, 2010)

8 Play must not be viewed as what happens when the work stops but where the real work of childhood takes place. (Samuelsson, 2004)

9 Play must be offered free of unnecessary interruption or limitations without predetermined outcomes. (Smidt, 2010)

10 Outdoor play, less confined by the boundaries and constraints experienced indoors, naturally delivers this powerful learning medium. (Maynard and Waters, 2007)

IDEAS FOR PRACTICE

Practical Project

Armed with Table 7.4 demonstrating the role of play in developing the features of Lifelong Learning, observe children playing both indoors and outdoors and identify where you are seeing these features being explored. If there are any features that you have not been able to identify, consider the reasons why this may be. Discuss your findings with the team and consider how you can open up the play activities you are offering to your children so that you incorporate them all.

Future Activities

Organise a day that allows the children to decide everything that happens. Invite them to discuss the nature of this day beforehand, considering what activities are followed, whether any routines are used, what features they would like included or not. As the day unfurls, observe what the children naturally want to do and identify what they have gained from it.

Work-based Tasks

Consider how you can help parents to understand the importance of playing with their child and how to offer them the guidance they may need. With National Play Day on the first Wednesday in August, you may wish to organise an event that celebrates the nature of play, inviting parents and staff to re-experience what it feels like to lose themselves in the world of play.

FURTHER READING

Brown, F. and Patte, M. (2013) *Rethinking Children's Play*. London: Bloomsbury Academic.

Using a playwork perspective, this book explores the idea that children's learning and development is derived from their opportunities to engage in play.

Brown, S. (2009) *Play, How it Shapes the Brain, Opens the Imagination and Invigorates the Soul*. London: Penguin.

Essential to developing social skills, adaptability, intelligence, creativity and ability to problem solve, this book looks at the blissful abandonment of play as necessary to not only our own health as much as sleeping and eating, but perhaps to the evolutionary survival of the species. In highly readable case studies looking at play from many angles, it suggests that play is the most important work we can do throughout our lives.

Sutton-Smith, B. (2009) *The Ambiguity of Play*. Cambridge, MA: Harvard University Press.

This book examines the importance of play and its key theories across many disciplines, considering it as having wider implications than child development, suggesting that play with its fluidity and adaptability might provide a model for 'natural' selection.

Whitebread, D. (2012) *The Importance of Play: A Report on the Value of Children's Play with a Series of Policy Recommendations*. Brussels: Toy Industries of Europe. Available at www.importanceofplay.eu/IMG/pdf/dr_david_whitebread_-_the_importance_of_play.pdf (accessed 6/4/16).

This report looks to counter the view that play is unimportant, trivial or lacking in serious purpose. It aims to demonstrate the rich variety of play, without which achievements in other areas would be impossible.

8

WORKING SPECIFICALLY WITH BABIES

THIS CHAPTER WILL

- consider the real learning objectives of the very young; understanding how this complex and fascinating world works and recognising their place within it
- explore how these learning objectives are recognised and achieved through the features of Lifelong Learning
- recognise that the process of preparing children for school and a lifetime of learning is embedded in every learning opportunity from birth, affecting the whole body (motor skills, sensory, vestibular and proprioceptive) from day one
- offer suggestions for developing these features of learning with appropriate delivery that will impact achievements and attitudes towards learning in later years.

Provision offered to very young children and the attitudes towards it can often be very different to that afforded to older children (Melhuish, 2003). Care must be taken to recognise and celebrate the first years of life, ensuring they are in no way undervalued or discounted. Rather than simply viewing a preverbal, pre-mobile dependent we must recognise that children during these time-sensitive years are developing at immense rates as they lay the foundations of all future growth (Waldfogel, 2004). This chapter will examine what it means to support the development of Lifelong Learning in these earliest years, considering practical delivery and the effect these secured features stand to have on the ongoing learning of our children.

Working with the very young

During these highly sensitive first years rapid growth and development takes effect throughout the body, strengthening muscles and developing the brain. During every afforded experience information bombards the senses to be processed across multiple regions of the brain as cumulative and explosive processes establish and reinforce visual, auditory and kinaesthetic neural networks. Experiences involving multiple senses involve more regions of the brain, widening the range of stimulation as the potential for learning becomes deeper and more effective.

The impact of pregnancy and early experiences on children's lifelong health and well-being are becoming increasingly evident (Waldfogel, 2004; DfCSF, 2009b), representing the most important determinant of children's success at school (Sylva et al., 2004) and by result their future economic status. If early experiences are inadequate there is every opportunity for learning and development to be put at risk, with enduring effects that later interventions are significantly less effective at redressing (Waldfogel, 2004). To reduce inequalities, appropriate experiences must be commonplace throughout the lives of children as the features of Lifelong Learning become established.

Care attuned to children's moods, their physical comfort as well as their need for responsive and emotive attention must be delivered by those with specialist training and understanding, mindful of the future emotional, intellectual and physical developments these experiences, relationships and environments are fuelling (Allen, 2011). Born highly reliant on the actions of those around them, babies require responsive, warm and consistent nurturing and care if they are to develop socially and emotionally (Munro, 2011). Able to consciously respond to consciously facial expressions from two months old (Trevarthen, 2011), emotional interplays are essential. Open engagement with sensitively animated smiles and facial expressions will be a joy and used as pre-verbal methods of connecting with the emotions, feelings and behaviours of others (Goldschmied and Selleck, 1996: Trevarthen, 1996), whereas distant, disinterested or closed-off behaviours will likely cause the infant stress (Tronick et al., 1978). As neuroscience illustrates, this requires positive, secure relationships (Roberts, 2011) and loving, stress-free environments (Thompson and Haskins, 2014).

As methods of communication and complexities of language develop, facial expressions alone will become insufficient and frustrating as children fail to see why their meaning is misunderstood (Forester and Cherington, 2009). As more mature techniques develop children will continuously imitate sounds, patterns and rhythms, so effective examples must surround them. The sequence of conversation participation and balanced interactions need to be modelled (Adamson et al., 2014; Forester and Cherington, 2009) with words and phrases embedded in meaningful contexts (Smidt, 2010) as familiar objects are named and routines vocalised. Those making the most utterances are not necessarily the most competent (Laevers et al., 2011) so all children, including the quieter ones, must be considered.

Value every opportunity for children to actively engage with the world and the people around them, using the experiences you share as you take time to recognise the monumental journey these infants are on. Enjoy a story with intonation, tone and pacing, experiencing repeated rhythms and patterns of language as literacy skills develop. Play with natural resources to offer multisensory, authentic opportunities for developing fine motor skills. Offer-first hand encounters with size, pattern and quantity as numeric understanding takes root, observing the complete concentration as children become absorbed in new experiences, their minds developing at rapid rates. Whilst they are mastering the skills characteristic of the age, their experiences of early learning are felt much deeper; children are also learning what it means to try to learn. Embrace and celebrate this wonderful age in its own right, not solely as preparation for children they are yet to come.

Developing the features of a Lifelong Learner

Equipped with the processes to learn since before they are born, features of Lifelong Learning are present in all children, but these need validating, encouraging and nurturing during these early days. As children look to adults seeking guidance and confirmation of their actions, these capabilities will be lost if eager attempts at learning are not valued (Kalliala, 2011). If children are denied opportunities to explore their instinctive urges to know and understand, if endeavours are limited, devalued or continuously interrupted, or if they become over stimulated and overwhelmed, they will learn that these attempts are not worth their efforts. Luckily children are very adept at demonstrating when their experiences are unmatched to their needs and within the hands of knowledgeable, experienced adults the features of Lifelong Learning can be seen to flourish.

Intrinsic qualities

Along with behavioural qualities, these core attributes within children enable them to pursue and access the experiences required to further their understanding, persisting through the time and inevitable setbacks faced on the way to mastery (see also Table 7.4). This is as true of learning to stand as it is of passing A-level physics.

Courageous

Courage within the early years requires being sufficiently comfortable to be uncertain within complex situations, to push limits and seek challenges that enable new learning experiences. This depends strongly on secure attachments and well-being. Developing alongside their increased mobility and impulse to move and explore, children should be permitted free exploration rather than confining them to bouncy chairs or segregated areas.

How can we develop this in our under-twos?

- Ensure that children are well attached to key people and comfortable in their surroundings.
- Allow children freedom to explore resources, make choices and try new things that challenge their existing physical and *cognitive* boundaries.
- Resist assisting too early or limiting their direction of enquiry.

Suggested delivery:

- Allow children the freedom they need to explore.
- Be aware of the potential for excessive frustrations making sure children feel protected and secure through reassuring interactions.

- Offer challenges that stretch their abilities – reaching out for objects, moving themselves into new areas and accessing new sensations.
- Games such as peekaboo, hiding objects under blankets or books with flaps introduce the pleasure of discovery as they build the courage to try something new.

Preparation for later learning:

- As children develop their courage to try new things, stretching their perceived limits and achieving the rewards experienced, courageous explorations will follow, provided these have been enjoyable experiences.

Self-motivated

Babies are born highly motivated to learn and will naturally display enthusiasm for new opportunities provided their basic needs are met. However, these self-motivated features will fade if persistence is met with obstructions or denied opportunities to experience the rewards of gaining new skills for themselves.

How can we develop this in our under-twos?

- Allow babies to explore their own enquiries, without routines over managing their time or being too quick to jump to their aid.
- Support discreetly so that they may focus on their chosen enquiries, unhampered by time and allowed to make mistakes.

Suggested delivery:

- Offer resources that react in unexpected ways, such as items that will not fit in all containers provided, requiring self-motivated persistence to discover solutions.
- Make things interesting with colour, texture and reactions, such as movement or noises they can manipulate.
- As mobility increases, self-motivated, active participation within the environment develops (Musatti and Mayer, 2011), so consider this when placing resources and interesting experiences.

Preparation for later learning:

- Pursuing self-directed exploration, accessing and fuelling current motivations brings its own reward, promoting desires to continue and embedding persistence even in the absence of external praise or reward.

Confident

Opportunities to trial their own investigations gives children a belief in their endeavours, raising confidence and self-esteem as abilities within tasks grow.

Having profound effects on emotional well-being, this sense of personal gratification must be promoted by careful selection of challenges, offering a sense of achievement without undermining confidence.

How can we develop this in our under-twos?

- Offer children activities that bolster their confidence whilst they contemplate more challenging opportunities, such as grasping and mouthing a toy while they consider how to make the car move.
- Through secure knowledge of children's abilities, offer a variety of tasks for them to select in their play.
- Develop confidence through repetition with familiar patterns of a favoured book and predictable experiences within routines.

Suggested delivery:

- Ranging from those they can succeed at, increase the complexity of tasks as their confidence grows.
- Bear in mind that confidence levels change throughout the day as children become tired; alternative options need to be as rewarding.
- Avoid completing tasks for them, allow them to persist.

Preparation for later learning:

- Confidence within their environment and with their own abilities fuels children's motivations to pursue more advanced learning, offering the self-assurance and enthusiasm to approach the next challenge.

Behavioural qualities

Along with intrinsic qualities, these core attributes enable children to approach new challenges in meaningful ways. Without needing to be led through every pursuit, children with these secure behaviours access their own learning from all available experiences. This is as true of learning how to make a chain rattle in a can as it is to designing chemical reactions.

Imaginative

Every time children are presented with new resources to manipulate, touch and mouth, they are given another opportunity to advance their imagination. Developing processes that began as instinct, children are drawn to new encounters, enhancing their bank of experiences. Considering what an opportunity will be like and whether they wish to have it will allow imagination to develop.

How can we develop this in our under-twos?

- Allow children opportunities to watch others at play, demonstrating experiences they can then try.
- Offer familiar experiences to utilise memories, imagining what it will be like.
- Care must be taken not to make assumptions, perceive early attempts as insignificant or stunt endeavours by denying access.

Suggested delivery:

- Allow children to explore resources and their many uses in their own way.
- Resist assuming conventional use of objects or conforming to expected outcomes.
- Take free exploration outside where more opportunity is permitted.
- Let art take many forms. Foods are excellent for imagining multisensory taste, feel and sound combinations.

Preparation for later learning:

- With imagination children embrace opportunities from many angles, learning more than the expected lessons. By testing and reaffirming ideas through every experience, imaginations are given opportunity to develop.

Intuitive

Patterns of intuitive behaviour are seen from birth, for example as children turn towards milk and use smiles to engage emotional reactions. To extend and strengthen this powerful skill of simply knowing something requires a bank of diverse and relatable experiences ready to be employed.

How can we develop this in our under-twos?

- Allow children to follow natural intuitions such as grasping and mouthing objects.
- Ensure that intuitive behaviours are not overlooked, disapproved of or devalued.

Suggested delivery:

- The mouth is full of sensory receptors children intuitively use to inform enquiries. Offer resources that can be safely explored in this way so that they may experience their intuitive instincts providing rich information rather than a source of upset or negative responses.
- Offer well-timed experiences similar to previous ones so they may apply their now instinctive response.

Preparation for later learning:

- The confidence and motivation to follow instincts enables children to seek out and access learning opportunities, drawing logical conclusions from them as they make the links in their learning.

Curious

Intensely interested in their world, children are naturally curious, seeking out opportunities to observe and investigate objects and people around them. To deepen understanding of new experiences they enthusiastically explore that within reach using all their senses, whether we want them to or not.

How can we develop this in our under-twos?

- Children need the opportunity to experiment in ways natural to them.
- Encourage and stimulate natural curiosity as mobility develops by providing interesting objects to reach for and mouth.
- Mindful of challenges this brings, manage the environment rather than stunting or denying opportunities.

Suggested delivery:

- Offer new, interesting resources and sensory-rich experiences safe for mouth exploration, such as real fruits and vegetables and creative projects that can be eaten.
- Present resources in different ways, for example slightly hidden in a treasure basket or under a blanket.
- Offer books with flaps, colours and textures.
- Objects concealed within sand or around the environment also encourage curious exploration.

Preparation for later learning:

- A powerful learning medium, curiosity will see children eager to seek out learning opportunities and supply a constant reward for their efforts.

Approaches to learning

With a range of approaches to learning, children will be able to acquire new knowledge and consider any problem from a variety of angles, finding the method that suits and ensuring that every learning opportunity is maximised and enjoyed.

Playful

Playful learning allows children to approach new situations in unthreatening ways. Using past experiences and observations of others, children will trial ideas and actions within safe environments. At their own pace and driven by their own needs, children experience complete emersion in satisfying learning experiences.

How can we develop this in our under-twos?

- Give babies opportunities to observe older children at play, where possible offering access to the same (or equivalent) resources.
- It is important for babies to wallow in play, so avoid breaking this essential practice with routine whenever possible.
- Consider if nappy changes and snacks can wait until the child indicates they have come to a natural pause in their play.

Suggested delivery:

- Offer a range of interesting resources, both familiar and new, to be freely played with using all senses.
- Take play outside as often as possible for increased stimulation and freedom.
- Provide sufficient resources so that sharing (a concept they are not ready for) is not an issue.
- Equip environments to accommodate differing needs and mobilities of the group.
- Avoid rushing or directing play, allowing it to take its own direction.

Preparation for later learning:

- Play offers children a safe environment in which to experience and rehearse ideas and concepts currently too complex to master whilst supplying a means of acquiring the skills needed for more advanced learning.

Sociable

Children are born into a highly sociable world able to use their natural abilities to motivate companionship and attention. Watching and interacting with those around them they observe interplays, behaviours and emotions as they rehearse language and facial expressions, trialling new ideas and learning from reactions enticed from others.

How can we develop this in our under-twos?

- Allow babies to watch others and participate with older minds (Trevarthen, 2011), motivating companionship (Roberts 2011).
- Encourage communication incorporating faces, hands and whole-body movements.
- Responding to facial expressions and voices from two months old (Trevarthen, 2011), children become easily distressed when responses are blocked (Allen, 2011), so sensitively manage their attempts.

Suggested delivery:

- Allow free movement towards social opportunities, avoiding segregated areas or prolonged securing in chairs.
- Provide opportunities to play alongside others, watching and participating within emerging social exchanges.
- Promote listening and experimentation of two-way babble by avoiding excessive background noise or overly distracting environments.
- Model warm, positive social interactions within stimulating environments that respond to children's reactions and attempts.
- Sit with children to provide a point of reference to their investigations (Musatti and Mayer, 2011), drawing them towards you.

Preparation for later learning:

- Social experiences are rewarding and exciting (Hurst, 1997); through them children learn to regulate emotions, demonstrating pride, shyness and showing off while recognising their effects on others (Murray and Trevarthen, 1985). Through warm, positive interactions language skills are developed and motor skills encouraged as they explore their world.

Independence

Permitted the thrill of independent discovery and motivated by previous experiences, children develop a sense of their own abilities. As they gain control of their bodies, grasping and releasing objects, supporting their head, their bodies and later mobility, greater possibilities for independence are presented. Hands no longer required for crawling are freed and more area can be covered, increasing fascinating, independent explorations, the rewards of which are clearly seen in their reactions.

How can we develop this in our under-twos?

- Know your children and their capabilities, resist the urge to make things easy.
- Whilst being mindful of creating frustrations, greater challenges offer a greater potential sense of reward, so present activities for children to access for themselves, allowing freedom of choice rather than presuming what they need.

Suggested delivery:

- As children independently engage with new environments, people, situations and skills, encourage their explorations with careful positioning of enticing opportunities.
- Consider spatial arrangement of environments to progress physical, *cognitive* and social abilities, allowing children to independently explore and rehearse skills.

- React to current achievements as you adjust the *scaffolding* you offer. Allowing room for independence to develop, being careful to offer the help required rather than the help that was needed yesterday.

Preparation for later learning:

- To maximise their learning children need the opportunity to do things for themselves, gaining the skills and freedoms to access that which is personally needed as they experience the satisfaction of independent achievement.

Practical

Children use their senses and the knowledge gained through movement to inform their learning. Access to ongoing practical experiences is instrumental in this process. Continually developing a sense of their own abilities, practical play informs these young learners how their world operates, equipping them with the tools to approach new problems.

How can we develop this in our under-twos?

- Provide familiar resources so that practical assumptions can be made based on previous experiences.
- Provide opportunities for children to effect practical change, for example moving things, grasping objects, causing sound and light effects.
- Introduce new elements with similar properties and new possibilities so their understanding can be used and challenged.

Suggested delivery:

- Avoid being too quick to change the experiences you offer. Allow children to return, building on their knowledge, exploring the practical possibilities of the objects at hand.
- Offer opportunities to develop practical trial and improvement techniques, such as making objects move or sound, fitting objects inside one another, pulling clothes off a doll or the cause and effect of splashing in water.

Preparation for later learning:

- Practical experiences provide the skills, manual dexterity and confidence to embrace future practical learning where these skills will be enhanced. It will have informed children's understanding of how objects work with one another as connections are made within their understanding.

Adaptable

Whilst babies need the security of familiar routines and processes, care must be taken to avoid becoming too rigid. Daily routines do not always run like clockwork and adaptability must be fostered to avoid high levels of stress in these situations.

How can we develop this in our under-twos?

- Routines and experiences should be flexible to children's current needs, allowing children to adapt to them.
- If play is deep and engaging, resist automatically breaking it to follow routine and instead consider whether a nappy change or bottle can wait until a natural break is reached.
- Ensure that your plans can be adapted, optimising and capturing opportunities as they present themselves.

Suggested delivery:

- Be aware of everything you could use as a learning opportunity, such as activities with older children you could observe or partake in, local events, weather you can feel as multisensory, whole-body experiences.
- Be organised so you can react to opportunities as adapting to them becomes a natural occurrence.

Preparation for later learning:

- Adaptable children are able to use many learning opportunities wherever they arise. Through these they will hear language of various styles to build vocabularies, see skills demonstrated and experience wide-ranging sensations. Being adaptable helps prevent stress levels that would otherwise restrict these opportunities for learning.

Reflective

Hands-on experiences are the beginning of deep learning. Children also need the opportunity to consider what has gone before, to try again, adapting their approach in order to achieve. Having observed others at play or experiencing new activities for themselves, children need opportunities to reflect on their experiences and experiment soon after the event.

How can we develop this in our under-twos?

- Children need to see people playing and engaging within a range of tasks, with time to consider what they have seen and emulate this for themselves.
- At this age children's focus remains on the present so direct, real experiences need to be provided for them to make meaning of.

Suggested delivery:

- Offer lots of opportunities to watch other children at play with opportunity to trial ideas they have seen demonstrated themselves with (where possible) the same resources.

- Allow the time it takes for children to ponder their actions and consider their observations.
- Resist giving cues or directives prematurely.

Preparation for later learning:

- Reflective skills allow children to consider alternative methods of achieving a task, even before they are aware of the process. Rather than giving up after a first attempt they become informed by the alternative approaches trialled and observed.

Modes of thought

Thought processes need to be established to ensure that children are able to manage information in whatever format it is gained, from any source, adapting their approach accordingly.

Think simultaneously

Babies' natural instinct is to simultaneously gather information from a range of sources, using their hands and mouths to inform their understanding.

How can we develop this in our under-twos?

- Provide opportunities for babies to explore in all ways natural to them.
- Extend play to consider spatial dimensions (under, over, inside, behind).
- Provide opportunities to play with relationships between objects as they simultaneously explore with their hands, feet and mouth, informed through all their senses.

Suggested delivery:

- Allow for objects to be accessed and moved between areas as children freely combine their thinking in different ways.
- Enable multisensory play by taking off socks and ensuring materials used can be safely put in the mouth.

Preparation for later learning:

- By simultaneously combining the areas of learning available to children, their banks of experiences are developed in deeper ways than discrete experiences would permit. As new experiences are encountered they are underpinned by these multifaceted, enriched foundations.

Think creatively

From the beginning we must balance adult scaffolding that directs children's focus and attention with that which guides and supports it to achieving greater creativity, enhancing children's inventiveness without imposing limits.

How can we develop this in our under-twos?

- Allow babies to pursue their ideas in ways that may be different to that expected.
- Fuelled by powerful curiosity, support and encourage new ways of exploring, resisting the urge to direct towards expectations.

Suggested delivery:

- Offer wide ranges of resources for exploration without predetermined expectations or direction.
- Allow observations of creative play inside and out to inform the style of resources that would most enhance this play without directing the end result.

Preparation for later learning:

- Having experienced the rewards of approaching new endeavours untethered, children are more open-minded towards learning opportunities of the future, more aware of and able to access the learning approaches right for them.

Think logically

In dealing with everyday encounters, predictable reactions will follow established patterns as children manipulate objects or recognise patterns in the shape of a face. The development of logical thought can be seen through the *schematic behaviours* they display, incorporating positioning and logical, repeated actions.

How can we develop this in our under-twos?

- Offer predictable logic in daily routines, such as collecting a nappy together before a change or getting out plates before a meal.
- Through established patterns children can find familiarity within new challenges.

Suggested delivery:

- Provide resources that behave in similar ways to each other, such as many different balls that roll when pushed in the same way.
- Offer resources that provide an expected outcome each time they are used, such as recordings accessed by pressing a button.
- Allow repeated play with open-ended resources so they can trial many options, discovering the logic within, such as water play with jugs and bottles with holes in the side.

Preparation for later learning:

- As learning becomes more complex, children need strategies to make sense of it. Establishing logical approaches to their enquiries, noticing and using pattern prepares them for this.

Think widely

As babies combine increasing mobility with natural instincts for exploration and investigation they become ready to engage in their wider surroundings, taking in information from all sources as connections are made in their learning.

How can we develop this in our under-twos?

- Offer environments free for exploring, with the encouragement of interesting discoveries to maximise children's access to wide ranges of experiences and learning opportunities.
- Ensure that this is delivered with the uninterrupted time children need to discover and explore.

Suggested delivery:

- Within stimulating environments, provide many opportunities to select so that interests can be followed and combined.
- Encourage free exploration with new and previously enjoyed resources found in a variety of places.
- Avoid having areas that are out of bounds, instead risk assess wide-ranging environments so children can freely trial and investigate.

Preparation for later learning:

- Before the perception of detail, children tend to follow *schematic behaviours* that embrace wider thinking (Broadhead, 2001), suggesting the need for broader approaches before the finer detail of future learning can be fully understood. By encouraging wider opportunities, children become bathed in experiences embedded in meaningful contexts as developing skills are given meaning.

CHAPTER SUMMARY

This chapter has considered how to develop the features of Lifelong Learning within our youngest children, instilling and nurturing these fundamental and underpinning principles of all learning from the very beginning.

(Continued)

(Continued)

Ten Key Concepts

1. Within securely attached relationships, encourage children without premature assistance that devalues their endeavours.
2. Whilst protected from excessive frustration, engage children with achievable challenges to creatively stretch their abilities, motivating active participation and promoting confidence.
3. Encourage children's natural methods of engagement, choosing, manipulating and combining resources freely to explore spatial dimensions, movement and effect, unafraid of making mistakes.
4. Allow children to set the pace, wallowing in whole-body experiences unrestricted by limiting routines or distractions.
5. Avoiding plastic, offer ample authentic, multisensory, unexpected and interesting resources presented in different ways.
6. Within familiar, accessible and encouraging environments, offer children opportunities to manipulate and adapt, to ponder and revisit, avoiding prematurely clearing away.
7. Know the children, their moods, fatigue and abilities so that scaffolding can easily adjust.
8. Offer opportunities to watch others, copying actions and participating with older children.
9. Take play outside for increased stimulation and freedom.
10. Whilst following familiar, logical patterns, ensure that planning remains adaptable, ready to react to opportunities.

IDEAS FOR PRACTICE

Practical Project

Consider how you actively promote the 16 features of Lifelong Learning with the babies you work with. Identify which features are being consistently demonstrated and nurtured, highlighting your successes and the ongoing benefits to your parents.

Future Activities

For each of the features of Lifelong Learning that you feel are not being adequately nurtured, consider how you can develop practice to incorporate them. You may use the suggestions given or take inspiration from these to inspire your own ideas. Following discussions with the team, focus on a new feature every week, adding to the depth of practice offered.

Work-based Tasks

Work with babies can often be undervalued. Produce literature such as pamphlets or posters to demonstrate the importance of the activities detailed above in a way to inform parents.

FURTHER READING

Durkan, M., Field, F., Lamb, N. and Loughton, T. (no date) *The 1001 Critical Days: The Importance of the Conception to Age Two Period*. Available at www.1001criticaldays.co.uk/1001days_Nov15.pdf (accessed 22/6/16).
This cross-party manifesto sees politicians from all parties acknowledging the crucial period of 1001 critical days from when a baby is conceived until age two. Highlighting the importance of early action on children's lifelong outcomes it recognises the moral, scientific and economic case for action within the early years being a focus of policy-making processes.

Movellan, J. (2015) 'Why babies smile', *Science Teacher*, 82 (8): 18.
This article looks at the natural instincts of babies to elicit responses from the adults around them. Using computer scientists, roboticists and developmental psychologists, it considers the impact of babies' smiles, their timing and the responses these elicit from adults.

Murray, L. and Andrews, L. (2005) *The Social Baby: Understanding Babies' Communication from Birth*. Glasgow: CP Publishing.
Based on evidence collected in research institutes around the world, this book uses picture sequences and engaging text to illustrate key aspects of the rich and complex social world of babies, showing how to relate more sensitively and responsively to the babies who depend on our care.

Rose, J. (2015) *Health and Well-being in Early Childhood*. London: Sage.
By looking at health and well-being from many fundamental and interrelated themes, this book brings together wide-ranging evidence on what matters to children's well-being in the early years, inviting reflection and implications for practice.

9

WORKING SPECIFICALLY WITH UNDER-THREES

THIS CHAPTER WILL

- consider the real learning objectives of 2-year-olds, navigating a minefield of demands and expectations as they become more familiar with this complex and fascinating world while navigating their place within it
- explore how these learning objectives are recognised and achieved in relation to the specific challenges and frustrations 2-year-olds face, progressing their learning with confidence and security through the features of Lifelong Learning
- recognise that the process of preparing children for school and a lifetime of learning is embedded in every learning opportunity throughout the early years
- offer suggestions for developing these features of learning with appropriate delivery to impact achievements and attitudes towards learning in later years.

To secure optimum foundations of learning, provision must focus on the distinctive needs of children as they turn two. Perhaps experiencing their first vertical transition away from secure attachment figures, this period sees mobility, vocabularies and cognitive abilities increasing at different rates, bringing monumental accomplishments as well as frustrations. With more 2-year-olds encouraged into early years settings it is imperative that specific understanding of this age group is maintained within the practitioners responsible for their care.

Holistic development of children's *cognitive* abilities, as well as initial explorations of the skills essential for developing more complex understanding, is rooted in the experiences offered to children in their early years (Sylva et al., 2004; Feinstein and Duckworth, 2006), with development scores at 22 months highly predictive of profiles at school entry (Sylva et al., 2004). This chapter will examine what it means to support children's development during this formative time, considering practicalities of delivery and the importance of securing confidence within each of the features of Lifelong Learning.

Working with under-threes

As recognised within the EYFS, developing key skills of all future areas of learning, including reading and writing, first requires security within the *prime areas* (Tickell, 2011). Children progress through their early years developing these key skills and establishing attitudes towards future learning, relationships and their self-belief. Heavily informed by all previous experiences, the brain will use familiar patterns within new experiences to predict and anticipate what may come next as situations are viewed with maturing abilities. Repetition is fundamental within this process and instinctively used throughout infancy to perfect skills, consolidating concepts and language (Smidt, 2010), but it needs recognising and promoting to enable further and more developed understanding.

Language and literacy are developing but will at times present frustration as children struggle to be understood. Opportunities to engage and experiment within authentic events will offer real purpose to their early efforts, especially when directed by their own interests and viewed as elements of larger social events, rather than as rules to master (Lynch, 2009). As vocabularies develop, more advanced forms of communication are possible as children engage in deeper learning, verbalising their needs and accessing what they require.

Books have already offered opportunities to play with concepts of rhythm, familiarity and predictability. Viewed as fun and comforting, they now begin to offer greater engagement and deeper understanding as children learn how to act like a reader. Turning pages, understanding how books work, the form and purpose of reading and writing establishes itself as children link fantasy and reality through the connections made between images on the page and real-life objects (Smidt, 2010).

At this time children undergo formative assessment by way of the *two-year development review*. Working collaboratively with health professionals, this review of attainment of the *prime areas* of learning is intended to monitor development and identify where additional support is required before the transition to school, by which time overcoming barriers to learning is much harder. With the understanding and cooperation of parents and families, timely, unified and well-informed interventions and effective, ongoing programmes of support can be offered (Allen, 2011), effectively addressing difficulties and helping children overcome specific obstacles to learning (Tickell, 2011).

Features of a Lifelong Learner

As the features of Lifelong Learning become more established, greater depths of understanding can flourish, provided we tune in to the specific needs and abilities of the age. As with younger children, all attempts at learning need supporting and encouraging in ways that promote children's individual journey. This year can incorporate many frustrations and needs to be viewed with the utmost understanding of the child, the motivations, capabilities and incentives characteristic of this time and with realistic expectations that both challenge and stimulate. Within the hands of experienced, knowledgeable adults, the features of Lifelong Learning will be seen to establish and thrive.

Intrinsic qualities

Along with behavioural qualities, these core attributes within children enable them to pursue and access the experiences required to further their understanding, persisting through the time and inevitable setbacks faced on the way to mastery. This is as true of learning to stand as it is of passing A-level physics.

Courageous

Mobility is improving greatly along with a sense of adventure and purpose. These initial attempts at courageous exploration must be met with support and encouragement within environments equipped for challenging, risk aware play.

How can we develop this in our under-threes?

- Children look for reassurance from trusted adults as courageous play develops, encourage their play without reprimand, allowing experimentation even if actions are not what you would choose or expect.
- As children become more comfortable and familiar within their own bodies allow them to set the pace, testing boundaries with the time, resources and opportunities required.
- Within appropriately rewarding challenges, promote the courage to persist.
- Avoid pushing directions they are not yet ready for or preventing that which they are.

Suggested delivery:

- Offer experiences that present challenges, such as climbing frames, beams or balancing on logs, aware that easily achieved goals will likely be insufficient.
- Allow children to access what they need when they need it, resisting premature aid or deferring the moment.
- Sometimes courage is not there immediately and may need the support of friends or a few return visits, so ensure that access to opportunities remain.

Preparation for later learning:

- As children grow and develop, their deep-rooted attitudes towards learning are forming. By gaining experiences of success in challenges significant to them and achieving where previously they could not, mindsets encouraging courageous behaviours are developed, allowing children to push through their own boundaries when future challenges are met.

Self-motivated

As abilities rapidly develop, children are motivated to access all manner of experiences. Keen to experience all they can, their ongoing self-motivations must be enabled through wide-ranging opportunities to trial new skills. Where their motivations are inappropriate, this must be handled sensitively and equally stimulating alternatives offered.

How can we develop this in our under-threes?

- Allow children to develop a sense of ownership within the activities available.
- Understand what currently motivates the children, offering opportunities to explore these ideas.
- Enable children to participate in ways that suit their motivations and abilities.
- Suggest activities that motivate the interests of wonderers, without misreading 'thinking time' as children mentally process their next move.

Suggested delivery:

- Ensure that resources are sufficient for all to become involved and left available for children to try again, demonstrating abilities to friends or trying different approaches having had time to ponder.
- Offer experiences in new and interesting ways that motivate new interest, ensuring that time is given for complete absorption.

Preparation for later learning:

- In deeply motivated play, new words and skills are required and developed as vocabulary increases, one of the most important indicators of future language and literacy success (Wasik et al., 2011). Self-motivated learning demonstrates to children their own possibilities in highly pleasurable and rewarding ways.

Confident

With confidence growing alongside ability it may take many knocks as explorations and interactions do not go as planned. With sensitive handling confidence levels will be preserved, nurtured and enhanced throughout the group.

How can we develop this in our under-threes?

- Ensure that activities are presented in ways to challenge whilst remaining in their grasp, offering a sense of achievement at varying levels of success.
- Recognise significant achievements in each child, offering relevant praise to show connections with their success.

Suggested delivery:

- Offer resources allowing children to demonstrate achievements, especially when unique to them and recognise it as such.
- Find confidence within familiar routines and patterns then follow up with trips to local shops or parks, safely gaining experiences outside their usual comfort zone.
- As language develops pronunciation may remain challenging, so avoid presumption or pressured environments from denting their confidence.

Preparation for later learning

- Building children's confidence stimulates self-belief. Less likely to avoid experiences, confident children are more likely to embrace new experiences, taking what they need to achieve, engaging with others and developing their identity as a confident individual.

Behavioural qualities

Along with intrinsic qualities, these core attributes enable children to approach new challenges in meaningful ways. Without needing to be led through every pursuit, children with these secure behaviours access their own learning from all available experiences. This is as true of learning how to make a chain rattle in a can as it is to designing chemical reactions.

Imaginative

Young children require hands-on experiences to develop understanding of concepts. Before they can process ideas mentally, rehearsing in their head, they need to develop imagination.

How can we develop this in our under-threes?

- Allow children to represent their ideas using resources in imaginative ways, not dependent on specified objectives.
- Allow opportunities to rehearse different roles through symbolic role play, pretending and creating scenarios based on previous experiences.
- Allow opportunities to imagine what will come next in their day.

Suggested delivery:

- Tell stories from your imagination; what do they think is going to happen next?
- Look at pictures together; what do they imagine it is, what is happening, what might come next?

- Allow opportunities to link fantasy to reality, connecting images to real life.
- Discuss what will happen next in their day so they can imagine this for themselves.

Preparation for later learning

- As children develop skills for mentally processing and linking that which they think about to that experienced, they are able to mentally rehearse possible outcomes and imagine new concepts, considering multiple outcomes before plans are made. These techniques allow them to consider their actions and responses, make sense of ideas being discussed and make more informed responses within their learning.

Intuitive

By now children are building banks of experiences to inform them how their world works. As these develop children become more able to make logical judgements and predictions about the things around them.

How can we develop this in our under-threes?

- Allow children to express ideas and receive adult and peer feedback.
- Let children see their free-forming ideas take shape.
- Allow activities today to echo that experienced yesterday so children can develop intuitive responses to their experiences.

Suggested delivery:

- If digging for treasure had been enjoyed yesterday, bury something else today, allowing children to build on knowledge gained and experience satisfaction from their intuitive success as new objects are discovered in similar ways.
- If a reward was offered yesterday, allow children to earn another if they naturally follow similar behaviours.

Preparation for later learning:

- To access the precise learning experience children require they need to have a level of intuition that drives explorations into the most beneficial areas, intuitively knowing what support they require and how best to receive it.

Curious

With added independence and mobility, curiosity can be more freely explored. Fuelled by previous rewards from curious explorations, children are keen to investigate their environment, understanding it on deeper levels.

How can we develop this in our under-threes?

- Give children free access to resources and environments, allowing access to areas that draw them, with permission to combine and manipulate as needed.
- Having risk-assessed environments, resist dampening curiosity or curtailing it with demands.

Suggested delivery:

- Reward curiosity with hidden treasures.
- Offer inquisitive exploration of different kinds of substances that react in different ways to their touch.
- Share detailed illustrations featuring areas of interest, such as jungle scenes full of wild animals.
- Resist the overuse of plastic, instead favour real materials that reward curiosity through all the senses.

Preparation for later learning:

- Developing a curious nature provides inbuilt incentives to approach and persist with learning activities. Curious to know and understand, children will be attracted to rich experiences, deepening and widening their learning experiences.

Approaches to learning

With a range of approaches to learning children will be able to acquire new knowledge and consider any problem from a variety of angles, finding the method that suits and ensuring that every learning opportunity is maximised and enjoyed.

Playful

As social and communication skills develop, different styles of play will be experimented with. Understand the intrinsic value of the emerging methods being trialled and allow space both inside and out so that activities do not become limited.

How can we develop this in our under-threes?

- Give children time, space and opportunity to react in childlike ways through play with minimum adult interaction.
- As emotions of joy, frustration, sadness and anger are expressed, become involved only when necessary, allowing children to use and experience these within their play.

Suggested delivery:

- Provide familiar resources such as authentic items within the home corner and dressing-up clothes representing people around them.
- Make sure sufficient resources, space and time are provided to minimise negative emotions and issues of space or sharing to derail play.
- Children need to experience rough-and-tumble play and social dominance, so find ways that these can be explored safely through physical play and games.

Preparation for later learning:

- As children play with ideas such as emergent mark-making and sharing stories within their play, they are becoming familiar with the purpose of writing and reading. While establishing the mechanics needed, the enjoyable and rewarding function of these activities is experienced, rather than simply acquiring skills to decode.

Sociable

Developing language, interactions and mobility are now allowing for greater sociability. Social interplays will also be aiding the exploration of differences in gender, race, skin colour, hair and facial features (Vandenbroeck, 1999).

How can we develop this in our under-threes?

- Offer wide-ranging communication methods, mindful of different abilities and recognising where frustrations or limitations may be felt.
- Emotions are not as developed as is often expected, so time and understanding must be given within situations.
- Allow children time to demonstrate ideas to peers within different social groupings, providing support where needed.
- To understand conversation sequencing children need to experience and then participate in it, learning to respond appropriately (Forester and Cherington, 2009).

Suggested delivery:

- Encourage sociable interactions and cooperation of the group by coordinating a point of interest through shared activities or a new focus.
- Begin connecting the language of emotions, feelings and behaviours through social interactions.
- Encourage language development by playing with new words during shared activities.
- Avoid doing everything in the same social groupings or key worker groups.

Preparation for later learning:

- Language ability is shown to be a strong determinant of group formation and togetherness (Oers and Hännikäinen, 2001). As children learn to react within complex relationships, engaging in social interactions, they are encouraged to develop their social skills. As they engage others in their interests, inviting flowing exchanges, interrelated skills develop around shared attention to objects or events, providing experience of interrelated techniques such as those required for more advanced learning (Lynch, 2009). The more experience children have of engaging, the more likely they are to focus on complex shared topics (Adamson et al., 2014).

Independence

Having been dependent on the actions of others for many things, liberation experienced through growing independence comes as a powerful realisation, encouraging greater confidence as abilities grow.

How can we develop this in our under-threes?

- Avoid doing too much for children. Allow skills of manual dexterity to develop so help is less required.
- Give children opportunities to practise required skills.
- Doing up coats and cutting up food may seem a kindness but this detracts from their attempts and removes a sense of achievement.
- Let children experience decision making, independently deciding on actions.

Suggested delivery:

- Encourage independent dressing, putting on shoes and coats and managing cutlery and resources as you support and celebrate growing confidence.
- Offer manageable situations to practise growing skills, such as playing with knives in modelling clay.
- Practise taking boots on and off when not in a hurry to get outside.
- Resist intervening too early or overly directing play, as this risks suggesting their endeavours are not worth their efforts.

Preparation for later learning:

- Children are learning constantly, but most profoundly where it has personal meaning, accessed at precisely the right level and in the right context. More likely to seek out and access their own learning opportunities, independent learners are informed by a growing understanding of their abilities, knowing what they can independently achieve and what needs to come next in ways onlookers are never fully privy to.

Practical

To develop practical skills children need many opportunities for hands-on experiences where resources inspire active participation, where ideas can be trialled and returned to free of directed expectation and efforts are rewarded with great personal satisfaction.

How can we develop this in our under-threes?

- Give children opportunities to engage with resources in ways they feel they need to without prescribing outcomes or expected results.
- Allow children to become immersed in explorations at a practical level, trialling properties of given materials, investigating and combining new ideas to see what they can achieve.

Suggested delivery:

- Establish environments for children to play with real events and resources for real purposes, such as ceramic plates, real food and utensils that work.
- Encourage practical responsibilities such as putting on boots before going outside, aprons on before painting and helping lay tables.

Preparation for later learning:

- Hands-on investigation gives children deeper understanding of how things work, ready for the more complex learning ahead. Muscle recall enables practical children to develop skills without needing to think about them, learning to perform tasks and manipulations with ease. Pencil grip will develop within hands that have established the muscle and fine motor skills to control utensils – core muscles that have strengthened through practical play will support children through the day.

Adaptable

As children bridge the gap between highly dependent situations and greater freedoms, adaptability helps them experience these transitions with less stress as they develop the flexibility to combine both approaches with ease.

How can we develop this in our under-threes?

- Encourage playful experiences that are open to adaptation so that children have opportunities to change things for themselves.
- Offer new experiences that may mean venturing out to new environments or joining new groups.
- Allow the day to follow a natural ebb and flow so that variation may be a natural occurrence, avoiding becoming too reliant on rigid routine.

Suggested delivery:

- Allow access to diverse selections of opportunities during the course of the day so that children can adapt their choice of activity as they feel the need.
- Allow children to adapt the intention of resources or activities, avoiding prescribed outcomes.

Preparation for later learning:

- As children progress their learning they need to make informed decisions and select a course of action, whether building a fort or solving a sum. Sometimes first ideas are not the most appropriate and children need to have learnt to adapt to changing situations, insufficient resources or methods that did not work. Adaptable children alter their course of action without losing motivation, ready to trial and learn from alternative approaches.

Reflective

Children are now beginning to develop their creative imagination (Bruce, 2011a), internalising thoughts and finding their own ideas. These will be continually informed by previous experiences but this reflective process needs time and space to take root and flourish.

How can we develop this in our under-threes?

- Offer opportunities for children to return to activities, having given their actions further thought.
- In order to reflect on mistakes, children need opportunities to make them. Allow this to happen so children can find meaning in their actions.
- Support children through offering repeated access to a range of materials.

Suggested delivery:

- Provide challenges that can be tackled in many ways rather than aiming for prescribed outcomes.
- Allow children to engage with something, leave it and return later without finding it packed away, assumed finished with.
- Provide opportunities for children to watch older children at play and adults performing tasks with resources left available for them to consider and trial.

Preparation for later learning:

- Children's banks of experiences are growing as is their capacity for imagination. Reflective children are developing processes to make connections between the two. Reflecting on previous tasks allows children to consider their approaches and fine-tune for next time. By reflecting on actions of others, children formulate ideas about observed practice, for example observing adults reading and writing. Through reflection on how others feel and observing their reactions, children develop empathy for others (Claxton, 2008a).

Modes of thought

Thought processes need to be established to ensure that children are able to manage information in whatever format it is gained, from any source, adapting their approach accordingly.

Think simultaneously

As children are more able to move around the environment they simultaneously access multiple experiences, sensations, activities and social groupings not possible before. Information is now gathered from all these sources to be evaluated simultaneously.

How can we develop this in our under-threes?

- Allow children simultaneous and free access to various areas inside and out wherever possible.
- Ensure that areas are not shut off or made inaccessible as children attempt to process their learning throughout the environment.
- Value and promote the act of seeking stimulation from wide-ranging sources, careful not to mistake 'flitting' for gaining information and ideas from multiple places.

Suggested delivery:

- To encourage an understanding of the potential learning within all different areas, provide interesting prompts within less popular locations inside and out.
- Reflect interests within a number of areas, providing different stimulation from each.
- Arrange games of 'teddy hunt', where multiple teddies are hidden in a variety of places.

Preparation for later learning:

- As more complex learning is undertaken, understanding will require information from multiple sources, all of which need evaluating at once. As children design a den they need to know what resources they have available, who is on hand to help, what the weather is likely to be and how previous techniques and methods have helped. Experiences of connecting areas in their thinking will underpin this.

Think creatively

As children's abilities and imaginations are developing the adult scaffolding directing their focus and attention needs to adjust, ensuring that children's creativity can shine through the guidance and support it offers.

How can we develop this in our under-threes?

- As more opportunities are available through their developing capabilities allow more creative approaches to activities.
- Ask children for creative solutions to the problems of the day, ensuring their creative responses can be facilitated.

Suggested delivery:

- Resist pre-designed art projects, such as Easter chicks, Mother's Day roses or hand-printed reindeers at Christmas.
- Within a wide range of resources and media allow opportunities for children's own creativity to flourish, documenting the journey as a demonstration of their achievements rather than relying on an end result.

Preparation for later learning:

- Provided their creative endeavours have been met positively and validated as worthwhile pursuits, children will have made wide-ranging connections within their learning. As creative thinkers they will approach the understanding of new concepts from a choice of angles, ready to embrace a range of creative solutions to new problems.

Think logically

As they develop logical approaches to everyday problems, making sense of their world, children want things to follow expected logical patterns, becoming concerned when they do not. If wrong names are used, or incorrect answers are given in a game, children can become frustrated and quick to correct (Forester and Cherington, 2009), demonstrating their need for logic within their arsenal of learning methods.

How can we develop this in our under-threes?

- Balance child-initiated and adult-initiated activities to combine intellectual challenge with the opportunity to play with ideas.
- Allow children to take investigations on their own tangents, repeating as often as necessary.

Suggested delivery:

- Allow children to play freely with resources that behave in logical ways, such as water flowing through pipes and gullies.
- Share familiar stories that follow logical patterns and expectations.
- Discuss logical routines, such as washing hands before we eat, boots on then we go outside.
- Display logical processes, such as preparing for lunch, pictorially around the room.

Preparation for later learning:

- Logical understanding is an established need within all children. As it develops we see practices such as self-invented counting systems and emergent mark-making displayed within children's play. These behaviours pave the way for more mature logical processes.

Think widely

As children's abilities and curiosities grow, opportunities are more readily accessed. All areas of learning should be represented throughout the environment, giving meaning in many different contexts rather than suggesting discrete skills.

How can we develop this in our under-threes?

- Offer exciting activities that lead children's focus around the environment.
- Link a number of areas with children's interests to encourage connections.
- Elaborate investigations by adding new dimensions and ideas.

Suggested delivery:

- Plan activities so that children need to access a number of areas.
- Finding 'things that roll' could be discovered in many areas inside and out, leading to ideas and investigations of their own.
- Leave pictorial cues and signs for treasure hunts around the wider environment.

Preparation for later learning:

- As children become familiar with the wider nature of knowledge they will take their understanding beyond that which is immediately presented, finding embedded words in meaningful contexts, developing skills of classification and recognising concepts wherever they are encountered. For example, knowing what represents a 'tree' takes more than one image.

CHAPTER SUMMARY

This chapter has considered how to develop the features of Lifelong Learning as children progress beyond the initial years, facing the frustrations and changes associated with this age as we continue to instil and nurture the underpinning features of all learning.

(Continued)

(Continued)

Ten Key Concepts

1. Supported through nurturing and reassuring relationships, encourage enquiry through rewarding, open-ended challenges where free ideas can be explored and sought out.
2. Whilst offering new experiences, allow repetition and the chance to revisit without packing opportunities away.
3. Avoid premature assistance or distraction, giving children time to immerse in activities and process ideas, unafraid of making mistakes.
4. Allow children to set the pace, testing their own boundaries within adaptable routines, activities and environments.
5. Offer sufficient, authentic, multisensory resources throughout the environment to support imaginative play as children adapt, manipulate and combine freely.
6. Within accessible environments allow children to feel a sense of ownership as they are freely drawn to what interests them, with the time and space to explore, adapting resources, learning new skills and rehearsing ideas as they make links with reality.
7. With realistic expectations, know the children so that individual success is recognised and motivations are encouraged through new and interesting experiences.
8. Offer opportunities to watch older children and trial the actions demonstrated, allowing experiences of emotions, rough-and-tumble play and social exchanges within different groups.
9. Take play outside for increased stimulation and freedom.
10. Balance familiar logical routines with opportunities for children to help plan with creative ideas and decision making as they imagine what comes next.

IDEAS FOR PRACTICE

Practical Project

Observe the actions of the children within the environment. What examples are you seeing of children exploring their ideas freely? Are they able to access and manipulate the experiences they need within the time-frames they require? Where this is not the case, identify what is limiting their actions.

Future Activities

Introduce some authentic resources that are new to the children, objects they may encounter visiting a friend, a nature ramble or a trip to a café or post office. Allow the children to explore and utilise these in their own way, revisiting and combining with other resources freely. Observe the actions of a particular child: how do they access the experience? How often do they go back to it? How is their interest raised and promoted?

Work-based Tasks

Having observed the richness of free exploration, consider the most significant stumbling block to this within your environment. Discuss your findings with colleagues and consider how you can address this issue.

FURTHER READING

Crowley, K. (2014) *Child Development*. London: Sage.
Focusing on the earliest years, this book looks at children's rapidly changing abilities to communicate, think and to interact and the effects this has on the care and education they require and the impact this has on their well-being. Looking at theories of development it considers the wide-reaching impact of policy and the role of the adult in care, sensitive to all children's health and development

Hansen, K. and Hawkes, D. (2009) 'Early childcare and child development', *Journal of Social Policy*, 38 (2): 211–239.
Using data from the UK Millennium Cohort Study, this paper looks at the effect on cognitive and behavioural development of 3-year-olds in non-maternal childcare whose mothers were working from when they were nine months old and the effects this has on school readiness measures.

Kington, A., Gates, P. and Sammons, P. (2013) 'Development of social relationships, interactions and behaviours in early education settings', *Journal of Early Childhood Research*, 11: 292.
With much research and policy regarding early years provision focusing on preschoolers, this UK study looks at the beneficial characteristics of a government pilot scheme for 2-year-olds in areas of social disadvantage. Showing increased confidence, communication and interaction, benefits were not limited to the development of cognitive skills.

10

WORKING SPECIFICALLY WITH UNDER-FIVES

THIS CHAPTER WILL

- consider the learning objectives of the under-fives; as personalities and abilities are growing the nature of support children need changes as they prepare for the transition into formal education
- explore the essential features of Lifelong Learning, challenging traditional tendencies to focus on discrete academic skills
- recognise that the process of preparing children for school and a lifetime of learning has been embedded in every experience since birth and will continue as children progress through the early years embracing the unique features, freedoms and possibilities it brings
- offer suggestions for developing these features along with appropriate delivery that will impact achievements and attitudes towards learning.

The claims are constant; children beginning formal schooling on strong foundations progress with favourable trajectories that result in repercussions felt for years. The strength of these foundations is, however, predominantly the result of experiences long before formal schooling begins (Grissmer and Eiseman, 2008). Children missing out on quality experiences during early childhood, especially those from disadvantaged backgrounds (Melhuish, 2003), tend to attain poorer social and emotional development, less auspicious academic achievement (Brooker, 2008) and disadvantaged health, well-being, happiness and resilience (Tickell, 2011; Allen, 2011; DfE and DH, 2011; Noel and Lord, 2014). There is no magic formula or set of coachable skills to be administered during the final stages of preschool; indeed, considering children's 'readiness' in the months prior to school transition is, in fact, many years too late.

Children demonstrating low cognitive skills at the end of the EYFS are six times more likely to still be doing so at Key Stage 1 (Tickell, 2011). Abilities at this time are the most important factor in predicting Key Stage 2 attainment across all subjects, with those behind in their development at age five being much more likely than their peers to be behind at age seven. Without quality foundations additional needs may also have been overlooked, further intensifying feelings of isolation and disadvantage (DfCSF, 2009c; Field, 2010). Schools are unable to effectively close this gap, and children arriving in the bottom range of ability tend to stay there (Field, 2010).

Children experiencing enriched early childhoods typically demonstrate school profiles four to six months ahead of their peers. With lasting effects on independence, confidence and social skills they are ready to take full advantage of school experiences from day one (Feinstein and Duckworth, 2006), typically showing improved levels of motivation and lower sense of failure (Melhuish, 2003). These effects are not fleeting but remain throughout Key Stage 1, as expectations in reading and maths are exceeded, promoting enhanced intellectual development (DfE, 2010a, 2010b) as concepts are accessed and understood more easily.

Working with under-fives

Moving towards school transition, the support and understanding of families becomes ever more pronounced. Children enjoying early childhoods steeped in vocabulary-rich experiences, practical activities and social play, sensitive to changing mediation, inspiration and support needs, will likely have developed greater confidence and higher intellectual, behavioural and social development (Sylva et al., 2004; DfE and DH, 2011). These practices over academic concerns must continue to be celebrated and encouraged.

Children's personalities and social behaviour traits are also developing (Sylva et al., 2004), and if negative these are linked to future under-achievement both directly and through their impact on attention skills, relationships, concentration and persistence (Feinstein and Duckworth, 2006). If these behaviours are met with detached, overly tolerant or overly reprimanding responses, they tend to see children make poorer progress than those nurtured within positive relationships (Sylva et al., 2004). To support and enrich children's social, emotional and *cognitive* achievements, emotions need to be positively managed. Rather than using distraction or directives to 'stop' (Sylva et al., 2004; Hamre et al., 2014), disputes need to be played out within safe environments, giving those involved and those watching opportunities they may not have elsewhere (Hayashi and Tobin, 2013), to trial techniques for solving their own problems, learning how to rationalise and talk through conflicts, as modelled by appropriate and well-informed reactions of practitioners with strong knowledge of child development (Bornstein et al., 2008). Children cannot be instructed how to behave or feel, this can only happen instinctively as emotions naturally arising in play are worked through.

Children must also feel positive about the effort they make. Meaningful, measured and focused praise is a necessary part of nurturing, supportive care; however, false boosting of self-esteem can be detrimental. To be meaningful, praise should arise from the effort children put in (a variable they are in control of). If instead we praise children for being good, because they are clever or because of talents (a variable they are not in control of), this can undervalue persistence, causing them to give up when greater challenges are faced as difficulties will, they assume, be because they are 'not clever enough' rather than because they need to apply more effort (Claxton, 2008b).

Gender differences are also presenting at this time. With greater cooperation, conformity, peer sociability and confidence, girls tend to show higher attainments in most areas at entry to preschool (Sylva et al., 2004). Perhaps because of these well-developed traits they tend to make greater gains in pre-reading and early number concepts, non-verbal reasoning and cognitive development than boys during preschool, suggesting gender differences found in school have already begun. Quality preschool experiences targeting required areas of development can impact boys' progress, helping to reduce the gender gap (Sylva et al., 2004)

Features of a Lifelong Learner

Children will all too soon be exposed to formal, de-contextualised learning that Katz (2010) suggests may only serve to introduce a sense of failure if we do not realise and use the styles of learning children need. The brain is not designed for demonstrated displays of knowledge but for learning how to get things done quickly in situations that matter (Claxton, 2008b: 99). These are not skills that scholarship and tests seek to measure, so we must find other ways of allowing children to demonstrate their capabilities. Within rich, experiential opportunities, foundations for all future learning, attitudes towards scholarly activity and children's belief in their own abilities are established.

Intrinsic qualities

Along with behavioural qualities, these core attributes within children enable them to pursue and access the experiences required to further their understanding, persisting through the time and inevitable setbacks faced on the way to mastery. This is as true of learning to stand as it is of passing A-level physics.

Courageous

Play is becoming divorced from adults and more in tune with peer groups. As directions of play are swiftly discussed, challenges considered and determined, children need courage to participate, voicing their views and accessing the opportunities required.

How can we develop this in our under-fives?

- Offer support, encouragement and guidance to ensure that opportunities are accessed at the right level.
- Enable positive experiences of setting themselves challenges and succeeding within them, developing courage to persist.
- Ensure that all children are able to find their voice within social interactions.

Suggested delivery:

- Understand how children are feeling about set tasks so you can develop courage in ways that are right for them.
- Talk to children. How do they view tasks and their role within them? What would they like to make happen?
- Offer opportunities to engage with diverse ranges of experiences and characters with resources, time and permission to try.

Preparation for later learning:

- Courage to engage with experiences and interact within social groupings is key when beginning school. Social groups form quickly and opportunities must be grasped within this new environment. A courageous outlook will fuel their attempts, allowing opportunities to be embraced.

Self-motivated

Belief in their ability affects children's emotional reactions, thought processes and self-motivation. If lacking they tend to behave ineffectively, even if they know what to do (Bandura, 1982). As children become more aware of their sense of self, motivations and experiences of success supported through appropriate opportunities enable children to persist even when external motivations are lacking.

How can we develop this in our under-fives?

- Let children take control of activity direction and intent rather than being governed by set objectives.
- Allow intrinsic motivations arising through play to drive the need for literacy, numeracy and other discrete skills.
- Ensure that motivated play is not derailed through interruption, expectation or unnecessary direction so children can follow motivations through to the end, demonstrating and realising their successes.

Suggested delivery:

- Offer sufficient, authentic resources to engage children within their chosen play.
- Allow children to self-direct and freely pursue motivations while being on hand to support if requested.
- Allow children to plan activities, discussing and gathering resources required, amending direction and intentions as freely as needed.

Preparation for later learning:

- Optimum cognitive development requires children's attention (Feinstein and Duckworth, 2006). To capture this consistently children need to be interested and self-motivated within an activity. Early experiences of pleasurable self-motivated discovery and achievement, where barriers have led to new understandings rather than disheartenment or relinquished efforts, encourage committed attention to future challenges.

Confident

At this age girls are shown to have higher confidence levels than boys. Arising perhaps from their sociability and desire to conform (Sylva et al., 2004) or from the value placed on skills they tend towards, either way this may demonstrate the origins of future gender differences.

How can we develop this in our under-fives?

- To develop the confidence of all children, abilities must be recognised and valued within a range of opportunities and peer groupings.
- Offer children safe environments to demonstrate their skills.
- No one approach suits the unique abilities of all children, so ensure that all can shine. To do anything less would suggest only specific skills are respected.

Suggested delivery:

- Organise activities that encourage and validate various skills.
- Offer different children the opportunity to take various roles within the group, valuing and celebrating unique abilities.
- Play games to build confidence and emotional security within social skills, such as sharing, cooperation, listening and voicing ideas.

Preparation for later learning:

- Confident sense of belonging and interpersonal support is associated with higher motivation and educational achievement (Feinstein and Duckworth, 2006). Confident children are able to access potential opportunities and social connections, forming bonds and attachments. Recovering quickly from setbacks, they are happy to embrace challenges of future learning, seeking the support and guidance required to make the most of new experiences.

Behavioural qualities

Along with intrinsic qualities, these core attributes enable children to approach new challenges in meaningful ways. Without needing to be led through every pursuit, children with these secure behaviours access their own learning from all available experiences. This is as true of learning how to make a chain rattle in a can as it is to designing chemical reactions.

Imaginative

As children's mental abilities are developing they are more able to process ideas mentally without needing it expressed in real terms. But these skills need rehearsing and exploring like any other.

How can we develop this in our under-fives?

- Ensure that the children's time is not overprescribed, allowing them to lose themselves in explorations, initiating new directions, following their imagination.
- Offer problems without immediate solutions, requiring imagination and child-initiated interactions to answer.
- Explore feelings and emotions within stories to imagine how things feel to others.

Suggested delivery:

- Offer an unfamiliar object; what could it be for, who might use it and how?
- Encourage their own stories, offering props or cliff-hangers if necessary.
- Use humour to promote imaginative use of language.
- Offer new materials to support and extend ongoing activities or posed problems.
- Ask questions to capture imagination, provoking new thinking.
- Introduce games they need to devise rules for.

Preparation for later learning:

- Having challenged and used diverse methods of thinking, children with good imagination are ready to mentally process new challenges. When difficulties arise within new learning, for example reading an unfamiliar word, they are able to mentally piece together information to arrive at solutions.

Intuitive

As children's abilities to make logical judgements develop they begin to initiate their own enquiries, predicting events and knowing intuitively how to proceed.

How can we develop this in our under-fives

- Give children opportunities to discuss and trial ideas, repeating with something similar soon so that the lessons learnt can be applied.
- Let them approach investigations how they feel they should, trialling intuition unafraid of being wrong.
- Even when you know something is unlikely to succeed, respect the thought processes displayed and talk through afterwards.

Suggested delivery:

- Allow children opportunities to consider activities and problems they are facing, considering solutions to their problems through previous experiences.
- Ask children to consider questions posed by previous experiences. What will happen if I mix different quantities? What will it be like when it dries? What made the tower fall?

Preparation for later learning:

- Intuitive skills suggest knowing something through logical predictions without requiring real experience. When learning new concepts, children need to take previous experiences together with new information to draw valuable, deeper conclusions.

Curious

Engaging in play more independent of adults and fuelled by their peers, curiosity can really bloom. Able to manage more complex manipulations independently, resources and opportunities can be staged to encourage curious enquiry.

How can we develop this in our under-fives?

- Give opportunities and permission to trial ideas as they occur.
- Let children approach investigations how they feel they need to.
- Encourage questions and find ways of exploring answers together.

Suggested delivery:

- Introduce strange objects they have little understanding of, inviting them to investigate and consider.
- Gradually reveal resources to tell the next element of a story.
- Encourage curiosity of interests though your knowledge, deepening thinking and understanding through open questions.

Preparation for later learning:

- Deep, rewarding knowledge requires curiosity: how does a battery work, how do aircraft stay in the sky, what is life like in a different country? Experience of rewarding investigations promotes children's natural curiosities.

Approaches to learning

With a range of approaches to learning children will be able to acquire new knowledge and consider any problem from a variety of angles, finding the method that suits and ensuring that every learning opportunity is maximised and enjoyed.

Playful

Play remains the most powerful learning vehicle and must not diminish, even in preparation for school when concerns regarding demonstrable learning achievements can see focus drawn to more traditionally academic pursuits. To continue laying foundations and making connections for later learning, children need meaningful play experiences. As understanding increases, more questions are raised, and play offers safe environments to explore these.

How can we develop this in our under-fives?

- Allow greater opportunities for genuine, authentic experiences as abilities develop. Where resources are heavier or bulkier, collaborative peer support is also encouraged.
- Validate children's play, ensuring that adults' understand and promote its purpose.
- Add greater authenticity through mark-making, communicating and problem solving within children's play.

Suggested delivery:

- Replicate practical uses of literacy and numeracy within play scenarios.
- Supply resources reflecting the backgrounds, homes and cultures of the children.
- Offer opportunity for dramatic play where speaking, listening and use of print are integrated.
- Supply fantasy and risky play, only intervening when needed.
- Allow sufficient time to explore ideas and tricky concepts, reaching conclusions.

Preparation for later learning:

- Play offers continual opportunity to trial ideas without fearing mistakes, experiencing processes and creating memories to underpin future learning experiences. Concepts such as weight and measure cannot be fully understood until they have been experienced; realities of peoples' lives, from Christopher Columbus to Mary Berry, cannot be considered until integral elements are trialled.

Sociable

Within the maturing social exchanges of play children discover their abilities, developing vocabularies and techniques for solving problems. Social skills developed now will remain relatively stable until adolescence (Stefan and Miclea, 2014), positively impacting on behaviours (Allen, 2011).

How can we develop this in our under-fives?

- Allow children to form their social groupings, with frequent opportunities to change.
- Allow collective problem solving, promoting social and cooperative relationships.

- Invite play scenarios with concepts of feelings, behaviours and emotions so that subtleties of behaviour can be responded to.
- Invite communication through thought-provoking questions.
- For those less talkative, promote social involvement through your responses, tone, actions and intonation with visual cues informing interactions.

Suggested delivery:

- Provide resources that synchronise children's interests, encouraging communication and participation.
- Offer resources to create shops, homes or adventures prompted by collective imaginations without prescribing what these should look like.
- Offer prompts suggesting collective problem solving; how will we build a space rocket? How can we lay out our shop and what should we stock it with?

Preparation for later learning:

- Effectively developed social, emotional and behavioural responses avoid antisocial behaviours restricting learning opportunities (Allen, 2011). Abilities to react to shared experiences within social exchanges allows children to explore distant and imagined concepts (Adamson et al., 2014) as companionable learning sees language ability and vocabularies grow (Hamre et al., 2014).

Independence

Children restless and seemingly exhausted through adult-led questions can become engaged and absorbed when constructing learning independently (Miller, 2010). Progressing understanding 'just in time' rather than 'just in case' (Claxton, 2008b), children acquire deep knowledge when it interests them rather than for future possibilities. This requires independent access to immediate, meaningful experiences without unnecessary interruptions to seek guidance or direction.

How can we develop this in our under-fives?

- Within stimulating environments, trust children's judgements regarding what they need or the intention of explorations.
- Resist dictating explorations or interrupting with unhelpful questioning.
- Observe children's pondering between activities without assuming disinterest or lack of understanding.

Suggested delivery:

- Allow children to plan and organise activities, individually and grouped.
- Encourage children to seek information and support as required so it is offered timely and driven by their interests, rather than being given the answers.

- Observe children's involvement before disturbing.
- Hold back from children's disagreements, allowing experience of emotion and conflict and responsibility for their behaviours to inform independent managing of situations.

Preparation for later learning:

- Security within their abilities and confidence independent of external elements will see children access future learning in powerful ways, independently pursuing learning without relying on or influenced by outside forces.

Practical

When granted free, diverse exploration, practical activities can offer concrete realism to difficult or abstract concepts. If valued, suitably resourced and supported practical explorations seen as 'tinkering' (Jane, 2006) can encourage and inspire scientific and technological ideas.

How can we develop this in our under-fives?

- Offer exciting experiments with real objects and tools, fuelled by current interests.
- Allow children to design investigations inspired by and supplied with authentic resources.
- Allow children to make mistakes and try again.

Suggested delivery:

- Offer authentic, practical elements to play that support imagination, such as slicing vegetables, undoing screws and using real tools to cut wood.
- Offer a range of resources so that practical decisions can be made – is string best for securing the den?
- Offer 'tinkering' in ways to appeal to all children.
- Avoid interrupting children's flow of thought and concentration by asking what they are doing or why. Allow it to unfurl naturally.

Preparation for later learning:

- Practical play allows repeated opportunities for trial and improvement as knowledge of difficult concepts develops, testing and reaffirming understanding. Experiences provide valuable techniques for future encounters, informing future mental analysis and confident persistence within future problems.

Adaptable

Children are becoming increasingly independent in their learning and play, with new opportunities, challenges and social exchanges occurring constantly. Adaptability aids stress-free flexibility as end results differ from that expected and children use opportunities to evolve their ideas and intentions.

How can we develop this in our under-fives?

- Promote children's sense of ownership within the environment so that learning opportunities are accessed as required.
- Ensure that different social groupings can form, offering different character mixes.
- Allow directives and ideas to come from various sources, promoting diversity without governing intention.

Suggested delivery:

- Avoid rigid planning, allow fluidity to mirror the interests of the children.
- Encourage children to initiate activities and enable them as closely as possible.
- Become aware of and respond to expected and unexpected opportunities for learning.

Preparation for later learning:

- Unexpected occurrences are commonplace throughout life. Adaptable children will embrace opportunities, optimising experiences to learn by them rather than becoming anxious or closed off to their potential.

Reflective

As imaginations develop, children no longer need to experience every possibility to make meaning of situations. Alternative realities can be conceived and considered as children move from a purely 'here and now' focus to considering past events and future possibilities, reflecting on actions and observations to inform understanding and increase acquired learning.

How can we develop this in our under-fives?

- Discuss past events, inviting children to consider approaches and actions.
- Use 'follow-up' discussions to consider conflicts, problem solving together rather than distracting or simply telling children to stop.
- Make connections between home and settings, repeating experiences so children can share the experience, considering what happened and how things could be different.

Suggested delivery:

- Allow repeated access to challenges over a number days, asking children to consider different approaches.
- Provide resources for children to record what they have learnt (photo, voice, video) and revisit.
- Share stories of children's experiences, adding purpose and authenticity to reflections.

- Use prop boxes to tell stories, offering children opportunities to re-tell and develop, and consider different outcomes.
- Offer visual cues and reminders around the environment, reflecting actions and consequences, linking events to emotions.

Preparation for later learning:

- With every experience informing future approaches to learning, reflective children do more than repeat experiences of the past – they learn from them, continuously improving and fine-tuning responses as they identify preferred styles of learning.

Modes of thought

Thought processes need to be established to ensure that children are able to process information in whatever format it is gained, from any source, adapting their approach accordingly.

Think simultaneously

As experiences grow, children become increasingly informed of information available to them. When presented with new challenges, this allows intuitive access to information from various, simultaneously presented sources, unlimited to those in front of them.

How can we develop this in our under-fives?

- Children need to access experiences and sources of information as required with realised permissions to do so.
- Help children realise that complete understanding is often provided through multiple senses and locations.
- Offer opportunities for gathering and combining information from various sources as connections are made.

Suggested delivery:

- Offer various instructive, adult-initiated, group and freely chosen activities, operating freely, for children to simultaneously access the direction and support required.
- Set tasks and invite participation in problems requiring information from various sources to solve.

Preparation for later learning:

- Children are expected to simultaneously access and process information from various sources throughout their schooling as they become familiar with their new environment, its expectations, social exchanges and learning objectives.

Think creatively

Creative thinking allows meaning to be accessed in many ways as children experiment with inventive solutions. Creative challenges need offering together with the means to approach them and process their ideas before progressing to graphic symbolism such as drawing, which girls will tend towards sooner (Adamson etal. 2004).

How can we develop this in our under-fives?

- Offer environments providing creative challenges rather than more obvious results.
- Encourage children to think creatively about resources and opportunities available.
- Allow children to adapt their environment and resources within it.

Suggested delivery:

- Ensure environments are adaptable by children, allowing them freedom to create new spaces and interesting projects.
- Engage children in sustained shared thinking to understand where creative inspiration is taking them, ensuring they have ample resources.
- Model creative solutions using ranges of resources, and demonstrate their use.

Preparation for later learning:

- Solutions to problems are not always straightforward and understanding does not always follow logical steps. Through positive experiences of creativity being respected and used, children gain an effective method of understanding.

Think logically

Logical approaches will prove valuable to children's thinking and problem solving, but methods of expressing their abstract, hidden and imagined ideas will now be required. Initially through language, symbolism will enhance as non-verbal reasoning, early number concepts and graphic representation develop (Adamson et. al., 2014).

How can we develop this in our under-fives?

- Encourage relevant and interesting independent problem solving and reflection.
- Support logical thought through developing key language within relevant topics.
- Encourage interest by playing with reactions (mixing cornflour and water) and mechanics (path of water through gullies), observing logical patterns.
- Follow logical steps to consider how things work, inviting children to identify connections.

Suggested delivery:

- Offer opportunities for tinkering and taking things apart.
- Demonstrate logical thought processes by demonstrating techniques such as mind maps.
- Demonstrate logical steps and approaches to a problem within group discussions.

Preparation for later learning:

- To derive meaning from letters and sounds, logical thought needs to connect theoretical understanding to the mechanics of writing. Maths skills without underpinning logic have no conceptual basis, limiting understanding. With logical thought comes the ability to process more complex, regulated principles and must be established from the start (Briars and Siegler, 1984; Fuson, 1988).

Think widely

Children are now ready and eager to embrace challenging investigations encompassing the whole environment, combining abilities and using varied skills. Once wide-thinking is embraced, the powerful potential of incidental learning found during everyday interactions can be exploited (Feinstein and Duckworth, 2006).

How can we develop this in our under-fives?

- Introduce resources that connect across wide areas to give children things to associate and talk about.
- Encourage children to push intellectual boundaries within wide-reaching challenges.
- Allow children to develop stories, plan with free reign, demonstrate thinking and prompt fresh ideas.

Suggested delivery:

- Invite the Tiger to Tea, but find out what tigers eat, how big they will be, if there is room to roam outside, and consider transportation. Information that needs to come from various sources. Stage a treasure hunt with messages and clues around the environment.
- With attention focused on specific interests, ask for many examples to encourage lateral thinking.

Preparation for later learning:

- Knowing how to combine techniques and access information from wide-ranging sources prevents learning becoming limited or directed in ways that constrain opportunities. As wider-reaching subjects are considered, the need to take on many opinions and sources of information will become essential.

CHAPTER SUMMARY

This chapter has considered how to develop the features of Lifelong Learning in the final years before transition to formal education. It has explored the vital importance of ensuring these underpinning features to all learning remain key in the minds and practices of all involved.

Ten Key Concepts

1. Support, encourage and guide all areas of learning without dictating expectations or interrupting motivated play.
2. Offer diverse ranges of practical, authentic experiences within different social groupings, promoting language as opportunities are offered to discuss, trial and approach new ideas where logical steps and lateral thinking can be explored.
3. Offer achievable, creative challenges and problems, giving opportunities for collective problem solving and decision making, demonstrating and celebrating individual success where children are unafraid of making mistakes and keen to try again.
4. Supply requested information rather than all the answers, enabling the children's voice within various roles and interactions, reflecting on their past actions and achievements.
5. Offer free access to adaptable, multisensory, authentic resources to promote and extend investigations reflecting home background and culture, synchronising interests and providing the right tools for the job.
6. Validate children's play by avoiding over-regulation of their time. Allow them to ponder and wallow, losing themselves in their enquiries as they explore ideas, concepts, feelings, emotions and behaviours within fluid social groupings.
7. Trust children's judgements regarding what they need, knowing the children well so that features can be uniquely developed and celebrated.
8. Offer resources and permissions to explore tricky concepts, fantasy and risky play, reacting to individual interests and unexpected occurrences.
9. Take play outside for increased stimulation and freedom.
10. Within flexible planning offer the time and opportunity for children to self-direct. Designing and planning activities and resources allow them to explore direction of enquiry, revisiting as often as needed.

IDEAS FOR PRACTICE

Practical Project

Within the freedom of the early year's curriculum there is great potential to explore effective new experiences. By considering each of the features of

Lifelong Learning and children's growing abilities, evaluate how you are maximising their opportunities.

Future Activities

Having identified a feature that is receiving limited attention, discuss possibilities with the children for an activity to address this. Consider the resources and planning that would enable this feature to flourish, being inspired through the interests and enthusiasms of the children.

Work-based Tasks

It is vital that parents recognise and appreciate the importance of the features of Lifelong Learning in the development of their children, especially at this crucial time. Organise an evening for parents to learn about the features. Have activities organised to demonstrate how these are developed within your practice and the importance of them on their child's onward learning trajectories.

FURTHER READING

Blanning, N. (2015) *School Readiness Today: A Report from the Pedagogical Section of the Goetheanum.* Spring Valley, NY: Waldorf Early Childhood Association North America.
Through international research and illustrated by children's drawings, this book demonstrates the importance of sensitively preparing children for the significant transition to school.

Desailly, J. (2015) *Creativity in the primary Classroom*, 2nd edn. London: Sage.
With the new curriculum permitting greater creativities within the primary classroom, this book highlights the influence of creativity and new ways of thinking to be expected when children transition to primary school.

UNICEF (2012) *School Readiness: A Conceptual Framework.* New York: UNICEF. Available at www.unicef.org/education/files/Chil2Child_ConceptualFramework_FINAL(1).pdf (accessed 22/6/16).
This paper looks at international evidence to ask what school readiness is, why it is important and what the consequences of inaction are. Looking at the broad concepts of children's readiness for school, schools' readiness for children, and families' and communities' readiness for school, it considers the importance of this concept on children's development and society.

11

AN ALTERNATIVE WAY FORWARD

THIS CHAPTER WILL...

- rethink traditional views of school readiness in light of the discussions of Lifelong Learning throughout the preceding chapters and consider an alternative way forward
- reflect on the features of Lifelong Learning and consider how these can be embodied within the logistics, environments and experiences of formal schooling
- consider the importance of the features of Lifelong Learning in preparing children for unknown futures within the 21st century.

Regardless of the label we affix to it, the early stages of a child's life sees children transition from a play-based curriculum to formal education. What this does not signify is the beginning of learning. If we move focus away from concerns regarding abilities within determined sets of discrete, uniformly set skills and instead celebrate children's plethora of realised achievements, the rich medium of learning, investigation, imagination and enquiry permitted in early childhood can be realised and built upon. It is a model so rich in potential for motivation, self-expression and deep and lasting achievement that it establishes the foundation for all future learning, and it is this that we must take every care to continue building.

How has the early years prepared children for their future learning?

Between the exit from neo-natal services shortly after birth and starting formal schooling, the early years encompasses a wide expanse of developmental phases. Within flexible, play-based curricula and with children's well-being, family involvement and social context at the core of early years policy, children's unique growth, agency and natural learning strategies have found a place to flourish (OECD, 2006). More than simply bestowing a set of skills, the foundation stage permits children an understanding of what they can achieve through their own developing abilities and persistence. By immersing children in environments rich in opportunity to explore and create, the purpose and enrichment of deeper understanding has been demonstrated. Through their investigative enquiries a sense of self has developed as multifaceted, enjoyable experiences of gaining knowledge have been embraced.

With one continual foundation stage, the transition into school should be straightforward, blending rich opportunities as ongoing features of learning rather than moving from one idea of 'best practice' to something startlingly new. However, expectations placed on children can differ dramatically between the two environments (Brooker, 2008). Coming from a place of permitted freedoms, where children have followed their developmental needs and interests, the more structured environment of school can be alarming: that is, a place children imagine will consist purely of study rather than pursuing interests or play (Margetts, 2013) as bodies and minds are disciplined into conformity and compliance (Brooker, 2008). As children progress their academic journey, rich, enquiry based experiences that were instrumental in developing cognitive and non-cognitive abilities through their early years must continue to influence approaches to learning. By treasuring collaborative, familiar methods of learning, transitions can be eased (Tickell, 2011) as schools become ready for all children (Whitbread and Bingham 2012), provided that adult, policy or curriculum agendas do not override.

Rethinking traditional views of school readiness

With international debate regarding school readiness focusing on lists of skills essential before children are 'ready to learn' (National Educational Goals Panel, 1991 cited in Neuman, 2001), and with delays proposed until proficiency is demonstrated, a number of key questions are raised:

- How has children's learning changed so that what enabled deep understanding before is no longer valid?
- Who decides on the skills and degree of competency required to suggest that children are now 'ready', and what agenda drives these decisions?
- Will the discrete list of attributes be favoured over equally valid achievements and abilities?
- How will children be prepared for meeting these requirements?
- What will the future impact be on children whose developments followed different rates or directions during the foundation years?

Readiness for learning is established years before formal education starts and encompasses practices, abilities and traits wider and deeper than quantifiable lists can demonstrate. Preparation for classroom learning must go beyond demonstrable abilities, looking at enduring features required for deep, meaningful learning beyond the classroom, focusing on the readiness of the new environment to embrace, challenge and support learning behaviours of all children. When realised by policy makers and curriculum authors, experiences and achievements of children will be better recognised and understood and increasing demands placed on them more relevant and manageable.

Looking abroad we can see examples of wider learning practices establishing within school preparation. The Ontario Institute for Studies in Education (OISE) use imagery, analysis and problem solving for children to generate their own answers to problems; the Hong Kong Institute of Education uses interactions with materials and people to encourage 'questioning, exploration and experience'; in China the child is recognised as an inventor and competent listener as creativity is encouraged alongside formal teachings. Where processes of facilitating and constructing knowledge are more valued than outcomes, children are unhampered by correct representation. By allowing exploration, creativity, self-expression and independent discovery to remain the primary concern, children's achievements are unimpeded by any current lack of vocabulary or print expertise, skills that will be sure to develop in time (Wong, 2008).

Some suggest that we do a disservice to children if we fail to concentrate on the rigors of formal academia during early childhood. Suggesting preparations for working within more formal environments and acquiring disciplines of reading and writing should take precedent over childhoods steeped in freedoms without pressures to perform. Whilst reading skills are intrinsic to any classroom practice and fundamental to ongoing understanding, school preparation can become centred on literacy skills of vocabulary, grammatical structure and language semantics, phonemic awareness, alphabet knowledge and concepts of print (Wasik et al. 2011). Familiarity introduced through shared books and print is a vital part of early childhood; however, to do so without meaning or relevance is futile at best and at worst frustrating and demotivating with lasting negative connotations. Holistic teaching methods familiar to early years must remain.

Taking the features of Lifelong Learning into the classroom

The ability to learn is the gateway to all development and children are born good at it (Claxton, 2008b), developing basic social, emotional, communication and language skills from birth that are now intrinsic to school success. However, powerful learning with its requirements for determination and self-discipline as much as intellect is not the same as being a model student and focus must centre on developing features of Lifelong Learning rather than conforming to expectations.

During their early years children were recognised as playing, learning individuals whose development and growth were understood to be as unique in direction and rate as the children themselves. Encouraged to enjoy learning through explorative play, their curiosities will have motivated their engagement in activities designed to promote abilities and skills as well as offering experiences to underpin all future learning, securing foundations for reading, writing and number manipulation. From this place of free expression and recognised achievements, their natural motivations for acquiring knowledge through experience will have deepened. Provided these motivations are appropriately challenged and sensitively guided, academic success will follow. If, however, we become preoccupied with the more academic stimulations that society often expects developing children to need (Entwisle and Alexander, 1998), these motivations can become unsatisfied or misdirected.

Used to actively pursuing learning through play, these two concepts have undergone symbolic separation through time and space. Once naturally active learners, a trait prized for its ability to access rich opportunities, children are now homogenously sitting on carpets or circulating through planned and prescribed activities, giving attention to uniform, pre-set learning objectives within regulated time-frames, unmatched to individual need. Dissuaded from authentically trialling abstract concepts or discussing their ideas as they occur, children can be misconstrued as fidgety, unfocused or disruptive within this environment, eliciting insensitive responses to natural learning impulses as 'playtime' becomes a reward for when 'learning' is complete.

By valuing early years principles, forging relationships with families and communities whilst conceiving of children as individuals, diverse goals and values can be respected (Brooker, 2008). Children do not learn in isolation: well-being and effects of background, family and community have an immense effect and must be recognised and accommodated, affording children responsibilities and rights befitting their age and understanding. However, school models following authoritarian traditions that afford little agency fly in the face of children's right to form their own views and express opinions within matters affecting them. By expecting passive compliance within pre-set lessons, children have diminished opportunity to actively participate, animate their ideas, resolve conflicts or manufacture and solve their own problems – a recipe for an oppressive and disrespectful environment (Jeffers, 2014).

Where outdated views of children as passive, 'empty boxes to be filled with knowledge' (Moss et al., 1999: 32) still exist, where social interactions and proactive learning from authentic experiences are discouraged, conformity becomes the prized characteristic as children become products of a system (Claxton, 1999 cited in Miller, 2010). For different children this experience of school can mean very different things, but with future success more dependent on self-belief than any measure of intellect or ability (Claxton, 2008b), all children's unique talents, abilities and passions must be given the opportunity to shine within curricula designed to meet all needs. To motivate deep learning, revealing motivations and capabilities unique to every child, we need to understand and utilise children's interests throughout their school experience. This requires teaching practices that include:

- knowing children as individuals, connecting through sensitive, genuine interest in their motivations
- understanding individual children's feelings and perspectives through verbal and non-verbal messages, avoiding the tendency to assume or overlook
- offering appropriate challenges to identify and access children's passions and talents whilst offering children a taste of their possibilities
- accommodating children's vast array of skills, competences and abilities, embracing their full potential and endless capacities

- collaborating and negotiating, steeped in shared meaning and discovery rather than requiring passive demonstration of pre-set learning objectives
- offering accessible learning environments that respect children's unique developmental needs.

With performance of even the brightest children from poorer homes overtaken by less gifted, richer peers by the time they are 10 years old (Field, 2010), the effect of school experiences on children must be considered. Curricula and timetables suitable to the learning needs of all children, including those whose less relatable experiences may affect social skills, self-belief, confidence and capacities to cope with formal learning, must provide engaging, adaptable, authentic and accessible approaches to learning if the life chances of all children stand to be enhanced. To do anything else risks a future of unprepared, disaffected and disengaged teenagers' mistrusting of education and their own abilities, a gross disservice to future generations when very different outcomes could have been realised had these abilities been recognised and passionately engaged.

Children are vulnerable to the decisions and best intentions of adults, often driven by wider agendas, potentially unfocused on the specific needs of and implications on the children they ultimately affect. By asking how we can shape children to fit the mould of the 'school-ready child' we stand to inflict great damage on the powerful practices permitted within quality early years environments. By focusing on 'reasonable expectations for what they should be able to do' (NAEYC, 2009: 1, quoted in Noel and Lord, 2014), we are in danger of losing characteristics and abilities not so easily measurable or clearly defined. A cycle of wasted potential and costly and damaging social problems leading to significant risk of later difficulties will follow (Allen, 2011) if suitable curricula and educational environments embracing the lifelong nature of learning for all children are not embraced.

The effect of school on children

Given quality experiences during early childhood, children tend to start school with many mastered skills, enthusiastic, eager and confident. With a high appraisal of their own competencies through the praise and encouragement received they also tend to have positive dispositions towards learning (Whitbread and Bingham, 2012). However, as playful approaches to learning diminish, children can quickly become 'disheartened' (Blenkin and Kelly,, 1994). Having experienced being partners within the preschool experience sharing their perspectives with others (Samuelsson, 2004), the primary classroom can feel dictated and uncomfortable where their perspectives and rights are less clearly valued (Samuelsson and Carlsson, 2008). Demands unmatched to inclinations can dishearten (Brooker, 2008) as pressures to succeed begin to narrow thinking (Moyles, 2010). Views of their ongoing abilities and the degree of difficulty they relate to future tasks are tightly linked to perceptions of their success or failure (Whitbread and Bingham, 2012) and the positive self-image, confidence and attitudes towards learning established during flexible early childhood experiences of learning how to learn is tarnished as children find themselves in a setting they feel distinctly unsuited to (Brostrom, 2002).

REFLECTION

Can you remember the last time you were put in a situation where you had no control, such as starting a new position, beginning a course or having dealings with Ofsted? How did this make you feel?

The transition to school also coincides with an important time in children's internal development as abilities within social interactions increase and independence is gained from key figures. Sensitively managed to support social competence, this can allow for increased capabilities and sense of achievement. Alternatively, this period of transition can leave children believing that the skills they possess and were celebrated for are no longer valued as disheartenment leads to disaffection. If deep levels of applied understanding gained throughout early childhood are underestimated, feelings of inadequacy and inferiority are likely to follow. With less expectation of deep thought, children begin to demonstrate only that which is expected of them, conforming to directives and required responses (Brooker, 2008; Margetts, 2013). This 'schoolification' (Moss, 2010: 9) can see children lose their ability to question (Claxton, 2008b) as acceptance supersedes deep-level thinking. With a sense of being lost in this new environment, children may also appear to lack involvement, interest or engagement, shying away from having a go in an attempt to mask their fear of failure of an approach to learning they do not understand. Easily misinterpreted and harshly judged, disruptive or disengaged behaviours fuelled by anxiety and distress can follow (Brooker, 2008) and the die is cast.

Discouraged by structured, more demanding school experiences of rules and routines, children are observed simply following the virtues of doing as prescribed in environments designed to promote attentive, orderly behaviours (Claxton, 2008b). As performance is more closely monitored and children's self-control is prized above self-expression (Ramey and Ramey, 1998), the freedom to approach experiences with creativity, initiative and challenge is replaced by requirements to follow instructions and stay on task. Difficulties handling this transition and 'following directions' are frequently observed as issues experienced with the transition to school (Rimm-Kaufman et al., 2000) and the rapid decline of school enjoyment over coming years (Entwisle and Alexander, 1998). With international studies showing children viewing school as being a place of study, not play or exploring interests (Margetts, 2013), they soon begin to consider themselves less capable, with confidence and enthusiasm for learning declining as demands progress from Key Stage 2 to Key Stage 3 (Claxton, 2008b).

REFLECTION

- Are calm, ordered environments always conducive to the highest level of learning?
- Are prolonged, teacher-led sessions on the carpet the most effective method of introducing highly kinaesthetic 5-year-olds to their new world of formal learning?

Nothing has gone wrong with these children, there is nothing lacking in their repertoire of skills or readiness for learning: they are, in fact, precisely at the stage that is right for them. What is different is that they have not yet learnt how to be school children, listening to instructions, raising their hand to verbalise, demonstrating understanding and waiting for teachers before offering responses (Samuelsson and Carlsson, 2008). But this model does not respect the developing, learning child whose verbal expressions will only ever be a small fragment of the ways they express their knowledge, and severely limits any evaluation of their abilities (Samuelsson, 2004).

To prepare children for a lifetime of deep understanding beyond acceptance of handed out knowledge we must continue developing their innate drives to question and challenge, but this is not achieved by operating within curricula and exam structures focusing on rehearsed answers and surface-level understanding, and fails to prepare future adults to advance understanding of the world or the people within it.

Creating a school environment conducive to promoting the features of Lifelong Learning

When contemplating the role of education, the needs of society as well as those of individual children must be considered through the experiences, knowledge and perspectives offered through any stated curricula (Pramling Samuelsson and Carlsson, 2003 quoted in Samuelsson, 2004; OECD, 2006). These needs include:

For society:

- A curriculum capable of equipping future adults with diverse skills and abilities ready to apply to any problem through experiences relatable to the challenges of an unknown future.
- Adults able to act in sociable ways, fulfilling active roles within society.

For our children:

- A curriculum that introduces young minds to a world of possibilities and sense of their own potential.
- Developing diverse and complementing skills and abilities of children in tune with their passions, understanding and knowledge.
- Developing abilities and attitudes that permit continued confidence, persistence and motivation within future endeavours.

In designing a curriculum for an unknown future, adaptability must take precedent over specifically itemised objectives to teach to and measure against. We must look to generic skills, abilities, traits, values and habits of mind as the focus rather than discrete facts relevant to a world that may no longer exist (Claxton, 2008b). Development of the highest quality early experiences must sit hand in hand with pedagogy accessible by all children and sustained over the long term as we develop the features of Lifelong Learning.

REFLECTION

In what ways has the world you lived in changed from when you were a small child? What experiences did you gain then that are still relevant to you today?

Intrinsic qualities

Whilst we may appreciate that children arrive at school with unique histories and cultures shaping their intrinsic motivations and fuelling confidence within their new environment, in reality they are often treated as uniform consumers of a pre-designed product (Katz, 2010). To actively develop intrinsically motivated, confident and courageous learners, a number of classroom ironies must first be addressed:

- Sustainable self-motivation must be encouraged so that persistence endures throughout periods of long- and short-term rewards, catering to differing desires for parental, verbal and intrinsic recognition.
- Confidence enabling the talents and diverse skills of all children to shine must be honoured while collaborative classroom communities are established that thrive on differing opinions.
- A balance must be struck between periods of apathy as children wait their turn and wild excitement that prevents planning, reflection or adjustments within environments that promote courageous involvement.

By tapping into and valuing inherent skills and talents, exposing children to and developing that which is inside, we can help them recognise the value of their intrinsic qualities. Always ready for new experiences, children's innate drive to learn is always present – perhaps not what we have in mind, but the desire is there. What children struggle to respond to is sitting still and being told what to do. By recognising themselves as strong, successful learners capable of working together, and independently solving problems and managing situations within changing environments, children develop the confidence and motivation to persist.

When engagement and interest are promoted, children's attention skills develop. Conceptually distinct and independent of a child's initial cognitive ability (McClelland et al., 2000; Yen et al., 2004), attention skills are predictive of later achievement with children spending more time engaged in higher quality pursuits (Alexander et al., 1993), continuing until mastery is gained. However, demotivated children within overly prescribed environments become reticent with diminished attention and motivations as lacklustre, ineffective actions without commitment become their regular practice (Claxton, 2008b).

Behavioural qualities

To develop behaviours of intuitive, curious, imaginative learner's, schools must permit free exploration of these learning behaviours when children feel compelled to indulge in them. To deny these instincts runs the risk of creating apathy within children having learnt that their natural instincts are somehow at fault. Alternatively, within classrooms welcoming explorers and adventurers, imaginative play encourages the necessary experiences underpinning future learning as empathetic practices are rehearsed and resilience developed.

When genuine, authentic experiences replace generic, predetermined activities and shared objectives, and children are permitted to freely explore and direct, the benefits are substantial:

- Children's own ideas are stimulated, permitted, celebrated and trialled, allowing intuitive responses and new directions of enquiry.
- Exposed to new ideas and genuine challenges, children identify, gain and combine endless transferable skills.
- With authentic resources and environments, greater practical understanding of complex concepts develops through self-facilitated and directed pursuits.
- With minimum facts and guidance, children's imaginative discoveries are encouraged and celebrated, leading towards greater personal challenge and exploration.
- As children formulate and modify projects they develop their views and ideas as techniques for identifying and seeking required additional knowledge are learnt.
- Projects can be given the necessary time for curiosities to mature and take shape without excessive interruptions or expectations.
- Permitted opportunities to wallow within a chosen pursuit, children can realise the purpose of their continued engagement as intuitive responses are given the time required to be realised.

Approaches to learning

When put in terms of matching children's level of understanding and introduced together with opportunities to trial for themselves, the foundations of any area of learning can be taught (Bruner, 1977). Once engaged, more complex ideas can be introduced to these secure foundations, advising and guiding learners rather than directing. If tendencies to pitch to average abilities are avoided, children's attention can instead be directed toward key concepts, offering specific information when requested as they gain greater depths of knowledge (Pramling Samuelsson and Sheridan, 1999 cited in Samuelsson, 2004). By avoiding premature solutions or undervaluing chosen pursuits, children's individuality can be taken account of. By avoiding thinking in terms of areas of weakness or cleverness and instead considering additional effort or information required, struggles experienced will not imply that limits have been reached.

Within a classroom alive with playful, practical, social and reflective learning, devoid of criticism or unrealistic expectations, children make rapid advances in their understanding. Supported through processes of reflection, children's developing independence will bring self-confidence and excitement towards the pursuit of greater depths of understanding. Directly linked to how relevant the learning experience is to the child (Moyles, 2010), cognitive understanding needs application. Whilst discrete skills are undoubtedly essential, providing support to all learning, taught in isolation without purpose they are decidedly less effective (Verhoeven and van Leeuwe, 2010):

- Children need to engage in playful investigations that allow exploration of new skills, playing with new ideas to trial their meaning, value and purpose.
- By understanding the social nature of teaching and learning, children must be offered opportunities for
  - collective reflection
  - sharing ideas, developing questioning and argument techniques
  - collaboration
  - thinking aloud
  - gaining and offering assistance with peers, experiencing being the most informed
  - forming mixed social groupings as interests and abilities coincide.
- Independent exploration promotes curiosity in ways that rote learning without motivation cannot. Take account of when children are most ready to learn, promoting children's agency as interruptions through demands of routine or demonstrating results are limited. Offer opportunities for children to select that
  - allow freely directed, spontaneous access to experiences
  - tempt them into challenges worthy of their pursuit
  - allow them to structure their own tasks, matching their understanding and making their own meaning
  - respond to independent thought and approaches to problems
  - offer opportunities to question and direct their experiences as they explore their wide-reaching potential.
- New knowledge must be relevant and practically useful otherwise it will soon be forgotten. Offer opportunities for children to trial for themselves, relevant in pitch, authenticity, purposefulness, transferable and worth the effort. Material taught in context will offer intellectual excitement to children unable to generalise more abstract concepts and will provide a structure for children

to secure new information as they experience transferring factual knowledge, theory and techniques to real applied problems.

- Children's processes of learning, experiences and environments need to be owned by them, adaptable, authentic and freely accessible to meet their learning needs. Supported through fluid timetables that avoid developing explorations being derailed, children can become deeply engaged in their pursuits, adapting and changing direction as they need rather than directed to follow a given path.
- Children require opportunities to reflect and re-approach experiences with the benefit of hindsight. This requires giving children opportunity and time to develop their understanding with resources left available to revisit and reflect upon when they are ready, even if this is some time later. By providing experiences for children to remember, this further enhances their long-term thinking.

Modes of thought

Thinking occurs in multifaceted dimensions. Requiring courage, skill, judgement and camradery, persistence and a belief in their abilities more than any innate characteristic (Claxton, 2008b), established patterns of thinking requires positive experiences of their own thinking endeavours, where logical and creative reasoning have combined to allow balanced systematic responses to creative problems and innovative solutions to analytical challenges.

Promoted through awareness, observation, decision making, interpretation and reflection, children's thinking enables them to make continual connections within their learning, allowing responses within unfamiliar situations. To develop a range of approaches to their thought processes, allowing informed intelligence to develop, learning and teaching experiences also need to be provided through blended approaches, embracing key pedagogical principles that enable children's logical, wide, simultaneous and creative thinking to enhance their depth of understanding as their needs dictate.

Direct instruction is not enough to provide the opportunities required. To develop interested, disciplined thinking, purposeful curiosity, imagination and scepticism are necessary. As skills develop and children are able to access and manipulate information, to the informed teacher their thinking becomes visible. By listening to and observing their actions, teachers can realise the impact of prior experiences on children's current thinking, responding to individual requirements and allowing misconceptions to be explored. By embracing authentic daily experiences that promote children's initiative and imagination, the rich connections required to formulate clear and effective ideas of their own are established. Through opportunities to manipulate and summarise new knowledge freely and within timeframes to suit the learner, children can make relationships within their existing knowledge allowing them to explore, reinforce, test and evaluate its validity and importance. As children rehearse methods of organising information in ways that can be understood and remembered, to reflect on and apply their experiences to new situations, formulating and recognising assumptions, their minds are awakening to a conscious understanding of their own power (Claxton, 2008b) as they begin to think of themselves as learners. However, by definition, this involves having the child rather than a curriculum at the centre.

CHAPTER SUMMARY

School preparations involving the home, school, wider community and national policy must embrace our understanding of children's learning from birth through every experience afforded so that where problems lie within the crossover from early years' pursuits of experiential knowledge and enquiry into more stipulated and governed deliveries, it is the national curriculum that becomes ready to embrace the learning methods of children, drawing on the strengths of the early childhood curriculum.

This chapter has looked at the importance of knowing individual children, to cultivate their mind without becoming dominated by adult ideas of desirable skills and traits, continuing to holistically develop children's learning in ways that can only be devised by those at the forefront of the subject and taught by thoughtful, unrestricted teachers inspiring children and embracing all they are.

Ten Key Concepts

1 School readiness stems from developing all features of Lifelong Learning and securing environments conducive to their continued development.

2 Deep school learning requires authentic, accessible, practical experiences with meaning, relevance and individualised challenge as much now as it did within the early years.

3 Curiosity, self-belief and engagement are more important to academic success than any definition of intelligence or image of the model student and must continue to be enhanced within play-rich curricula adaptable to the needs of all children.

4 Naturally active modes of learning must continue to be proactively embraced as children verbalise and action their thought processes, ideas and opinions.

5 Verbal and non-verbal engagement must be continuously used to understand children's thinking, misconceptions and well-being without preconceived ideas of limits or capabilities.

(Continued)

(Continued)

6. Children's agency must be recognised and celebrated within environments unrestricted by set objectives, promoting exploration as children direct their own enquiries, questioning accepted ideas and requesting information as needed.
7. Children continue to need opportunity for social collaboration, reflection and negotiation within naturally forming social groupings.
8. Curricula must embrace generic skills and abilities within enduring features of learning rather than focusing on discrete facts, information children do not currently see the need for, premature solutions to potentially rich problems or devaluing direction of children's choosing.
9. By allowing children to construct and modify their own projects, structuring their own learning, seeking answers to their own questions, ideas are promoted sustaining self-motivation, confidence and persistence within genuine challenges.
10. With time and opportunity to reflect and revisit without unnecessary interruption or pre-determined expectations, concepts are given the opportunity to mature within children's thinking.

IDEAS FOR PRACTICE

Practical Project

Focus on the actions of three primary school children. Observe their involvement with the activities on offer throughout the day and their engagement where active responses are permitted. Where are their own ideas and learning needs best voiced and supported?

Future Activities

With a small group of children, ask them what skills, abilities and knowledge they would like if you were able to transport them 20 years into the future. From their ideas of an unknown future, consider what the responses of children and adults may have been 20 years ago. How different would this be from the reality we now know, and how relevant were the skills bestowed?

Work-based Tasks

Consider how you can embody the features of Lifelong Learning, free exploration and self-initiated enquiry into the experiences of the children you work with. Devise and enable a change to practice that will have real impact on children's learning.

FURTHER READING

Dockett, S. and Perry, B. (2004) 'Starting school: perspectives of Australian children, parents and educators', *Journal of Early Childhood Research*, 2 (2).

This article looks at the issues facing 300 children, 300 families and 300 teachers in Australia as school is begun. Looking at perceived requirements for knowledge, social adjustment, skills, dispositions and physical abilities, their relative value to the three groups questioned is examined.

Halle, T., Hair, E., Wandner, L. and Chien, N. (2012) 'Profiles of school readiness among four-year-old head start children', *Early Childhood Research Quarterly*, 27 (4): 613–26.

This study investigates the degree to which child, family, classroom, teacher and Head Start programme characteristics are related to children's school readiness and continued development over the 4-year-old Head Start year based on the USA Family and Child Experiences Survey (FACES) data from 1997.

Wasik, B.A., Karweit, N., Bond, M.A., Woodruff, L.B., Jaeger, G. and Adee, S. (2011) 'Early learning in CRESPAR', *Journal of Education for Students Placed at Risk (JESPAR)*, 5: 1–2, 93–107.

This study looks at teachers' ideas of school readiness from the perspectives of children requiring additional support.

GLOSSARY

Baseline assessments Introduced from September 2016, this non-compulsory national testing of reception-aged children aims to assess the level of development at the beginning of formal schooling in order to record progression by the time they leave primary school. Provided through three approved providers, the Baseline Assessment will replace the EYFS Profile. Correct at the time of writing.

Bilingualism The use of more than one language being spoken.

Characteristics of effective learning (CofEL) The CofEL consist of playing and exploring, active learning, and creating and thinking critically. By considering the ways children engage with other people and their environment, they underpin learning and development across all areas of learning within the EYFS (England) with the aim of supporting children's effective and motivated learning.

Cognitive Cognitive development considers specific aspects of children's brain development, such as processing of information, their understanding of concepts, their perceptual skills and language learning.

Cultural expectations Cultural expectations imply a drive for academic excellence. These can be related to gender issues that see different ideas of what is expected of girls and boys.

Cumulative Success at one level provides the abilities to be more successful at the next. For example, children with more established speech can ask the questions needed, and better reading abilities allow for quicker mastering of future texts.

Cyclical Learning that is returned to as approaches are reconsidered and abilities strengthened.

Discrete abilities The unconnected tasks that children can perform. For example, counting to 10 without any real understanding of what these words relate to.

Every Child a Talker Funded by the DCSF across all local authorities on a three-year rolling programme between 2008 and 2011, Every Child a Talker (ECAT) was designed to help practitioners and parents create a developmentally appropriate, supportive and stimulating environment for children to enjoy experimenting with and learning language, becoming confident and skilled communicators before they start school.

Explicit That which is stated clearly rather than implied or open to interpretation such as legislation.

Family Nurse Partnership Introduced in England in 2007, The Family Nurse Partnership (FNP) is a voluntary home visiting programme. Regularly visiting first-time young mothers from the early stages of pregnancy until their child is two, it aims to enable them to have a healthy pregnancy, improve their child's health and development, plan their own futures and achieve their aspirations.

Formative assessment A process of formal and informal assessments throughout the learning process to inform future planning, this will consist of observations, informed knowledge about the child and information given by others involved in the child's development.

Foundation years The years from birth until the September following a child's fifth birthday.

Free entitlement A government initiative to offer free childcare hours to working parents.

Free-flow Opportunity to move freely between environments, including accessing the indoor and outdoor space as they wish.

Healthy Child Programme Published under the 2005–2010 Labour government, this programme covering pregnancy and the first five years focused on a universal preventative service, providing screening, immunisation, health and development reviews, supplemented by advice around health, well-being and parenting.

Hierarchical One skill building on another. For example, learning to stand before you can run.

Holistic learners Children learn from all things at all times, enabling them to make connections in their learning.

Horizontal transitions Moving environments during the course of the day. For example from home, to setting, to the outdoors.

Implicit That which is not necessarily written down but is commonly understood.

Insignificant practices Little changes that can have great effect, such as turning the radio off in the car to have a conversation, taking the time for a toddler to walk short distances even though a pushchair would be quicker, or using dummies only for sleep time.

Intergenerational Factors affecting the older generations of a family naturally impacting on the experiences and expectations of the children, which is in turn passed on to their own families.

Key worker Intrinsic within the EYFS (England), a key person (or key worker) is a named member of staff with care and development responsibilities for a small group of children. Through attending to physical and intimate needs, care is tailored to individual children, nurturing feelings of security. An accessible point of contact, relationships are built with children and their families as detailed records are kept and shared.

Linear learners Learning that follows a straight sequential path with each element building on the one before.

Metaphysical The world that exists in the child's mind – not limited by the realities of the environment or resources that are available.

Microsystems The child's immediate surroundings.

Multidimensional A highly complex environment full of new things to cope with that we may not fully appreciate and cannot underestimate.

Multidisciplinary That which brings together the opinions and knowledge of relevant professions working within early years including health, care and education.

Multifaceted Having many different features and roles to play.

Nuances of speech The subtle differences in speech.

Ofsted Childcare Register A register of providers who are registered by Ofsted to care for children from birth to 17 years. In addition to the Early Years Register that covered those looking after children within the foundation stage, this has two parts: compulsory for those caring for children under age eight, and a voluntary part for those wishing to register for older children.

Oxymoron A figure of speech where the two terms used seem to contradict each other.

Parent forums Meetings to discuss the setting attended by parents and staff so that a representative view can be considered.

Parity The experiences offered to children cannot be the same as they must be tailored to individual need. However, care must be taken so that the level of quality and accessibility is always equivalent.

Pedagogies The methods and practices of teaching.

Peripheries The information gained from all around us, not solely that which we focus on.

Plasticity The brain's ability to change and adapt itself as a result of learning experiences.

Prime areas Communication and language, physical development, and personal, social and emotional development. These form the focus for working with the youngest children to build a basis for successful learning in the specific areas, with more equal focus on all areas of learning as children grow in confidence and ability.

Proprioception The sense of self, of knowing where your body is without needing to look. Coming from the central nervous system, this allows us to drive without looking at our feet and to find our mouth without looking at the fork.

Pupil profiles These EYFS Profiles (EYFSPs) are an assessment of children's developments at the end of the EYFS across the 17 Early Learning Goals.

Qualified Teacher Status (QTS) The professional status that must be held to take a teaching post in a maintained school in England.

Resource packs A selection of resources that deliver an idea or activity through various media or approaches. This could include a book of the Three Little Pigs, three toy or puppet pigs and a wolf, masks or costumes so that the children can play the parts, representative pieces of hay, straw and brick and a fact sheet that draws attention to the learning potential of the activity.

Rote delivery An approach to teaching and working with children that is heavily planned and delivered as intended without being reactive to the children's needs or the experiences of the day.

Scaffolding A temporary support given to children as they acquire new skills that will gradually be removed as these skills are mastered.

Schematic behaviours Driven by children's interests and needs, this deeply powerful learning mechanism involves repeated, sometimes compulsive actions and behaviours enabling children to discover underpinning structures of the world around them.

Self-efficacy How much we believe in our own abilities to achieve a task or succeed in an endeavour. A measure of our own self-worth.

Self-initiated Opportunities for children to explore the experience they wish to, rather than being directed into one of someone else's choosing.

Social mobility The ability to move oneself or one's family from one social grouping to another, for example out of poverty.

Specific areas As prime areas are secured these are strengthened and applied through the specific areas of literacy, mathematics, understanding the world and expressive arts and design.

Stay and play Opportunities for parents to attend a session, spending time with their child whilst gaining an understanding of the practices and activities taking place.

Subsidised Financial support from state funds.

Summative assessment Assessed at the end of a key period of time to provide a summary of progress, this takes place with the prime areas between the ages of 24 and 36 months and at the end of the EYFS in the EYFS Profile (or baseline assessment).

Sure Start A government area-based early intervention programme providing a range of integrated support services for children under five and their families at accessible community locations. Offering a broad range of services that focus on family health, early years care and education and improved well-being programmes, it aims to support disadvantaged families from pregnancy to give children the best start in life.

Synapses How information is passed through the connections within the nervous system.

Tangible Real examples that children can experience, touch and manipulate.

Two-year development review A requirement of the EYFS (England), this one-to-one meeting with parents and follow-up written summary assesses their child's learning and development, identifying strengths and the need for extra support. Accompanied by the integrated NHS development review at 27 months, the aim is to promote positive outcomes in health and well-being, learning and development by facilitating appropriate intervention and support for children and families where it is needed.

Vertical transitions Progressive movements through rooms in the setting, from the baby room, to toddlers, to preschool and then up to school.

Windows of developmental opportunity Critical periods when positive experiences may be most beneficial in the developmental process.

REFERENCES

Adamson, L.B., Bakeman, R., Deckner, D.F. and Brooke Nelson, P. (2014) 'From interactions to conversations: the development of joint engagement during early childhood', *Child Development*, 85 (3): 941–55.

Alexander, K.L., Entwisle, D.R. and Dauber, S.L. (1993) 'First grade classroom behavior: its short- and long-term consequences for school performance', *Child Development*, 64: 801–814.

All Party Parliamentary Sure Start Group (2013) *Best Practice for a Sure Start: The Way Forward for Children's Centres*. London: All Party Parliamentary Sure Start Group. Available at www.4children.org.uk/Files/cffc42fe-49eb-43e2-b330-a1fd00b8077b/Best-Practice-for-a-Sure-Start.pdf (accessed 31/3/16).

Allen, G. (2011) *Early Intervention: The Next Steps. An Independent Report to Her Majesty's Government*. London: Cabinet Office. Available at www.gov.uk/government/uploads/system/uploads/attachment_data/file/284086/early-intervention-next-steps2.pdf (accessed 21/6/16).

Asmussen, K. and Weizel, K. (2010) *Evaluating the Evidence: Fathers, Families and Children*. London: King's College, National Academy of Parenting Research.

Association of Teachers and Lecturers (ATL) (2015) 'Early years experts unite in the call to block baseline assessment', press release, 15 July. Available at www.atl.org.uk/media-office/2015/early-years-experts-block-baseline-assessment.asp (accessed 30/6/16).

Atkinson, M., Jones, M. and Lamont, E. (2007) Multi-agency Working and its implications for practice: A review of the literature. CfBT Education Trust. Available at www.nfer.ac.uk/nfer/publications/MAD01/MAD01.pdf (accessed 30/6/16).

Bain, J., James, D. and Harrison, M. (2015) 'Supporting communication development in the early years: a practitioner's perspective', *Child Language Teaching & Therapy*, 31 (3): 325–36.

Baker, M., Gruber, J. and Milligan, K. (2008) 'Universal childcare, maternal labor supply and family well-being', *Journal of Political Economy*, 116 (4): 709–745.

Ball, C. (1994) *Start Right: The Importance of Early Learning*. London: RSA.

Bandura, A. (1982) 'Self-efficacy mechanism in human agency', *American Psychologist*, 37 (2): 122–47.

Bertram, T. and Pascal, C. (2002) *Early Years Education: An International Perspective*. London: QCA.

Biggs, B. (1996) 'Western misperceptions of the Confucian-heritage learning culture', in *The Chinese Learner: Cultural, Psychological and Contextual Influences*, D.A. Watkins and J.B. Biggs (Eds.), Hong Kong: Comparative Education Research Centre/ Melbourne: Australian Council for Educational Research. pp. 45–67.

Bilton, H. (2002) *Outdoor Play in the Early Years*. London: David Fulton.

Bjorklund, S., Mard-Miettinen, K. and Savijarvi, M. (2014) 'Swedish immersion in the early years in Finland', *International Journal of Bilingual Education and Bilingualism*, 17 (2): 197–214.

Blakemore, S.J. (2000) *Early Years Learning*. London: Parliamentary Office of Science and Technology.

Blanden, J. (2006) '"Bucking the trend": What enables those who are disadvantaged in childhood to succeed later in life?', *DWP Working Paper* No. 31. London: Department for Work and Pensions.

Blanning, N. (2015) *School Readiness Today: A Report from the Pedagogical Section of the Goetheanum*. Spring Valley, NY: Waldorf Early Childhood Association North America.

Blenkin, G.M. and Kelly, A.V. (Eds) (1994) *The National Curriculum and Early Learning*. London: Paul Chapman.

Board of Education (1905) *Reports on Children under Five Years of Age in Public Elementary Schools by Women Inspectors of the Board of Education*. London: HMSO.

Board of Education (1908) *Report of the Consultative Committee upon the School Attendance of Children below the Age of Five*. London: HMSO.

Boivin, M. and Bierman, K. (Eds.) (2014) *Promoting School Readiness and Early Learning: Implications of Developmental Research for Practice*. New York: Guilford Press.

Boone, T. (no date) 'Jean-Jacques Rousseau', *Representing Childhood*. Available at www.representingchildhood.pitt.edu/rousseau.htm (accessed 28/6/16).

Bornstein, M.H., Tamis-LeMonda, C.S., Hahn, C.S. and Haynes, O.M. (2008) 'Maternal responsiveness to young children at three ages: longitudinal analysis of a multidimensional, modular and specific parenting construct', *Developmental Psychology*, 44: 867–74.

Bradley, R.H. and Corwyn, R.F. (2007) 'Externalizing problems in the fifth grade: relations with productive activity, maternal sensitivity and harsh parenting from infancy through middle childhood', *Developmental Psychology*, 43: 1390–1401.

Briars, D. and Siegler, R.S. (1984) 'A featural analysis of preschoolers counting knowledge', *Developmental Psychology*, 20: 607–618.

Broadhead, P. (2001) 'Investigating sociability and cooperation in four and five year olds in reception class settings', *International Journal of Early Years Education*, 9 (1).

Bronfenbrenner, U. (Ed.) (2005) *Making Human Beings Human: Biological Perspectives on Human Development*. London: Sage.

Brooker, L. (2002) *Starting School: Young Children Learning Culture*. Buckingham: Open University Press.

Brooker, L. (2008) *Supporting Transitions in the Early Years*. London: McGraw Hill.

Brookes, G., Gorman, I., Harman, J., Hutchinson, D., Kinder, K., Moor, H. and Wilkin, A. (1997) *Family Literacy Lasts*. London: Basic Skills Agency.

Brostrom, S. (2002) 'Communication and continuity in the transition from kindergarten to school', in H. Fabian and A-W. Dunlop (Eds), *Transitions in the Early Years*. London: RoutledgeFalmer.

Brown, C.P. (2010) 'Balancing the readiness equation in early childhood education reform', Journal of Early Childhood Research, 8 (2).

Brown, F. and Patte, M. (2013) *Rethinking Children's Play*. London: Bloomsbury Academic.

Brown, S. (2009) *Play, How it Shapes the Brain, Opens the Imagination and Invigorates the Soul*. London: Penguin.

Browne, A. (1998) 'Provision for reading for four year old children', *Reading*, 32 (1): 9–13.

Bruce, T. (2011a) *Cultivating Creativity For Babies, Toddlers and Young Children*, 2nd edn. London: Hodder Education.

Bruce, T. (2011b) *Learning Through Play: For Babies, Toddlers and Young Children*, 2nd Edn. London: Hodder Education.

Bruner, J. (1977) *The Process of Education*. Cambridge, MA: Harvard College.

Brzeziska, A.I., Matejczuk, J. and Nowotnik, A. (2012) 'Wspomaganie rozwoju dzieci w wieku od 5 do 7 lat a ich gotowo do radzenia sobie z wyzwaniami szkoły', *Edukacja*, 1 (117): 7–22, cited in Margetts, K. (2013) *International Perspectives on Transition to School: Reconceptualising Beliefs, Policy and Practice*. London: Routledge.

Cameron, C. and Moss, P. (2007) *Care Work in Europe: Current Understandings and Future Directions*. London: Routledge.

Centre for Longtitudinal Studies (CLS) (2015) 'Welcome to the Millennium Cohort Study'. Available at www.cls.ioe.ac.uk/page.aspx?sitesectionid=851 (accessed 27/6/16).

Child Trends DataBank (2013) *Parental Involvement in Schools: Indicators on Children and Youth*. Bethesda, MD: Child Trends DataBank. Available at www.childtrends.org/wp-content/uploads/2012/10/39_Parent_Involvement_In_Schools.pdf (accessed 5/4/16).

Clarke-Stewart, K.A. (1992) 'Consequences of child care for children's development', in A. Booth (Ed.), *Child Care in the 1990s: Trends and Consequences*. Hillsdale, New Jersey: Lawrence Erlbaum. pp. 63–82.

Clarkson, R. and Sainsbury, M. (2007) *Attitudes to Reading at Ages Nine and Eleven: Full Report*. Slough: National Foundation for Educational Research. Available at www.nfer.ac.uk/publications/RAQ01/RAQ01.pdf (accessed 30/6/16).

Claxton, G. (1999) 'Playing for life: laying the foundations for lifelong learning', paper delivered at BAECE Conference Sure Start–Brighter Future, London, 9 June.

Claxton, G. (2008a) 'Cultivating positive learning dispositions', in H. Daniels, H. Lauder and J. Porter (Eds), *Routledge Companion to Education*. London: Routledge.

Claxton, G. (2008b) *What's the Point of School? Rediscovering the Heart of Education*. London: Oneworld.

Crowley, K. (2014) *Child Development*. London: Sage.

Dahlberg, G. and Moss, P. (2005) *Ethics and Politics in Early Childhood Education*. London & New York: RoutledgeFalmer.

Dahlgaard-Park, S.M. (2006) 'Learning from east to west and west to east', *TQM Magazine*, 18 (3): 216–37. Available at http://emeraldinsight.com/Insight/viewPDF.jsp?Filename=html/Output/Published?EmeraldFullTextArticle/Pdf/1060180301.pdf (accessed 26/6/16).

Dau, E. (1999) *Child's Play: Revisiting Play in Early Childhood Settings*. Sydney: Maclennan Petty.

Davis, R. and O'Hagan, F. (2014) *Robert Owen*. London: Bloomsbury Academic.

Deák, G.O. and Wiseheart, M. (2015) 'Cognitive flexibility in young children: General or task-specific capacity?', *Journal of Experimental Child Psychology*, 138 (2015): 31–53.

Dearing, E., Berry, D. and Zaslow, M. (2006) 'Poverty during early childhood', in K. McCartney and D. Phillips (Eds.) *Blackwell Handbook of Early Childhood Development*. London: Blackwell.

Degioia, K. (2009) 'Parent and staff expectations for continuity of home practices in the child care setting for families with diverse cultural backgrounds', *Australasian Journal of Early Childhood*, 34 (3): 9–17.

Department for Children, Schools and Families (DfCSF) (2003) *The Impact of Parental Involvement on Children's Education*. London: DfCSF. Available at http://webarchive.nationalarchives.gov.uk/20130401151715/www.education.gov.uk/publications/eOrderingDownload/DCSF-Parental_Involvement.pdf (accessed 15/7/15).

Department for Children, Schools and Families (DfCSF) (2009a) *Every Child a Talker: guidance for Consultants and Early Language Lead Practitioners*. Nottingham: DCSF Publication. Available at www.foundationyears.org.uk/files/2011/10/ecat_guidance_for_practitioners_31.pdf (accessed 21/6/16).

Department for Children, Schools and Families (DfCSF) (2009b) *Healthy Child Programme: Pregnancy and the First Five Years of Life*. London: Department of Health. Available at www.gov.uk/government/uploads/system/uploads/attachment_data/file/167998/Health_Child_Programme.pdf (accessed 21/6/16).

Department for Children, Schools and Families (DfCSF) (2009c) *Next Steps for Early Learning and Childcare: Building on the 10-year Strategy*. London: DfCSF.

Department for Education (DfE) (2010a) 'Achievement of children in the Early Years Foundation Stage Profile', RR-034. London: DfE.

Department for Education (DfE) (2010b) 'Early Years Foundation Stage Profile Results in England, 2009/2010', SFR 28/2010. London: DfE.

Department for Education (DfE) (2013) *More Great Childcare: Raising Quality and Giving Parents More Choice*. London: DfE.

Department for Education (DfE) (2014) *Statutory Framework for the Early Years Foundation Stage: Setting the Standards for Learning, Development and Care for Children from Birth to Five*. London: DfE.

Department for Education (DfE) (2015) *2010–2015 Government Policy: School and College Funding and Accountability*. London: DfE.

Department for Education (DfE) and Gyimah, S. (2015) 'Help to up-skill childcare staff before the reach the frontline', Press Release, 1 July. Available at https://www.gov.uk/government/news/help-to-up-skill-childcare-staff-before-they-reach-the-frontline (accessed 28/6/16).

Department for Education and Department of Health (DfE and DH) (2011) *Supporting Families in the Foundation Years*. Available at www.gov.uk/government/publications/supporting-families-in-the-foundation-years (accessed 15/7/15).

Department for Education and Standards and Testing Agency (DfE and STA) (2014) *Early Years Foundation Stage Profile: Exemplification Materials*. London: DfES. Available at www.gov.uk/government/publications/eyfs-profile-exemplification-materials (accessed 22/6/16).

Department for Education and Standards and Testing Agency (DfE and STA) (2016) 'Reception baseline comparability study published', Press release. Available at www.gov.uk/government/news/reception-baseline-comparability-study-published (accessed 22/6/16).

Department for Education and Employment (DfEE) (1998a) *National Literacy Strategy: Framework for Teaching*. London: DfEE.

Department for Education and Employment (DfEE) (1998b) *National Numeracy Strategy: Framework for Teaching*. London: DfEE.

Department for Education and Employment (DfEE) (1998c) 'Meeting the Childcare Challenge' Green Paper. Norwich: The Stationery Office.

Department for Education and Skills (DfES) (2002) *Birth to Three Matters*. Norwich: The Stationery Office.

Department for Education and Skills (DfES) (2005) *Departmental Report 2005*. Norwich: The Stationery Office. Available at www.gov.uk/government/uploads/system/uploads/attachment_data/file/272106/6522.pdf (accessed 30/6/16).

Department for Education and Skills (DfES) (2007) *The Early Years Foundation Stage*. London: DfES.

Desailly, J. (2015) *Creativity in the Primary Classroom*, 2nd edn. London: Sage.

Desforges, C. and Abouchaar, A. (2003) 'The *Impact of Parental Involvement, Parental Support and Family Education on Pupil Achievement and Adjustment: A Literature Review*', Research Report RR443. London: DfES.

Diamond, A. and Lee, K. (2011) 'Interventions shown to aid executive function development in children 4 to 12 years old', *Science*, 333: 959–64.

Dockett, S. and Perry, B. (2004) 'Starting school: perspectives of Australian children, parents and educators', *Journal of Early Childhood Research*, 2 (2).

Dombey, H. (2010) 'It all starts with /c/ /a/ /t/ – or does it? Foundation phonics', in S. Smidt (Ed.), *Key Issues in Early Years Education*. London: Routledge.

Donaldson, M. (2004) *Children's Minds*. London: Fontana.

Dowling, M. (1995) *Starting School at Four: A Joint Endeavour*. London: Paul Chapman.

Drummand, M. (1997) 'An undesirable document', *Coordinate*, January: 7–8.

Drummand, M.J. (2010) 'Under the microscope', in S. Smidt (Ed.), *Key Issues in Early Years Education*. London: Routledge.

Dunlop, A. and Fabian, H. (Eds.) (2007) *Informing Transitions in the Early Years*. London: McGraw Hill.

Dunlop, A-W., Lee, P., Fee, J., Hughes, A., Grieve, A. and Marwick, H. (2008) *Positive Behaviour in the Early Years*. Strathclyde: Department of Childhood & Primary Studies, University of Strathclyde. Available at www.gov.scot/resource/doc/238252/0065411.pdf (accessed 5/4/16).

Dunn, J. (1988) *The Beginnings of Social Understanding*. Blackwell: Oxford.

Durkan, M., Field, F., Lamb, N. and Loughton, T. (no date) *The 1001 Critical Days: The Importance of the Conception to Age Two Period*. Available at www.1001criticaldays.co.uk/1001days_Nov15.pdf (accessed 22/6/16).

Early Years Interboard Panel (no date) *Learning Through Play in the Early Years*. Belfast: CCEA. Available at www.nicurriculum.org.uk/docs/foundation_stage/learning_through_play_ey.pdf (accessed 21/6/16).

Ebbeck, M. (1996) 'Children constructing their own knowledge', *International Journal of Early Years Education*, 4 (2): 5–27.

ECEC (2004) *National Curriculum Guidelines on Early Childhood Education and Care in Finland.* Paris: UNESCO. www.ibe.unesco.org/curricula/finland/fi_ecefw_2004_eng.pdf (accessed 22/6/16).

Education and Manpower Bureau (2005) 'Quality assurance inspection 2004–2005: annual report for kindergartens'. Hong Kong: EMB. Available at www.emb.gov.hk/FileManager/TC/Content_756/kg_annualreport_0405.pdf (accessed 20/12/06).

Edwards, C., Gandini, L. and Forman, G.E. (Eds) (2011) *The Hundred Languages of Children: The Reggio Emilia Experience in Transformation*, 3rd edn. Westport, CT: Greenwood Press.

Edwards, R., Gillies, V. and Horsley, N. (2016) 'Early intervention and evidence-based policy and practice: framing and taming', *Social Policy and Society*, 15: 1–10.

Ellyatt, W. (2015) 'Towards an integrated understanding of the child', Save Childhood Movement. Available at www.toomuchtoosoon.org/uploads/2/0/3/8/20381265/towards_an_integrated_understanding_march_2015_8_(1).pdf (accessed 6/4/16).

Entwisle, D. and Alexander, K. (1998) 'Facilitating the transition to first grade: the nature of transition and research on factors affecting it', *Elementary School Journal*, 98(4): 351–64.

Evangelou, M., Sylva, K., Kyriacou, M., Wild, M. and Glenny, G. (2009) *Early Years Learning and Development Literature Review*. London: DfCSF.

Evans, M. (2011) 'What does "ready for school" mean?', *Nursery World*, 111 (4255): 10–11.

Fabian, H. (2002) 'Empowering children for transitions', in H. Fabian and A-W. Dunlop (Eds), *Transitions in the Early Years: Debating Continuity and Progression for Children in Early Education*. London: RoutledgeFalmer.

Faust, H. (2010) 'Mathematical development in the Early Years Foundation Stage: problem-solving, reasoning and numeracy', in S. Smidt (Ed.), *Key Issues in Early Years Education*. London: Routledge.

Feinstein, L. and Duckworth, K. (2006) 'Development in the early years: its importance for school performance and adult outcomes', Wider Benefits of Learning Research Report No. 20. Available: at eprints.ioe.ac.uk/5970/1/Feinstein2006Development.pdf (accessed 28/7/15).

Field, F. (2010) *The Foundation Years: Preventing Poor Children Becoming Poor Adults. The Report of the Independent Review on Poverty and Life Chances*. London: Cabinet Office.

Finnegan, J. (2016) *Lighting Up Young Brains: How Parents, Carers and Nurseries Support Children's Brain Development in the First Five Years*. London: Save the Children. Available at www.savethechildren.org.uk/sites/default/files/images/Lighting_Up_Young_Brains1_0CSCupdate.pdf (accessed 6/4/16).

Fisher, D. and Frey, N. (2009) *Background Knowledge: The Missing Piece of the Comprehension Puzzle*. Portsmouth, NH: Heinemann.

Fisher, J. (2011) 'Building on the Early Years Foundation Stage: developing good practice for transition into Key Stage 1', *Early Years: An International Journal of Research and Development*, 31 (1): 31–42.

Fisher, K., McCulloch, A. and Gershuny, J. (1999) 'British fathers and children', Working Paper, Institute for Social and Economic Research, Essex, cited in M. O'Brien and I. Shemilt (2003) *Working Fathers: Earning and Caring*. Manchester: Equal Opportunities Commission.

Fleer, M. (2009) 'Supporting scientific conceptual consciousness or learning in "a roundabout way" in play-based contexts', *International Journal of Science Education*, 31 (8): 1069–89.

Flouri, E. (2006) 'Parental interest in children's education, children's self-esteem and locus of control, and later educational attainment: Twenty-six year follow-up of the 1970 British birth cohort', *British Journal of Educational Psychology*, 76: 41–55.

Forester, M.A. and Cherington, S.M. (2009) 'The development of other-related conversational skills: a case study of conversational repair during the early years', *First Language*, 29 (2): 166–91.

Frith, U., Bishop, D. and Blakemore, C. (2011) *Brain Waves Module 2: Neuroscience: Implications for Education and Lifelong Learning*. London: The Royal Society.

Frost, J. (2009) *A History of Children's Play and Play Environments*. London: Routledge.

Fuson, K.C. (1988) *Children's Counting and Concepts of Number*. New York: Springer.

Gardner, H. (2011) *Creating Minds: An Anatomy of Creativity Seen Through the Lives of Freud, Einstein, Picasso, Stravinsky, Eliot, Graham, and Ghandi*. New York: Basic Books.

Gasper, M. (2010) *Multi-agency Working in the Early Years: Challenges and Opportunities*. London: Sage.

Gehris, J., Gooze, R. and Whitaker, R. (2015) 'Teachers' perceptions about children's movement and learning in early childhood education programmes', *Child: Care, Health and Development*, 41 (1): 122–31.

Goldman, R. (2005) *Fathers' Involvement in their Children's Education*. London: National Family and Parenting Institute.

Goldschmied, E. and Selleck, D. (1996) *Communication Between Babies in their First Year*. London: National Children's Bureau.

Grauberg, J. (Ed.) (2014) *Early Years: Valuable Ends and Effective Means*. London: CentreForum. Available at www.centreforum.org/assets/pubs/early-years.pdf (accessed 17/7/15).

Greene, V., Joshi, P., Street, C., Connor, J., Soar, S. and Kurtz, A. (2014) *Two year olds in schools: summary of delivery approaches and support needs: Baseline survey of schools, Research Report*. London: DfE. Available at www.gov.uk/government/uploads/system/uploads/attachment_data/file/307281/RR348_-_Two_year_olds_in_schools_baseline_survey.pdf (accessed 5/4/16).

Greene, V., Joshi, P., Street, C., Connor, J., Soar, S. and Kurtz, A. (2015a) *Two-year-olds in Schools: A Case Study of Eight Schools*. London: DfE. Available at www.gov.uk/government/uploads/system/uploads/attachment_data/file/398996/RR389_-_Two-year-olds_in_schools_A_case_study_of_eight_schools.pdf (accessed 5/4/16).

Greene, V., Joshi, P., Street, C., Connor, J., Soar, S. and Kurtz, A. (2015b) *Process Evaluation of the Two-year-olds in Schools Demonstration Project: Research Report*. Available at www.gov.uk/government/uploads/system/uploads/attachment_data/file/

399000/RR390_-_Process_and_cost_evaluation_of_the_two_year-olds_in_schools_demonstration_project.pdf (accessed 5/4/16).
Grissmer, D.W. and Eiseman, E. (2008) 'Can gaps in the quality of early environment and non-cognitive skills help explain persisting Black–White achievement gaps?', in K.A. Magnuson and J. Waldfogel (Eds.), *Steady Gains and Stalled Progress: Inequality and the Black-White Test Score Gap*. New York: Russell Sage Foundation. pp. 139–80.
Grissmer, D., Grimm, K.J., Aiyer, S.M., Murrah, W.M. and Steele, J.S. (2010) 'Fine motor skills and early comprehension of the world: two new school readiness indicators', *Developmental Psychology*, 46 (5): 1008–1017.
Guha, M. (1994) 'Play in school', in G. Blenkin and A.V. Kelly (Eds), *The National Curriculum and Early Learning*. London: Paul Chapman.
Gutman, L.M. and Akerman, R. (2008) 'Determinants of Aspirations', Centre for Research on the Wider Benefits of Learning Research Report 27. London: Institute of Education.
Hall, J. (2005) 'Neuroscience and education: a review of the contribution of brain science to teaching and learning', Research Report No.121. Glasgow: SCRE.
Halle, T., Hair, E., Wandner, L. and Chien, N. (2012) 'Profiles of school readiness among four-year-old head start children', *Early Childhood Research Quarterly*, 27 (4): 613–26.
Haller, E. (2013) *The Reflective Early Years Practitioner*. London: Sage.
Hamre, B., Hatfield, B., Pianta, R. and Jamil, F. (2014) 'Evidence for general and domain specific elements of teacher–child interactions with preschool children's development', *Child Development*, 85 (3): 1257–74.
Hansen, K. and Hawkes, D. (2009) 'Early childcare and child development', *Journal of Social Policy*, 38 (2): 211–239.
Hargreaves, L. (2010) 'How children learn at home', *Early Years: An International Research Journal*, 30 (1): 100–101.
Harris, P. (1990) Quoted in *Oxford Today*, 2: 18–19.
Harris, Y.R. and Schroeder, V.M. (2012) 'What the Berenstain bears can tell us about school readiness: maternal story grammar style and preschool narrative recall', *Journal of Early Childhood Research*, 10 (2).
Hayashi, A. and Tobin, J. (2013) 'The power of implicit teaching practices: continuities and discontinuities in pedagogical approaches of deaf and hearing preschools in Japan', *Comparative Education Review*, 58 (1).
Hibel, J. (2009) 'Roots of assimilation: generational status differentials in ethnic minority children's school readiness', *Journal of Early Childhood Research*, 7 (2).
Hicks, D. (1996) 'Contextual inquiries: a discourse-oriented study of classroom leaning', in D. Hicks (Ed.), *Discourse, Learning and Schooling*. Cambridge: Cambridge University Press. pp.104–141.
Hirsch, E.D. (2003) 'Reading comprehension requires knowledge-of words and the world', *American Educator*, 27 (1): 10–13, 16–22, 28–48.
HM Government (2015) *Working Together to Safeguard Children: A Guide to Inter-agency Working to Safeguard and Promote the Welfare of Children*. London: DfE. Available at www.gov.uk/government/uploads/system/uploads/attachment_data/file/419595/Working_Together_to_Safeguard_Children.pdf (accessed 21/6/16).
HM Government (2016) *Childcare Act 2016*. Norwich: The Stationery Office. Available at www.legislation.gov.uk/ukpga/2016/5/enacted (accessed 5/4/16).
HM Treasury (1998) *Modern Public Services for Britain: Investing in Reform – Comprehensive Spending Review: New Public Spending Plans*. London: Stationery Office.
HM Treasury (2004) *Choice for Parents, the Best Start For Children: A Ten Year Strategy for Childcare*. London: DfES.
Home Office (2015) *Multi Agency Working and Information Sharing Project 2014*. London: Home Office. www.gov.uk/government/uploads/system/uploads/attachment_data/file/338875/MASH.pdf

House of Commons Education Committee (2013) *Foundation Years: Sure Start Children's Centres, Fifth Report of Session 2013–14*. Available at www.publications.parliament.uk/pa/cm201314/cmselect/cmeduc/364/364.pdf (accessed 07/08/2015).

Hurst, V. (1997) *Planning for Early Learning: Educating Young Children*, 2nd edn. London: Paul Chapman.

Ingleby, E. (2012) *Early Childhood Studies: A Social Science Perspective*. London: Bloomsbury Academic.

Irwin, J. (2012) *Paulo Freire's Philosophy of Education: Origins, Developments, Impacts and Legacies*. London: Continuum.

Isaacs, S. (2013) *The Educational Value of the Nursery School*. London: British Association for Early Childhood Education.

Jane, B.L. (2006) 'Online reflection about tinkering in early childhood: a socio-cultural analysis', *Asia-Pacific Forum on Science Learning and Teaching*, 7 (1): n1.

Jeffers, G. (2014) 'Schooling through a Human Rights lens', in M. Thomas (Ed.), *A Child's World: Contemporary Issues in Education*. Aberystwyth: CAA, Aberystwyth University.

Johansson, E. and Pramling Samuelsson, I. (2006) Lek och la¨roplan. Mo¨ten mellan barn och la¨rare I fo¨rskola och skola (Play and curriculum), Göteborg Studies in educational Sciences 249. Gothenberg: Acta Universitatis Gothoburgensis.

Kalliala, M. (2011) 'Look at me! Does the adult truly see and respond to the child in Finnish day-care centres?', *European Early Childhood Education Research Journal*, 19 (2): 237–54.

Karweit, N.L. (1998) *Maryland Kindergarten Survey Report*. Baltimore: Johns Hopkins University, Centre for Research on the Education of Students Placed At Risk.

Katz, L. (2010) 'A developmental approach to the curriculum in the early years', in S. Smidt (Ed.), *Key Issues in Early Years Education*. London: Routledge.

Kiernan, G., Axford, N., Little, M., Murphy, C., Greene, S. and Gormley, M., (2008) 'The school readiness of children living in a disadvantaged area in Ireland', *Journal of Early Childhood Research*, 6 (2).

Kington, A., Gates, P. and Sammons, P. (2013) 'Development of social relationships, interactions and behaviours in early education settings', *Journal of Early Childhood Research*, 11: 292.

Kirkup, C. (2016) 'Baseline assessment', *Research Insights*. Available at www.nfer.ac.uk/schools/baseline-assessment.pdf (accessed 21/6/16).

König, A. and Van der Aalsvoort, G. (2009) 'Attitudes of Dutch and German preschool teachers towards professional childcare: a cultural comparison', *Early Years: Journal Of International Research & Development*, 29 (3): 249–60.

Krogh, S.L. and Morehouse, P. (2014) *The Early Childhood Curriculum: Inquiry Learning Through Integration*, 2nd edn. London: Routledge.

Laevers, F., Buyse, E., Willekens, A. and Janssen, T. (2011) 'Promoting language in under 3s: assessing language development and the quality of adult intervention', *European Early Childhood Education Research Journal*, 19 (2): 269–98.

Lamb, M.E., Sternberg, K.J. and Prodromidis, M. (1992) 'Nonmaternal care and the security of the infant–mother attachment: a reanalysis of the data', *Infant Behavior and Development*, 15: 71–83.

Levin, D. (1996) 'Endangered play, endangered development: a constructivist view of the role of play in development and learning', *Topics in Early Childhood Education*, 2.

Lindon, J. (2012) *Understanding Child Development: 0–8 Years*, 3rd edn. London: Hodder Education.

Lindon, J. and Brodie, K. (2016) *Understanding Child Development 0–8 Years: Linking Theory and Practice*, 4th edn. London: Hodder Education.

Lipscomb, S., Pratt, M., Schmitt, S., Pears, K. and Kim, H. (2013) 'School readiness in children living in non-parental care: impacts of head start', *Journal of Applied Developmental Psychology*, 34 (1) 28–37.

Lynch, J. (2009) 'Preschool teachers' beliefs about children's print literacy development', *Early Years: An International Research Journal*, 29 (2), 191–203.

MacBlain, S. (2014) *How Children Learn*. London: Sage.

Margetts, K. (2013) *International Perspectives on Transition to School: Reconceptualising Beliefs, Policy and Practice*. London: Routledge.

Marton, F. and Booth, S. (1997) *Learning and Awareness*. Mahwah, NJ: Lawrence Erlbaum.

Marzano, R.J. (2004) *Building Background Knowledge for Academic Achievement*. Alexandria, VA: Association for Supervision and Curriculum Development.

Mathers, S. and Smees, R. (2014) *Quality and Inequality: Do Three- and Four-year-olds in Deprived Areas Experience Lower Quality Early Years Provision?* London: Nuffield Foundation.

Maynard, T. and Waters, J. (2007) 'Learning in the outdoor environment: a missed opportunity?', *Early Years: An International Research Journal*, 27 (3): 255–65.

McClelland, M., Morrison, F.J. and Holmes, D.L. (2000) 'Children at risk for early academic problems: the role of learning-related social skills', *Early Childhood Research Quarterly*, 15: 307–329.

McMillan, M. (1923) *What the Open Air Nursery School Is*. London: The Labour Party.

Melhuish, E.C. (2003) *A Literature Review of the Impact of Early Years Provision on Young Children, with Emphasis Given to Children from Disadvantaged Backgrounds*. London: National Audit Office.

Melhuish, E.C. (2004a) 'A literature review of the impact of early years provision upon young children, with emphasis given to children from disadvantaged backgrounds', Report to the Comptroller and Auditor General. London: National Audit Office. Available at www.nao.org.uk/publications/nao_reports/03-04/268_literaturereview.pdf (accessed 24/6/16).

Melhuish, E.C. (2004b) *Child Benefits: The Importance of Investing in Quality Childcare*. London: Daycare Trust.

Melhuish, E.C., Quinn, L., McSherry, K., Sylva, K., Sammons, P., Siraj-Blatchford, I., Taggart, B. and Guimares, S. (2000a) *The Effective Pre-School Provision Northern Ireland (EPPNI) Project: Technical Paper 1 – Characteristics of Pre-School Environments in Northern Ireland: An Analysis of Observational Data*. Belfast: Stranmillis University College.

Melhuish, E.C., Quinn, L., Sylva, K., Sammons, P., Siraj-Blatchford, I., Taggart, B. and Shields, C. (2000b) *The Effective Pre-School Provision Northern Ireland (EPPNI) Project: Technical Paper 5 – Progress of Cognitive Development at the Start of P1*. Belfast: Stranmillis University College.

Mensah, F. and Kiernan, K. (2011) 'Maternal general health and children's cognitive development and behaviour in the early years: findings from the Millennium Cohort Study', *Child: Care, Health & Development*, 37 (1): 44–54.

Miller, L. (2010) 'Shaping early childhood through the literacy curriculum'. *Early Years: An International Research Journal*, 21 (2): 107–116.

Mills, C. and Mills, D. (1998) *Dispatches: The Early Years*. London: Channel Television.

Montessori, M. (1996) *The Secret of Childhood*. New York: Random House.

Moss, P. (2010) 'We cannot continue as we are: the educator in an education for survival', *Contemporary Issues in Early Childhood*, 11 (1): 8–19.

Movellan, J. (2015) 'Why babies smile', *Science Teacher*, 82 (8): 18.

Moyles, J. (2005) *The Excellence of Play*, 2nd edn. Milton Keynes: Open University Press/McGraw-Hill Education.

Moyles, J. (2010) 'Play: the powerful means of learning in the early years', in S. Smidt (Ed.), *Key Issues in Early Years Education*. London: Routledge.

Munro, E. (2011) *The Munro Review of Child Protection: Final Report. A child-centred system*. London: Department for Education. Available at www.gov.uk/government/uploads/system/uploads/attachment_data/file/175391/Munro-Review.pdf (accessed 6/8/15).

Murray, L. and Andrews, L. (2005) *The Social Baby: Understanding Babies' Communication from Birth*. Glasgow: CP Publishing.

Murray, L. and Trevarthen, C. (1985) 'Emotional regulations of interactions between two-month-olds and their mothers', in G. Allen (2011) *Early Intervention: The Next Steps. An Independent Report to Her Majesty's Government*. London: Cabinet Office.

Musatti, T. and Mayer, S. (2011) 'Sharing attention and activities among toddlers: the spatial dimension of the setting and the educator's role', *European Early Childhood Education Research Journal*, 19 (2): 207–222.

National Association for the Education of Young Children (NAEYC) (2009) 'Developmentally Appropriate Practice in Early Childhood Programs Serving Children from Birth through Age 8', a position statement of the National Association for the Education of Young Children. Washington, DC: NAEYC. Available at www.naeyc.org/files/naeyc/file/positions/position%20statement%20Web.pdf (accessed 30/6/16).

National Education Goals Panel (1991) *The National Education Goals Report*. Washington, DC: National Education Goals Panel.

National Research Council (2001) *Eager to Learn: Educating Our Preschoolers*. Washington, DC: National Academy Press.

Neaum, S. (2016) *Child Development for Early Years Students and Practitioners*, 3rd edn. Exeter: Learning Matters.

Neuman, M. (2001) *Early Childhood Education: Critical Perspectives*. Paris: OECD.

Neuman, S. (2010) 'Sparks fade, knowledge stays: The National Early Literacy Panel's report lacks staying power', *American Educator*, 34 (3): 14–39.

Noel, A.M. and Lord, K.M. (2014) 'Early Childhood teachers', care providers', and administrators' perceptions of dispositions toward learning, social emotional maturity, general knowledge, physical size and maturity, and age at school entry as factors in school readiness', paper presented at the annual conference of the European Early Childhood Educational Research Association, 8 September.

Nutbrown, C. (1998) 'Early assessment – examining the baselines', *Early Years*, 19 (1).

Nutbrown, C. (2011) *Threads of Thinking: Schemas And Young Children's Learning*, 4th edn. London: Sage.

Nutbrown, C. (2012) *Foundations for Quality: The Independent Review of Early Education and Childcare Qualifications, Final Report*. London: Department for Education.

Nutbrown, C. (2015) 'We must scrap new baseline tests for primary school children', *The Conversation*, 21 January. Available at https://theconversation.com/we-must-scrap-new-baseline-tests-for-primary-school-children-36558 (accessed 30/6/16).

O'Brien, M. and Shemilt, I. (2003) *Working Fathers: Earning and Caring*. Manchester: Equal Opportunities Commission.

O'Connor, D. and Angus, J. (2014) 'Give them time – an analysis of school readiness in Ireland's early education system: a Steiner Waldorf Perspective, Education 3–13', *International Journal of Primary, Elementary and Early Years Education*, 42 (5): 488–97.

Oberhuemer, P. (2005) 'Conceptualising the early pedagogue: policy approaches and issues of professionalism', *European Early Childhood Education Research Journal*, 13 (1): 5–16.

OECD (2006) *Starting Strong II: Early Childhood Education and Care*. Paris: Organisation for Economic Co-operation & Development.

Oers, B.V. and Hännikäinen, M. (2001) 'Some thoughts about togetherness: an introduction', *International Journal of Early Years Education*, 9 (2): 101–108.

Ofsted (2014a) *Early years annual report: 2012/13*. Manchester: Ofsted. Available at www.gov.uk/government/publications/ofsted-early-years-annual-report-201213 (accessed 5/4/16).

Ofsted (2014b) Helping disadvantaged children start school. Manchester: Ofsted. Available at www.gov.uk/government/publications/are-you-ready-good-practice-in-school-readiness (accessed 21/6/16).

Ofsted (2014c) *Are You Ready? Good Practice in School Readiness*. Manchester: Ofsted. Available at www.gov.uk/government/publications/are-you-ready-good-practice-in-school-readiness (accessed 22/6/16).

Peeters, J. (2008) *The Construction of a New Profession: A European Perspective on Professionalism in Early Childhood and Care*. Amsterdam: SWP.

Peisner-Feinberg, E.S. and Burchinal, M.R. (1997) 'Relations between preschool children's child care experiences and concurrent development: the cost, quality, and outcomes study', *Merill-Palmer Quarterly*, 43 (3): 451–77.

Peisner-Feinberg, E., Burchinal, M., Clifford, R., Culkin, M., Howes, C., Kagan, S. and Yazejian, N. (2001) 'The relation of preschool child care quality to children's cognitive and social developmental trajectories through second grade', *Child Development*, 72 (5): 1534–53.

Pelligrini, A.D. (2005) *Recess: Its Role in Development in Education*. Mahwah, NJ: Lawrence Erlbaum.

Peters, M., Seeds, K., Goldstein, A. and Coleman, N. (2008) *Parental Involvement in Children's Education 2007: Research Report*. London: DCSF.

Pilling, D. and National Children's Bureau (1990) *Escape from Disadvantage*. Lewes: Falmer.

Pirard, F. (2011) 'From the curriculum framework to its dissemination: the accompaniment of educational practices in care facilities for children under three years', *European Early Childhood Education Research Journal*, 19 (2): 255–68.

Pluckrose, H. (1987) *What Is Happening in Our Primary Schools?* Oxford: Blackwell.

Pound, L. (2008) *How Children Learn: Book 2*. London: Step Forward.

Pound, L. (2013) *Quick Guides for Early Years: Cognitive Development*. London: Hodder Education.

Pramling Samuelsson, I. (2005) 'Can play and learning be integrated in a goal-oriented early childhood education?', *Early Childhood Practice: The Journal for Multi-Professional Partnerships*, 7 (1): 5–22.

Pramling Samuelsson, I. and Asplund Carlsson, M. (2003) Det lekande lärande barnet—en utvecklingspedagogisk teori [The playing learning child – in a developmental pedagogic theory]. Stockholm: Liber.

Pramling Samuelsson, I. and Sheridan, S. (1999) *Lärandets grogrund. Perspektivoch förhållningssätt i förskolans läroplan [The basis of learning]*. Lund: Studentlitteratur.

Purcell-Gates, V. (2001) 'Emergent literacy is emerging knowledge of written, not oral, language', *New Directions for Child and Adolescent Development*, 92: 7–22.

Qualifications and Curriculum Authority (QCA) (2000) *Curriculum Guidance for the Foundation Stage*. London: QCA Publications.

Ramey, S. and Ramey, C. (1998) 'Commentary: The transition to school: opportunities and challenges for children, families, educators and communities', *Elementary School Journal*, 98 (4): 293–5.

Rayna, S. and Laevers, F. (Eds) (2014) *Understanding the Under 3s and the Implications for Education*. London: Routledge.

Read, J. (2015) 'Transformation and regulation: a century of continuity in nursery school and welfare policy rhetoric', *Journal of Education Policy*, 30 (1): 39–61.

Rimm-Kaufman, S., Pianta, R. and Cox, M. (2000) 'Teachers' judgments of problems in the transition to kindergarten', *Early Childhood Research Quarterly*, 15 (2): 147–66.

Rinaldi, C. (2005) *In Dialogue with Reggio-Emilia: Contestualising, Inerpreting and Evaluating Early Childhood Education*. London: RoutledgeFalmer.

Roberts, R. (2011) 'Companionable learning: a mechanism for holistic well-being development from birth', *European Early Childhood Education Research Journal*, 19 (2): 195–206.

Rose, J. (2015) *Health and Well-being in Early Childhood*. London: Sage.

Roulstone, S., Law, J., Rush, R., Clegg, J. and Peters, T. (2011) 'The role of language in children's early educational outcomes', Research Brief 134. London: DfE.

Sammons, P., Sylva, K., Melhuish, E., Siraj-Blatchford, I., Taggart, B., Barreau, S. and Grabbe, Y. (2007) *Influences on Children's Development and Progress in Key Stage 2: Social/Behavioural Outcomes in Year 5*, Research Report RR007. London: Institute of Education, University of London.

Samuelsson, I.P. (2004) 'How do children tell us about their childhoods?', *Early Childhood Research and Practice*, 6 (1).

Samuelsson, I.P. and Carlsson, M.A. (2008) 'The playing learning child: towards a pedagogy of early childhood', *Scandinavian Journal of Educational Research*, 52 (6): 623–41.

Schaub, M. (2015) 'Is there a home advantage in school readiness for young children? Trends in parent engagement in cognitive activities with young children, 1991–2001', *Journal of Early Childhood Research*, 13 (1).

School Curriculum and Assessment Authority (SCAA) (1996) *Desirable Outcomes for Children's Learning on Entering Compulsory Education*. London: DfEE.

Schweinhart, L.J., Montie, J., Xiang, Z., Barnett, W.S., Belfield, C.R. and Nores, M. (2005) *Lifetime Effects: The HighScope Perry Preschool Study through Age 40*, Monographs of the HighScope Educational Research Foundation, 14. Ypsilanti, MI: HighScope Press.

Sharp, C. (2002) School Starting Age: European Policy and Recent Research. Paper presented at LGA Seminar, November 2002.

Sharp, C., Keys, W. and Benefield, P. (2001) *Homework: A Review of Recent Research*. Slough: NFER.

Shildrick, T. and Rucell, J. (2015) *Sociological Perspectives on Poverty*. York: Joseph Rowntree Foundation. Available at www.jrf.org.uk/sites/default/files/jrf/sociological-perspectives-poverty-full.pdf (accessed 7/4/16).

Shin, S.J. (2010) 'Teaching English language learners: recommendations for early childhood educators', *Dimensions of Early Childhood*, 38 (2): 13–21.

Sijthoff, E. (2014) 'Exercising rights and "active" citizenship: children, physical activity and learning – in the classroom and beyond', in M. Thomas (Ed.), *A Child's World: Contemporary Issues in Education*. Aberystwyth: CAA, Aberystwyth University.

Sims, M. and Ellis, E. (2015) 'Raising children bilingually is hard: why bother?', *Babel*, 49 (2): 28–35.

Smidt, S. (Ed.) (2010) *Key Issues in Early Years Education*. London: Routledge.

Smith, P.K. (1988) 'Children's play and its role in early development', in A.D. Pellegrini (Ed.), *Psychological Bases for Early Education*. Chichester: Wiley.

Snyder, J., Cramer, A., Afrank, J. and Patterson, R.G. (2005) 'The contributions of ineffective discipline and parental hostile attributions of child misbehaviour to the development of conduct problems at home and school', *Developmental Psychology*, 41: 30–41.

Sommer, D. (2003) *Barndomspsykologiske facetter—en artikelsamling* [Childhood psychological facets]. Århus: Systimic Academic.

Standards and Testing Agency (STA) (2016) Reception Baseline Comparability Study: Results of the 2015 Study. London: Standards and Testing Agency. Available at www.gov.uk/government/uploads/system/uploads/attachment_data/file/514581/Reception_baseline_comparability_study.pdf (accessed 21/6/16).

Stefan, C.A. and Miclea, M. (2014) 'Effectiveness of the social-emotional prevention program as a function of children's baseline risk status', *European Early Childhood Education Research Journal*, 22 (1): 14–44.

Suggate, S. (2007) 'Research into early reading instruction and Luke effects in the development of reading', *Journal for Waldorf/R. Steiner Education*, 11 (2): 17.

SureStart (2003) *Full Day Care: National Standards for under 8s Day Care and Childminding*. Nottingham: DfES Publications. Available at www3.imperial.ac.uk/pls/portallive/docs/1/46973696.PDF (accessed 30/0/16).

Sutton-Smith, B. (2009) *The Ambiguity of Play*. Cambridge, MA: Harvard University Press.

Swaminathan, S., Byrd, S., Humphrey, C., Heinsch, M. and Mitchell, M. (2014) 'Beginnings learning circles: outcomes from a three-year school readiness pilot', *Early Childhood Education Journal*, 42 (4): 261–9.

Sylva, K., Melhuish, E., Sammons, P., Siraj-Blatchford, I. and Taggart, B. (2004) *The Effective Provision of Pre-School Education (EPPE) Project. Technical Paper 12 The Final Report: Effective Pre-School Education*. London: Institute of Education, University of London.

Sylva, K., Melhuish, E., Sammons, P., Siraj, I. and Taggart, B. (2014) *The Effective Pre-school, Primary and Secondary Education Project (EPPSE 3-16) Students' Educational and Developmental Outcomes at Age 16*, Research Report 354. London: DfE.

Tang, F. and Adams, L. (2010) '"I have f-rien-d now": how play helped two minority children transition into an English nursery school', *Diaspora, Indigenous & Minority Education*, 4 (2): 118–30.

Thomas, M. (2014) 'Empowering parents to work in partnership with schools to improve child learning, health and well-being', in M. Thomas (Ed.), *A Child's World: Contemporary Issues in Education*. Aberystwyth: CAA, Aberystwyth University.

Thompson, R.A. (1991) 'Infant day care: concerns, controversies, choices', in J.V. Lerner and N.L. Galambos (Eds.), *Employed Mothers and their Children*. New York: Garland. pp. 9–36.

Thompson, R.A. and Haskins, R. (2014) 'Early stress gets under the skin: promising initiatives to help children facing chronic adversity', *The Future of Children Policy Brief*, 24 (1): 1–6.

Tickell, C. (2011) *The Early Years: Foundations for Life, Health and Learning. An Independent Report on the Early Years Foundation Stage to Her Majesty's Government*. London: DfE.

Tovey, H. (2007) *Playing Outdoors: Spaces and Places, Risk and Challenge*. Milton Keynes: Open University Press.

Trevarthen, C. (1996) 'First contracts of mutual understanding', Goldschmieds Association for Early Childhood Conference Report, Goldsmiths' College, London.

Trevarthen, C. (2011) 'What young children give to their learning: making education work to sustain a community and its culture', *European Early Childhood Education Research Journal*, 19 (2): 173–94.

Tronick, E., Als, H., Adamson, L., Wise, S. and Brazelton, T.B. (1978) 'The infant's response to entrapment between contradictory messages in face-to-face interaction', *Journal of Child Psychiatry*, 17: 1–13.

UNESCO (2011) *EFA Global Monitoring Early Childhood*. Paris: UNESCO.

UNICEF (2012) *School Readiness: A Conceptual Framework*. New York: UNICEF. Available at www.unicef.org/education/files/Chil2Child_ConceptualFramework_FINAL(1).pdf (accessed 22/6/16).

Urban, M. (2008) 'Dealing with uncertainty: challenges and possibilities for the early childhood profession', *European Early Childhood Education Research Journal*, 16 (2): 135–52.

Vandenbroeck, M. (1999) *The View of the Yeti: Bringing Up Children in the Spirit of Self-awareness and Kindredship*. The Hague: Bernard Van Leer Foundation.

Veale, F. (Ed.) (2013) *Early Years for Levels 4 & 5 and the Foundation Degree*. London: Hodder Education.

Verba, M. (1994) 'The beginnings of collaboration in peer interaction', *Human Development*, 37.

Verhoeven, L. and van Leeuwe, J. (2010) 'The simple view of second language reading throughout the primary grades', *Reading and Writing*, 25: 1805–1818

Vogler, P., Crivello, G. and Woodhead, M. (2008) 'Early childhood transitions research: A review of concepts, theory, and practice', Working Papers in Early Childhood Development No. 48. The Hague: Bernard van Leer Foundation. Available at http://library.bsl.org.au/jspui/bitstream/1/4282/1/Early_childhood_transitions_research_A_review_of_concepts_theory_and_practice.pdf (accessed 4/7/16).

Waldfogel, J. (2004) 'Social mobility, life chances, and the early years', CASE Paper 88. London: London School of Economics.

Wang, X., Bernas, R. and Eberhard, P. (2002) 'Variations of maternal support to children's early literacy development in Chinese and American Indian families: implications for early childhood educators', *Internal Journal of Early Childhood*, 34 (1): 9–23.

Wasik, B.A., Karweit, N., Bond, M.A., Woodruff, L.B., Jaeger, G. and Adee, S. (2011) 'Early learning in CRESPAR', *Journal of Education for Students Placed at Risk (JESPAR)*, 5: 1–2, 93–107.

West, J., Germino-Hausken, E. and Collins, M. (1993) *Readiness for Kindergarten: Parent and Teacher Beliefs*. Washington, DC: Department of Education, National Center for Education Statistics.

Whitbread, D. and Bingham, S. (2012) *School Readiness: A Critical Review of Perspectives and Evidence*. London: TACTYC Association for the Professional Development of Early Years Educators.

Whitebread, D. (2012) *The Importance of Play: A Report on the Value of Children's Play with a Series of Policy Recommendations*. Brussels: Toy Industries of Europe. Available at www.importanceofplay.eu/IMG/pdf/dr_david_whitebread_-_the_importance_of_play.pdf (accessed 6/4/16).

Wollens, R. (Ed.) (2000) *Kindergartens and Cultures: The Global Diffusion of an Idea*. New Haven, CT: Yale University Press.

Wong, M.N.C. (2008) 'How preschool children learn in Hong Kong and Canada: a cross cultural study', *Early Years*, 28 (2): 115–133.

Wong, N.C. (2003) 'A study of children's difficulties in transition to school in Hong Kong', *Early Child Development and Care*, 173 (1): 83–96.

Wood, E. (2008) 'Towards a critical pedagogy of play', Play Colloquium paper. Leeds: Leeds Metropolitan University.

Woodhead, M. (1986) 'When should children go to school?', *Primary Education Review*, 25 (Spring): 10–14.

Woodhead, M. (1989) 'School starts at 5 ... or 4 years old? The rationale for changing admission policy in England and Wales', *Journal of Education Policy*, 4: 1–22.

World DataBank (2016) 'Official entrance age to primary education (years) 2011–2015'. Washington, DC: World Bank Group. Available at http://databank.worldbank.org/data/reports.aspx?source=2&country=&series=SE.PRM.AGES&period= (accessed 22/6/16).

Yen, C., Konold, T.R. and McDermott, P.A. (2004) 'Does learning behavior augment cognitive ability as an indicator of academic achievement?', *Journal of School Psychology*, 42: 157–69.

INDEX

Added to a page number 'f' denotes a figure, 't' denotes a table and 'g' denotes glossary.